C0-AUC-201

VOLUME 482 NOVEMBER 1985

THE ANNALS

of The American Academy *of* Political *and* Social Science

RICHARD D. LAMBERT, *Editor*
ALAN W. HESTON, *Associate Editor*

CHANGING PATTERNS OF POWER IN THE MIDDLE EAST

Special Editors of this Volume

THOMAS NAFF

Director
Middle East Research Institute
University of Pennsylvania
Philadelphia

MARVIN E. WOLFGANG

President
American Academy of Political and Social Science
Professor of Sociology and Law
University of Pennsylvania
Philadelphia

SAGE PUBLICATIONS *BEVERLY HILLS LONDON NEW DELHI*

THE ANNALS

© 1985 *by* The American Academy *of* Political *and* Social Science

ERICA GINSBURG, *Assistant Editor*

Editorial Office: 3937 Chestnut Street, Philadelphia, Pennsylvania 19104.

For information about membership (individuals only) and subscriptions (institutions), address:*

SAGE PUBLICATIONS, INC.
275 South Beverly Drive
Beverly Hills, CA 90212 USA

From India and South Asia, write to:
SAGE PUBLICATIONS INDIA Pvt. Ltd.
P.O. Box 4215
New Delhi 110 048
INDIA

From the UK, Europe, the Middle East and Africa, write to:
SAGE PUBLICATIONS LTD
28 Banner Street
London EC1Y 8QE
ENGLAND

**Please note that members of The Academy receive THE ANNALS with their membership.*

Library of Congress Catalog Card Number 85-050651
International Standard Serial Number ISSN 0002-7162
International Standard Book Number ISBN 0-8039-2486-0 (Vol. 481, 1985 paper)
International Standard Book Number ISBN 0-8039-2485-2 (Vol. 481, 1985 cloth)
Manufactured in the United States of America. First printing, September 1985.

The articles appearing in THE ANNALS are indexed in *Book Review Index; Public Affairs Information Service Bulletin; Social Sciences Index; Monthly Periodical Index; Current Contents; Behavioral, Social Management Sciences;* and *Combined Retrospective Index Sets.* They are also abstracted and indexed in *ABC Pol Sci, Historical Abstracts, Human Resources Abstracts, Social Sciences Citation Index, United States Political Science Documents, Social Work Research & Abstracts, Peace Research Reviews, Sage Urban Studies Abstracts, International Political Science Abstracts,* and/or *America: History and Life.*

Information about membership rates, institutional subscriptions, and back issue prices may be found on the facing page.

Advertising. Current rates and specifications may be obtained by writing to THE ANNALS Advertising and Promotion Manager at the Beverly Hills office (address above).

Claims. Claims for undelivered copies must be made no later than three months following month of publication. The publisher will supply missing copies when losses have been sustained in transit and when the reserve stock will permit.

Change of Address. Six weeks' advance notice must be given when notifying of change of address to insure proper identification. Please specify name of journal. Send change of address to: THE ANNALS, c/o Sage Publications, Inc., 275 South Beverly Drive, Beverly Hills, CA 90212.

The American Academy of Political and Social Science

3937 Chestnut Street Philadelphia, Pennsylvania 19104

Origin and Purpose. The Academy was organized December 14, 1889, to promote the progress of political and social science, especially through publications and meetings. The Academy does not take sides in controverted questions, but seeks to gather and present reliable information to assist the public in forming an intelligent and accurate judgment.

Meetings. The Academy holds an annual meeting in the spring extending over two days.

Publications. THE ANNALS is the bimonthly publication of The Academy. Each issue contains articles on some prominent social or political problem, written at the invitation of the editors. Also, monographs are published from time to time, numbers of which are distributed to pertinent professional organizations. These volumes constitute important reference works on the topics with which they deal, and they are extensively cited by authorities through-out the United States and abroad. The papers presented at the meetings of The Academy are included in THE ANNALS.

Membership. Each member of The Academy receives THE ANNALS and may attend the meetings of The Academy. Membership is open only to individuals. Annual dues: $26.00 for the regular paperbound edition (clothbound, $39.00). Add $9.00 per year for membership outside the U.S.A. Members may also purchase single issues of THE ANNALS for $6.95 each (clothbound, $10.00).

Subscriptions. THE ANNALS (ISSN 0002-7162) is published six times annually—in January, March, May, July, September, and November. Institutions may subscribe to THE ANNALS at the annual rate: $50.00 (clothbound, $66.00). Add $9.00 per year for subscriptions outside the U.S.A. Institutional rates for single issues: $10.00 each (clothbound, $15.00).

Second class postage paid at Philadelphia, Pennsylvania, and at additional mailing offices.

Single issues of THE ANNALS may be obtained by individuals who are not members of The Academy for $7.95 each (clothbound, $15.00). Single issues of THE ANNALS have proven to be excellent supplementary texts for classroom use. Direct inquiries regarding adoptions to THE ANNALS c/o Sage Publications (address below).

All correspondence concerning membership in The Academy, dues renewals, inquiries about membership status, and/or purchase of single issues of THE ANNALS should be sent to THE ANNALS c/o Sage Publications, Inc., 275 South Beverly Drive, Beverly Hills, CA 90212. *Please note that orders under $20 must be prepaid.* Sage affiliates in London and India will assist institutional subscribers abroad with regard to orders, claims, and inquiries for both subscriptions and single issues.

THE ANNALS

of The American Academy *of* Political *and* Social Science

RICHARD D. LAMBERT, *Editor*
ALAN W. HESTON, *Associate Editor*

FORTHCOMING

RELIGION AND THE STATE:
THE STRUGGLE FOR LEGITIMACY AND POWER
Special Editor: Robert J. Myers
Volume 483 — January 1986

THE LAW AND MENTAL HEALTH:
RESEARCH AND POLICY
Special Editor: Saleem A. Shah
Volume 484 — March 1986

FROM FOREIGN WORKERS TO SETTLERS?
TRANSNATIONAL MIGRATION AND
THE EMERGENCE OF NEW MINORITIES
Special Editors: Martin O. Heisler and Barbara Heisler
Volume 485 — May 1986

See page 3 for information on Academy membership and purchase of single volumes of **The Annals**.

CONTENTS

BOOK DEPARTMENT CONTENTS

SOCIOLOGY

ECONOMICS

PREFACE

The Middle East is an area of great importance and considerable danger in world politics. Abundant in a resource vital to the economies of nations, the Middle East is also beset with multiple conflicts whose repercussions are felt throughout the globe: the unresolved problem of the Palestinians, continuing wider Arab-Israeli hostility, the war in the Gulf, the invasion of Afghanistan, the ongoing tragedy in Lebanon. As a region in which the boundaries between the superpowers are not clearly marked, it is also an area for active competition for influence by the United States and the Soviet Union as well as a source of potential confrontation between them. Although many of the problems of the area are of long duration, the Middle East appears to be entering a period of change that will alter many of the underlying power relationships. It is on these changes, which are taking place at several levels, that the present volume focuses.

Discerning signs of movement toward solution of the Palestinian problem, the Egyptian ambassador to the United States, El Sayed Abdel Raouf El Reedy, expresses mild optimism that the peace process begun at Camp David will go forward. Progress on this difficult issue could, he argues, eventually open the way to peace between Israel and the Arab states. For there to be a real chance for negotiations to take place, however, the United States must be actively involved. Philip H. Stoddard agrees that the United States is in a unique position to act as a catalyst, but he sees a necessity for this country to define clearly its concept of engagement in the Middle East. Does the administration want to try to shape the process of resolving the Arab-Israeli conflict, or does it wish to stand aside? Pointing to one of the difficulties that inhibit the formulation of effective policy, Jack G. Shaheen analyzes the stereotype of the Arab in Western media and asserts that fair portrayals and accurate information are essential to appropriate foreign policy decisions.

The Soviet Union also has a major interest in the Arab-Israeli conflict and is seeking to expand its role throughout the Middle East. According to Robert O. Freedman, the Soviet Union has engaged in what it perceives to be a zero-sum competition with the United States for influence. However, despite the provision of arms aid on a large scale, the USSR has so far been unable to realize the objective of creating an enduring anti-imperialist Arab alignment, and its influence remains limited.

Although the Arab-Israeli conflict has long dominated politics in the Middle East, water is emerging as a problem that Frederick W. Frey and Thomas Naff predict is likely to become a major disruptive issue unless changes in current patterns of use and management of this resource are altered quickly and significantly. Water can be a potent source of conflict or of cooperation among the region's actors, depending on whether or not present policies are altered. Drawing from examples of several river systems in the region, Frey and Naff construct a theoretical framework for analyzing this complex issue.

Important changes have also been transforming relationships of power within several states in the region. In Iran direct rule by Islamic clerics constitutes a new phenomenon with far-reaching implications. Marvin Zonis examines the ideology and foreign-policy themes of the clerical regime and assesses the likelihood that the Iranian pattern will spread to other countries in the region. In Lebanon, under the impact of recent economic, political, and social changes, the Shiite community, once a downtrodden part of the population, has emerged as a powerful force. According to Augustus Richard Norton, the Shiites are now a major factor that must be taken into account.

In a number of Middle Eastern countries elections have recently taken place. The role of elections as devices for legitimizing governments is examined by Dankwart A. Rustow, who analyzes the experience of two democracies, Israel and Turkey, and presents comparisons with the legitimizing process in other forms of government. Power relationships in the economic sector are also undergoing evolution in several states of the region. Robert Bianchi traces the emergence of private business associations in both Turkey and Egypt and explores the role they play in influencing national economic policy.

Finally, a note on the transliteration system used in this volume is in order. Although a consistent system for Middle Eastern languages is often of utility to specialists, there are times when such transliteration is not necessary. In this issue of *The Annals,* the editors deem the topics to be so current, the readers so accustomed to reading about them in the popular press, that scientific transliteration would be an unnecessary encumbrance, and we have therefore opted for a simpler style—even though this leads to some inconsistencies. The specialist will know the non-English words that appear in the text.

THOMAS NAFF
MARVIN E. WOLFGANG

ANNALS, *AAPSS*, **482**, November 1985

New Opportunity for Peace in the Middle East

By EL SAYED ABDEL RAOUF EL REEDY

ABSTRACT: The Middle East is one of the most dangerous regions of the globe, with ongoing conflicts in Lebanon, the West Bank, the Gulf, and Afghanistan. Over the last 40 years, the Arab-Israeli conflict has been the single most important factor shaping the history of the region and preventing the emergence of a more stable order. The first successful step toward a peaceful solution of this issue was taken with the Egyptian initiative of 1977, which resulted in the Camp David accords. While these accords led to the 1979 Egyptian-Israeli peace treaty, no agreement resulted on the Palestinian question. Further peace initiatives were stalled by the Israeli invasion of Lebanon; however, recent developments have created a more favorable climate for dealing with the Israeli-Palestinian problem. Resolution of this issue would clear the way toward solving the entire Arab-Israeli conflict. The United States has a central role to play in maintaining the current momentum. Uniquely able to act as a catalyst, it must help achieve a settlement that would strengthen moderates in the region and reduce the risk of Soviet-American confrontation. Such a settlement would create many dividends for the United States.

El Sayed Abdel Raouf El Reedy, ambassador of Egypt to the United States, has been in the diplomatic service of his country for the past 30 years. He has represented Egypt in several capacities at the United Nations and from 1980 to 1983 was ambassador and permanent representative to the United Nations in Geneva. He also participated in the peace negotiations with Israel at Camp David. At the Egyptian Foreign Ministry he was director of the Department of Research and Policy Planning from 1977 to 1979, prior to his appointment as Egyptian ambassador to Pakistan from 1979 to 1983. From 1983 to 1984 he was director of the Department of Internal Organizations.

IT is no great source of satisfaction for a Middle Easterner, like me, to refer to this region as one of the most dangerous, if not the most dangerous, region of the present-day world. It is sufficient to glance at the daily headlines to realize what is going on in this part of the world: in Lebanon, on the West Bank, in the Gulf, in Afghanistan, and elsewhere. In these places there are active conflicts of all kinds. Many young men and women are both the victims and the instruments of these conflicts. So are many innocent civilians, regardless of their age or associations.

There can be no doubt that the United States is involved in the Middle East. It is, therefore, essential that American policymakers, diplomats, and political scientists understand both the causes and the current politics of the region in order to determine guidelines for an American approach to the region.

HISTORY SINCE 1945

If we review the four decades from 1945 to 1985, which is by no means a long span of time in the history of nations, we would find that much has happened over these years. There was the establishment of the Arab League, the independence of Syria and Lebanon from France, and the first Arab-Israeli war in 1948. Old regimes disappeared, new revolutionary and military governments took over, and, on the heels of the Suez war, Arab nationalism rose to an even higher level. The Soviet Union entered the region through arms deals and its role in building the High Dam. There followed the unity between Egypt and Syria, the American-British expedition in Lebanon in 1958, the revolution in Yemen, the departure of the British from east of the Suez to the Persian Gulf, the collapse of Egyptian-Syrian unity, the triumph of the Algerian revolution, the reemergence of a Palestinian national movement, the War of Attrition, and the emergence of the Qaddafi phenomenon in the Arab world. Then came the 1967 war, the 1973 war, the dramatic rise in oil prices, the beginning of the Lebanese tragedy, the Egyptian peace initiative, and the Camp David accords and the Egyptian-Israeli peace treaty. The rest of the Arab world reacted to the Egyptian-Israeli agreements and attempted to isolate Egypt; they failed to create an Arab system without Egypt. Finally, we have Israel's invasion of Lebanon, the decline of oil prices, the failure of the Israeli campaign in Lebanon, and, most recently, the Jordanian-Palestinian agreement to join the peace process.

These events were never divorced from factors external to the Middle East. But I submit that the Arab-Israeli conflict has been a major, if not the central, factor in most of these events. Indeed, the Arab-Israeli conflict has been the most important single factor in the shaping of history in the Middle East during the past four decades. Had it not been for that conflict, we would have been able to see in that area a much more stable order, the orientation of which would have been liberal and rational. We would have been saved from much upheaval and destruction.

Certainly there have been numerous attempts to find a peaceful solution to that conflict. These attempts never succeeded until 1977, when Egypt undertook a major historic initiative under the leadership of President Anwar el-Sadat that shattered all obstacles and resulted in the conclusion of the Camp David accords and the Egyptian-Israeli peace treaty of 1979.

The Camp David accords rested on the basic principle of exchanging peace for territory and aimed at the final resolution of the Arab-Israeli conflict, which entailed the solution of the Palestinian problem in all its aspects. The most complex area of the conflict pertained, naturally, to the West Bank and Gaza. The Camp David accords envisaged a solution that would lead to a transitional period in which the Palestinian people in those territories would elect a Palestinian self-governing authority that would exercise full autonomy over the territories pending negotiations that would determine the territories' final status. While the Camp David accords successfully led to the conclusion of the Egyptian-Israeli peace treaty, no agreement was reached on the Palestinian question, due to the narrow Israeli negotiating position on the definition of autonomy, despite three years of negotiations between Egypt and Israel.

This disappointment was soon followed by a series of unfavorable events in the area culminating in the Israeli invasion of Lebanon in June 1982. Aside from its disastrous consequences in Lebanon, the invasion resulted in the diversion of attention from the Palestinian question to the newly created problem in Lebanon. The years 1983 and 1984 were consumed in that exercise, and Egypt's endeavors to pursue its peace initiative had to be delayed until the emergence of a favorable climate. Now, in 1985, we believe that such a climate is emerging and deserves a new round of activities that, by necessity, should involve the United States as the catalyst.

NEW MOVEMENT TOWARD PEACE

I wish to refer to some of the encouraging signs of this new, favorable climate for peace. Let us begin with the recent elections in Israel, which led to the formation of a new government whose position on the peace process is obviously more flexible than that of the previous government. First, the present Israeli government does not reject one of the important peace proposals on the table, namely, President Reagan's peace initiative of 1 September 1982. Second, this government made the decision to withdraw its forces from Lebanon, thus bringing to an end a situation that has obstructed the pursuit of negotiations regarding the Palestinian question. We must make sure that this withdrawal is complete, genuine, and final.

A third development came from the United States. President Reagan's election to a second term of office by an impressive landslide has given him the authority to enable him to engage the United States in a bold policy for peace in the Middle East.

Fourth, there have been developments on the Arab side. I refer, first, to the restoration of diplomatic relations between Egypt and Jordan, both with special responsibility to the West Bank and Gaza. Second was the restoration of relations between Egypt and the Palestine Liberation Organization (PLO), symbolized by the visit of Chairman Yasir Arafat to Egypt late last year. Then came the meeting of the Palestine National Council in Amman last November in which King Hussein of Jordan launched a peace initiative based on the underlying principle of exchanging peace for territory, an initiative that was not rejected by the PLO. The meeting of the Palestine National Council led to a series of negotiations between the Palestinian and Jordanian leadership, which culminated in the Palestinian-Jordanian agreement of 11 February 1985.

We believe that this agreement could be a watershed. Here we have at long last an Arab position in which the official, organized Palestinian leadership is formally committed to negotiate jointly with Jordan a settlement of the Palestinian question in all its aspects. The PLO also agreed that the right to self-determination, to which the Palestinian people, like any other people in the world, are entitled, is to be exercised in the form of establishing a confederate relationship with Jordan. No less important is the provision to form a Palestinian-Jordanian delegation as the interlocutor of the Arab side.

Egypt viewed these positive developments in the region with a sense of appreciation and a sense of urgency. We felt that such developments, long awaited, deserved to be employed within a plan of action that would strengthen the rhythm of progress toward peace. We do not think that the momentum created should be allowed to fade away, nor that the Palestinian-Jordanian agreement should be allowed to constitute merely one more paper in a large pile of documents and missed opportunities on the shelf of the Palestinian question.

It was for this reason that when President Hosni Mubarak came to the United States in April 1985 he urged the United States to make use of that newly emerging opportunity for peace, no matter how fragile it was. The glimmer of emerging hope should never be ignored. We fully realize the difficulties, the obstacles, the hardships, and the pains involved in the pursuit of the peace process. But we equally believe that the promise is worth the endeavor, particularly since the alternative to the pursuit of peace is even bleaker than what we see today in the Middle East and would certainly be more menacing for world peace.

In an endeavor to keep the momentum alive and to generate a sense of confidence and reassurance with the people who have long been victimized by that problem, namely, the Palestinian people, President Mubarak proposed as an initial step that the United States commence a dialogue with a Jordanian-Palestinian delegation. Such a dialogue would not be a substitute for negotiations nor would it be a form of prenegotiations. It would only be a confidence-building measure intended to break through the wall of isolation and mistrust behind which the Palestinians have been living for generations. We do feel that the United States has received this proposal with a measure of understanding and appreciation.

The choice between war and peace in the Middle East is all too evident. There are on the one hand the moderates, who are eager to find appropriate solutions to the conflicts that are causing so much suffering for the people concerned and that are condemning the countries involved in more arms spending rather than development. On the other hand, there are those who are all too eager to exploit existing problems to destabilize the area even more. In our view, a solution of the Israeli-Palestinian conflict would have monumental impact in achieving a final solution of the entire Arab-Israeli conflict and decisively steering the area toward a course of moderation and development.

I also believe that the parties in the conflict are today more prepared and willing to be engaged in a search for peace. The two parties most directly involved are the Palestinians and the Israelis. Obviously, the majority of the Palestinians wish to put an end to the occupation and, in association with Jordan, to be able to assume responsibility for their own affairs. They have explicitly committed themselves to that course, through the signing of the Palestinian-Jordanian agreement. I would say that the majority of the Israelis are also eager to have a settlement.

THE INVOLVEMENT OF THE UNITED STATES

In these circumstances, the United States cannot afford to sit back and let events, in a critical area such as the Middle East, merely take their course. On the contrary, the United States should intervene to shape events.

There is no substitute for the United States in this regard. For a variety of reasons, the United States enjoys a predominant position in the area, particularly when it comes to the peace process. No other country or group of countries enjoys such a position. I was a member of the Egyptian delegation at Camp David, and I would confidently say that had it not been for the active and persistent role of the United States, it would have been impossible for the parties to reach an agreement.

Active participation by the United States in bringing about a peaceful settlement of the Arab-Israeli conflict would be a most significant contribution to world peace. No doubt, the Middle East, as is almost universally recognized, constitutes today the most dangerous region of the globe. The United States recognized this fact when it entered into bilateral talks with the Soviet Union on questions related to the Middle East. These talks are aimed at reducing the possibility of confrontation—planned or accidental—between the superpowers. For the situation in the Middle East carries with it the seeds of wider conflicts. One can think of various scenarios in which events could lead to superpower confrontations, which obviously would constitute serious threats to world peace.

I also believe that the United States would stand to benefit from an investment in peace in the Middle East. The United States has many stakes—political, strategic, economic, and others—in that critical region. Nothing could serve U.S. interests better than a peaceful solution of the Arab-Israeli conflict. Such an achievement would enhance the position of the moderates in the Middle East. It would vindicate them. It would prove that the policy of reason and moderation pays off. A failure to move on the peace front would tend to strengthen the rejectionists and extremists on both sides.

The Palestinians and Jordanians have gone a long way to meet the requirements for entering negotiations. It would, indeed, be a setback for the moderates if the present momentum is wasted and they are left out in the cold.

It has been said that the history of the Middle East is a history of missed opportunities. The blame has always fallen on the parties in the region. But this time the parties are prepared to engage in movement toward peace. It is up to the one great power, which is uniquely positioned to play the role of a catalyst. We do not believe that the United States can afford to let that opportunity slip away.

* * *

QUESTIONS AND ANSWERS

Q (Bianchi): On what is your optimism for the prospect of peace based? Considering the missed opportunities in the last few years and the reluctance of Americans to play the positive role that you wish for them, why do you think the future will be any different?

A: I am certain that this time is going to be better. I am not a prophet, but we are now witnessing some positive developments and these positive developments have taken place on all sides with all the actors in the play. It is up to the United States to use these circumstances to push the peace process forward. The parties have displayed a certain measure of willingness to be engaged, and I would say that there are also encouraging signs on the part of the United States, such as the visits by Ambassador Richard W. Murphy and Secretary of State George Shultz to the Middle East. I think these are positive elements that we hope would continue, would multiply, would be further used and exploited to the point where we can have a settlement. I am not minimizing the difficulties. I think the road is full of difficulties, but quite frankly I do not see an alternative to peace. The alternative to peace would be something that I would never wish to envision.

Q: Would it be possible to achieve a permanent peace?

A: The desire of the Soviet Union to join the peace process would be a positive development. It would be something that everybody would welcome. It is up to the Soviet Union to engage itself in the search for peace. But the United States has the pivotal and central role. Peace has been achieved between Egypt and Israel without the Soviet Union; the United States was the big force behind that peace.

Q (Harold Saunders, American Enterprise Institute of Public Policy, Washington, D.C.): It is important to identify the elements in the situation that created the obstacles to progress in a diplomatic process. On the other hand, there are policymakers whose job it is to move the situation forward, if at all possible, against the odds; therefore, they are willing to proceed with anything they can find to work with. I think that the ambassador is not voicing unanalytical optimism; rather, there is more to work with in early 1985 than there was in 1984, 1983, 1982, or 1981. We have the first significant multiparty Arab initiative since the 1973 war. It is the first Arab effort since Anwar el-Sadat's visit to Jerusalem. We cannot discount this development even though anyone could very reasonably say the odds are against us. The ambassador is certainly aware of the analytical problems and obstacles to establishing peace in the Middle East, so he is being optimistic in a sense, but not unreasonable. He is simply saying that he, as a representative of a government that has invested a lot in this process, against a lot of odds, sees something to work with and hopes that he will find an American partner in the process, and in that I applaud him.

The pieces that are part of this process will not be neatly lined up before the process begins. I think the American government at this point is sitting back and looking for two lives to be in order, in the Arab world and in Israel, before it engages in the process.

The issue is not whether the United States engages but in what part of the process it engages. The United States today has its choice about the extent to which it will engage in getting the process started. No country has committed itself to negotiations; therefore, we are not asking the American government to engage in the negotiation process. We are asking it what the United States is uniquely able to contribute at the very beginning of this political process that might lead ultimately to the kinds of negotiation in which the United States could serve as a catalyst. What can the United States throw into the pot now, in this early political stage, that would help those who are involved to move the process forward a little bit?

A: We have suggested that the United States can begin by having a dialogue with a joint Palestinian-Jordanian delegation. This type of dialogue is important because the Palestinians—together with the Israelis—are the central factor in this problem. It is in a way a Palestinian-Israeli conflict. The United States, of course, is having a normal, natural, multidimensional dialogue with Israel as it is having that dialogue with Egypt and any other country in the world. But unfortunately the Palestinians throughout their history have never really been given the chance to make up their own mind, to speak for themselves, really to be consulted. I think this is one of the sad aspects of the Palestinian problem, beginning from the Balfour Declaration to present-day affairs. We do not suggest negotiations between the United States and the Palestinians. What is needed is a dialogue to make the Palestinians feel that they are equally legitimate and that they are recognized as an equal party in the situation.

Quite frankly, I think one of the discouraging phenomena of today is that so many people are unaware of the significance of the Palestinian-Jordanian agreement. Anybody who has studied the history of the Arab-Israeli conflict and the Palestinian question would think that this agreement is a monumental achievement; it can be a watershed. So let us not allow this opportunity to slip away; let us build on it, let us engage it before it evaporates.

Q: How can the Israeli government get assurances that any further negotiations on the principles of the Camp David accords would not result in a cold peace and could result in a warmer relationship with its neighbors?

A: I think peace in itself—hot, warm, or cold—is a very important achievement. The relationship between Egypt and Israel today is a full, meaningful relationship between two sovereign states. The borders between Israel and Egypt are peaceful. Some 200,000 Israeli tourists cross the borders to see the antiquities in upper Egypt. They come to Egypt and are welcomed in Egypt as good tourists.

Egypt has opened itself to Israel. Israel buys oil from us. Israel has an embassy with a full-fledged and able ambassador in Cairo. It also has a cultural center that has a full complement of activities. It was mentioned that there is only an Egyptian ambassador who is not today in Israel. But there is in Israel a full Egyptian diplomatic mission headed by a chargé d'affaires and the ambassador can go there anytime. There are contacts between Shimon Peres and Hosni Mubarak for reviewing all kinds of problems between the two countries.

We see that Israel and Egypt are building good relations. But let me also tell you that Lebanon was a big disappointment for the Egyptians. Egypt is an Arab country and the Egyptians look at themselves as part of the Arab people. When I was in Cairo in the summer of 1982, I saw how the Egyptians were shocked when they saw on television the scenes of Israel's aerial bombardment of civilian quarters in Beirut and the massacres in the Sabra and Shatila camps. Any responsible leader of a government must weigh the public opinion in his or her own country. For Egypt, that evaluation resulted in the temporary withdrawal of its ambassador from Israel. Unfortunately the events in Lebanon were compounded by Israel's nonwithdrawal from Taba, which is a piece of Egyptian territory.

So we have a disappointment, but we are looking ahead to the future. Since Lebanon, there have been elections in Israel and a new government. The government is withdrawing now from Lebanon, a development that we have always looked forward to. The withdrawal has been coupled with what we think is the beginning of movement on the peace process and also contact between our two leaders concerning various issues. I am hopeful that there will be a settlement of the Palestinian-Israeli conflict. A settlement would dramatically change the whole situation because the Palestinian-Israeli conflict is a source of the problem. Egypt got involved in that problem because of the Palestinian question. If that question is solved, I guarantee that there will be peace. Let us not just look at the situation from one particular angle, but let us see the whole picture. I continue to be hopeful that peace will be established.

ANNALS, *AAPSS*, **482**, November 1985

U.S. Policy and the Arab-Israeli Conflict: Observations on the Current Scene

By PHILIP H. STODDARD

ABSTRACT: The United States will have to define its concept of engagement in the Arab-Israeli peace process. Will it try to shape this process or will it wait until Arab leaders make enough concessions to interest Israel? The Reagan administration does not view the Arab-Israeli conflict as a serious threat to American interests. It sees no crisis to manage. Instead, it encourages Jordanians and Egyptians to clear the way for direct talks with Israel. In the current prenegotiation period, both sides of the conflict will have to decide to negotiate. This decision will require major changes in the political environment, as well as internal coalition building in support of concessions. Neither side is likely to negotiate unless the United States acts as a catalyst. The Reagan administration is moving toward doing something to stimulate the peace process, but it is reluctant to get out in front until it concludes that its role will be both painless and successful.

Philip H. Stoddard received his graduate degrees at Princeton; he joined the Department of State in 1963. When he retired in 1983, he was a deputy assistant secretary in the Bureau of Intelligence and Research. He then became executive director of the Middle East Institute. His publications include Change and the Muslim World *(coeditor, 1981) and "The U.S. Approach Today," in Michael C. Hudson's* Alternative Approaches to the Arab-Israeli Conflict: A Comparative Study of the Principal Actors *(1984).*

NOTE: This article reflects the views of the author and not those of the Middle East Institute or its board of governors. The author is indebted to Lois Houghton for her valuable assistance.

SUCCESSIVE American administrations over the past 18 years have ranked the peaceful resolution of the Arab-Israeli conflict high among U.S. national interests in the Middle East. The reason for this consistency is not hard to find: resolution of the conflict has long been seen as holding the key to achieving other U.S. objectives in the Middle East. Under Secretary of State for Political Affairs Michael H. Armacost recently summed up the U.S. position:

> We have a vital stake in peace between Israel and its neighbors. Conflict in the Middle East risks Great Power confrontation, the security of Israel, disruption of oil supplies, expanded political and military opportunities for the Soviet Union, and the growth of Islamic radicalism and other threats to friendly governments.[1]

Similarly, it has long been said that the issue for the United States in the Middle East is not whether it will be involved in the resolution of the conflict, but how. In present circumstances, this means that the United States will have to define its concept of engagement in the Arab-Israeli peace process. Does the Reagan administration want to shape the process or does it want to stand aside? At the moment, it seems to be trying to do both. This task is difficult. As the Turkish proverb puts it, "Two watermelons cannot be carried under one arm."

Middle East specialists in the Reagan administration are cautious about the posture the United States should adopt. Some seem to think that Secretary of State George Shultz is moving too slowly. They point to the diplomatic record—four times in the past 12 years the United States has brokered peace arrangements in the Middle East—and note that the high-water mark of the peace process—the Camp David accords of 1978 and the Egyptian-Israeli treaty of 1979—required vigorous American involvement.

These experts seem hopeful that the situation in the Middle East may be moving toward an opportune moment for a more active U.S. role. They note that such moments do not happen by accident; they tend to be made. Indeed, as observed earlier this year by Harold H. Saunders, former assistant secretary of state for Near Eastern and South Asian affairs,

> If we had not pushed, in 1977, for a return to Geneva, Sadat would never have come to Jerusalem. Exploring and pressing in order to determine whether there is a ripe moment, or even working to precipitate such a moment, can lead to unexpected consequences and opportunities.[2]

Other specialists, although cautiously optimistic, advocate continued restraint to avoid the backlash that developed after the Camp David agreements. They urge the administration not to blind itself to the remaining difficulties and the likelihood of failure. They also allege that when the United States gets out in front in the Middle East, its Arab interlocutors sit back and expect the United States to deliver Israeli concessions.

While hoping to keep the momentum going by talking about stepping up efforts to revive the peace process, many administration experts remain cautious. "You need a process to keep things going that would involve negotiations," according to an unidentified State Depart-

1. Michael H. Armacost, "U.S. Diplomacy and the Search for Peace: Address before the Baltimore Council on Foreign Affairs, 24 Apr. 1985," *Current Policy*, no. 696 (May 1985).

2. Harold H. Saunders, "America and the Middle East," *New Outlook* 28(4):28 (Apr. 1985), based on a discussion at the U.S. embassy in Tel Aviv, 12 Feb. 1985.

ment official. "And as we keep up the momentum . . . , we tend to get more drawn into it. Yet we don't want to be centrally involved and become the motor instead of the gasoline."[3]

THE ADMINISTRATION'S APPROACH

Several themes have run through administration pronouncements on the Arab-Israeli conflict in recent months. According to these statements, the possibilities for promoting peace are more encouraging than they have been for some time. For example, Ambassador Richard W. Murphy, the able and experienced assistant secretary of state for Near Eastern and South Asian affairs, early this year cited several "small but significant steps" in the pursuit of an Arab-Israeli peace:[4]

1. Israeli Prime Minister Shimon Peres, in his inaugural address to the Knesset in September 1984, offered to negotiate with Jordan without preconditions.
2. In November 1984, at the meeting of the Palestine National Council in Amman, King Hussein proposed a coordinated Palestinian-Jordanian approach based on U.N. Resolution 242 and the convening of an international conference.[5] The United States supports Jordan's entry into negotiations with Israel as the "essential next step in the peace process," but Washington believes that the proposal for holding an international conference is "neither realistic nor productive."
3. The Arab states that support a peaceful settlement are now "more cohesive," as evidenced by the resumption of formal relations between Jordan and Egypt.

Against the backdrop of these hopeful signs, Assistant Secretary Murphy reiterated administration policy: "The U.S.," he said, "is ready to resume its role as a full partner in the search for peace whenever the parties are prepared to negotiate." The negotiations should be based on U.N. Security Council Resolution 242. Meanwhile the United States "remains committed to the positions set forth in Reagan's September 1982 initiative."

The Reagan initiative, however, was an early casualty of the failure of U.S. policy in Lebanon. It is a statement of lofty principles with no practical effect.[6] Still, as Ambassador Armacost com-

3. Charlotte Saikowski, "U.S. Making Effort to Keep Peace Initiative Alive in Middle East," *Christian Science Monitor,* 9 Apr. 1985.

4. Richard W. Murphy, "Statement before the Subcommittee on Europe and the Middle East of the House Foreign Affairs Committee, Washington, D.C., January 30, 1985," *Current Policy,* no. 651 (Feb. 1985).

5. Resolution 242, adopted by the U.N. Security Council on 22 Nov. 1967, "affirms" the need for "a just and lasting peace in the Middle East"; "withdrawal of Israel armed forces from territories occupied in the recent conflict"; and "termination of all claims or states of belligerency and respect for and acknowledgement of the sovereignty, territorial integrity, and political independence of every State in the area and their right to live in peace within secure and recognized boundaries free from threats or acts of force." Also asserted are three other requirements: "freedom of navigation through international waterways in the area; . . . a just settlement of the refugee problem; . . . [and] the territorial inviolatility and political independence of every State in the area." The resolution also asks for (1) the appointment of "a special representative" to foster relationships with various Middle Eastern countries in order to reach "a peaceful and accepted settlement in accordance with the provisions and principles in [the] resolution"; and (2) a report "as soon as possible" by the U.N. secretary-general on the representative's "efforts." See *Christian Science Monitor,* 27 Feb. 1985, p. 32.

6. For my views of President Reagan's proposal, see Philip H. Stoddard, "The U.S. Approach Today," in *Alternative Approaches to the Arab-Israeli Conflict: A Comparative Analysis of*

mented on 24 April 1985, "Once negotiations are joined, the positions we will take will be those set forth in President Reagan's September 1, 1982, speech on the Middle East."[7]

In April 1985, Assistant Secretary Murphy found additional "encouraging developments":[8]

1. Israel had proposed negotiations with Jordan without preconditions. On 31 March Prime Minister Peres told *Al-Quds,* the Arabic newspaper in Jerusalem, that "we are prepared to negotiate unconditionally with a joint Jordanian-Palestinian delegation, a Jordanian delegation, or a Palestinian delegation in our efforts toward an immediate peaceful solution or a solution in steps."[9]

2. Jordan and the Palestine Liberation Organization (PLO) had agreed on a joint approach that could be a helpful step toward direct negotiations between Israel and Jordan, with Palestinian participation.

3. Egypt was actively seeking steps toward direct negotiations.

4. High-level contacts between Egypt and Israel had intensified. For example, Israeli Minister without Portfolio Ezer Weizman had returned recently from a private visit to Cairo. The trip, however, touched off a major controversy in Israel's national unity government, indicating that Labor Party leader Peres has a long way to go in his dealings with Likud Party leader Foreign Minister Yitzhak Shamir if he is to enjoy the influence on foreign policy exercised by his predecessors.[10]

As a result, Ambassador Murphy concluded, Israelis and Arabs "have imparted new momentum" to the peace process. The momentum is tentative, however. It must be maintained and built upon by achieving "the near-term goal of direct negotiations between Israel and Jordan with the participation of representative Palestinians." Mr. Armacost would consider other auspicious developments to be furthering this momentum, including the Israeli withdrawal from Lebanon; King Hussein's defiance of intimidation from hostile states—such as Syria—to work with Palestinians toward eventual negotiations with Israel; and Iraq's development of closer relations with its moderate Arab neighbors and its reestablishment of full diplomatic relations with the United States.[11]

Two events lie behind the relative optimism of Murphy and Armacost: the agreement of 11 February 1985 between King Hussein and PLO leader Yasir Arafat, and Egyptian President Hosni Mubarak's proposal of late February, followed by his visit to Washington in March.

THE 11 FEBRUARY AGREEMENT: "A FRAMEWORK FOR COMMON ACTION"

According to the 11 February agreement, which resulted from contentious discussion, Jordan and the PLO agreed

> to move together towards the achievement of a peaceful and just settlement of the Middle East crisis and the termination of Israeli occupation of the occupied Arab territories, including Jerusalem, on the basis of five principles:
>
> —Total Israeli withdrawal from the territories occupied in 1967 [in return] for

the Principal Actors, ed. Michael C. Hudson (Washington, DC: Center for Contemporary Arab Studies, 1984), pp. 175-201.

7. Armacost, "U.S. Diplomacy."

8. Murphy, "Statement before the Subcommittee."

9. Ibid.

10. C. Robert Zelnik, "Israel's Unity Government and Peace," *Christian Science Monitor,* 6 May 1985.

11. Armacost, "U.S. Diplomacy."

comprehensive peace as established in United Nations Security Council Resolutions.

—Right of self-determination for the Palestinian people: Palestinians will exercise their inalienable right of self-determination when Jordanians and Palestinians will be able to do so within the context of the formation of the proposed confederate Arab states of Jordan and Palestine.

—Resolution of the problem of Palestinian refugees in accordance with United Nations resolutions.

—Resolution of the Palestine question in all its aspects.

—On this basis, peace negotiations will be conducted under the auspices of an International Conference in which the five Permanent Members of the Security Council and all the parties to the conflict will participate, including the Palestine Liberation Organization, the sole legitimate representative of the Palestine people, with a joint Jordanian-Palestinian delegation.[12]

Ambassador Murphy characterized this framework as constructive thinking that could serve as an important step forward in the peace process. However, he faulted it for lacking a specific reference to Security Council Resolution 242—the territory-for-peace formula that has long been the basis for U.S. policy toward resolving the Arab-Israeli conflict—and he noted that it contained "unrealistic elements," specifically the idea of an international conference. The United States, Murphy said, strongly supported the king's efforts to move toward negotiations, "but only time will tell whether the agreement will ultimately enable him to do so."

12. Jordan and the Palestine Liberation Organization, A Framework for Common Action, Amman, 11 Feb. 1985 (Washington, DC: Jordan Information Bureau, 25 Feb. 1985).

The PLO's interpretation raised the question of exactly what Arafat and Hussein had agreed on. Shortly before the agreement's publication in Amman, the PLO Executive Committee repeated its standing opposition to Resolution 242, a resolution not mentioned—but implied—in the 11 February agreement.

The reactions of the West Bank Palestinians themselves have not been ascertained in detail, even though their views are ultimately more important than those of King Hussein and Yasir Arafat. Many West Bankers seemed to view the 11 February framework as a significant and beneficial development. Presumably, many others expected nothing to come of it, and a minority probably opposed it. In any case, the Palestinians, not surprisingly, can be expected to say that they should decide who negotiates for them. And their choice seems to be the PLO, no matter who is leading the process.

What is wrong with the 11 February agreement, other than the idea of an international conference? Several points are vague. For example, is the PLO willing—in the context of a negotiating process—to recognize Israel's right to exist within secure and recognized borders? Does the PLO still insist on an independent Palestinian state? How will the PLO's views be represented in a Jordanian-Palestinian delegation? At first, the Jordanians seemed to be saying that the PLO would not be included, but King Hussein has since declared that it must be. Indeed, a press report of early May 1985, citing a "senior Jordanian official," alleged that Jordan and the PLO had agreed on a list of non-PLO members to be part of a joint negotiating team. However, PLO spokesmen later said that the Palestinians on the joint delegation had to be PLO representatives.[13]

En route to the Middle East, Secretary Shultz asserted on 19 May 1985 in Lisbon that Palestinian participation in direct talks with Israel was "essential" to a settlement "that will hold." He also said he would discuss with Arabs and Israelis the names of Palestinians who might be acceptable to all sides, including the United States, the PLO, and Israel, for participation in direct talks about the future of the West Bank.[14] Of course, it is a giant leap from talks between the United States and a joint delegation, whoever its members, to talks between that delegation and Israel. It is likely, as the *New York Times* noted, that American experts are not optimistic about an early breakthrough. Moving the process forward a little, as Mr. Shultz said he hoped to, is hard in any circumstances, but progress is further complicated by divisions within the PLO between those who think the United States can help and those who do not. Arafat, after all, has only a paper-thin mandate from the PLO Executive Committee.

Mr. Shultz told the Israelis on 11 May that "the gains are being made by inches" and that several months may be needed to reach a decisive point.[15] But who talks to whom about what is still up in the air. Israelis do not want the United States to engage in prenegotiations with Arabs about issues that Israel thinks should be discussed with it. Still, an Israeli official seemed willing to accept U.S. discussions with a joint Jordanian-Palestinian delegation if they might advance the peace process.[16]

These are crucial issues for the United States, Israel, and the Palestinians. Acceptance of Resolution 242 is a basic requirement for Israel. For the Palestinians, it is their major bargaining chip. They do not want to play it as the price of getting a negotiating process started unless there are reasonable assurances that the Israelis are willing to compromise. They certainly would not want to play it merely for the privilege of talking with the United States.

MUBARAK'S PROPOSALS

In late February, President Mubarak probed the prospects for negotiations and the United States' seriousness of purpose by offering to host direct talks between Israel and a joint Palestinian-Jordanian delegation. He also urged the Reagan administration to invite Israelis and members of a joint Jordanian-Palestinian delegation to Washington for discussions, with Egyptian participation as as the first step in preparing for direct negotiations. Furthermore, Mubarak said, the Palestinian contingent could be made up of non-PLO Palestinians.

Prime Minister Peres reacted favorably to Mubarak's call for direct negotiations. The plan, he said, "deserves a careful and positive study" by Israel.[17] Jordan and the PLO, however, rejected Mubarak's offer to host peace talks in

13. Mary Curtius, "Jordan and PLO Agree on Team to Negotiate with U.S.," *Christian Science Monitor,* 7 May 1985.

14. Bernard Gwertzman, "Shultz Urges a Palestinian Role in Talks," *New York Times,* 10 May 1985.

15. Don Oberdorfer, "Shultz Calls Progess on Mideast Talks Slow," *Washington Post,* 12 May 1985.

16. Ibid.; see also "Shultz's Reluctant Mission," *Christian Science Monitor,* 10 May 1985; "Shultz Treads Lighly to Pull Mideast Factions Together," ibid.

17. Charlotte Saikowski, "U.S. Awaits Clearer Arab Peace Bid," *Christian Science Monitor,* 27 Feb. 1985.

Cairo and described the plan as not helpful. Presumably, they wondered how much of the plan was intended to impress the United States on the eve of Mubarak's Washington visit. Indeed, hardly was the ink dry on Mubarak's proposal when he changed course. First, he said that the United States would have to talk separately to a joint Palestinian-Jordanian delegation. Second, he hedged on the issue of whether the PLO could be excluded.

Peres's favorable attitude toward the proposal was understandable. Mubarak had called for the direct talks that Israel advocates; and he had not demanded PLO participation in the discussions, long anathema to Israelis. For these reasons, it has been seen as a more attractive scheme for Israel and the United States than the Hussein-Arafat agreement, which included, among other deficiencies, emphasis on an international conference that would include the Soviets.

The PLO leaders rejected parts of Mubarak's proposal on grounds that he had left the PLO out completely or had relegated its concerns to the sidelines. Nevertheless, the Mubarak and Hussein-Arafat proposals are connected. Indeed, it has been argued that Mubarak's plan saved the Jordanian-PLO framework from "swift self-destruction." Surprisingly, Washington seemed to be less enthusiastic than Israel about Mubarak's scheme, which it called "premature."[18]

By the time Mubarak arrived in Washington on 9 March, there was little left of his bold new idea. By then it had come down to a discussion about peace between Arabs and Americans; the Israelis would not be there. The result was disappointment in Israel and a certain amount of gloom in Washington that the diplomatic flurry of the past few months was leading nowhere and that time might be slipping away. Nevertheless, Mubarak's trip was seen as a positive occasion for a discussion of practical steps toward peace. The United States, according to Mr. Murphy, remained open to Egyptian proposals, "including the suggestion that the United States meet with a Jordanian-Palestinian delegation, provided this would lead to direct negotiations between Israel and an Arab partner."[19]

President Reagan also had kind words for Mubarak's idea: it was a "positive contribution," he noted, but "the parties were still a long way from the negotiating table."[20] Support from the United States would be limited for now to helping Egypt and others find an acceptable formula based on Resolution 242. The president gave no sign of eagerness to involve himself in the peace process. Instead, the United States was pressing Mubarak to push Hussein to talk directly with Israel. Reagan obviously did not welcome the idea of a Jordanian-Palestinian delegation landing on his doorstep, nor did he want to mediate between Israel and Jordan.[21]

In short, Mubarak's effort in mid-March fell short of his goal of getting the

18. Judith Miller, "Mubarak Tries to Jump Start Stalled Mideast Peace Talks," *New York Times,* 3 Mar. 1985.

19. Richard W. Murphy, "Statement before the Subcommittee on Europe and the Middle East of the House Foreign Affairs Committee, Washington, D.C., April 4, 1985," *Current Policy,* no. 683, p. 1 (Apr. 1985).

20. David B. Ottaway, "Mubarak Call for Talks Wins Reagan's Praise," *Washington Post,* 13 Mar. 1985.

21. Charlotte Saikowski, "U.S. Urges Mubarak to Bring Israel, Jordan to Peace Table," *Christian Science Monitor,* 13 Mar. 1985.

Americans back in the game. Questioned closely during his talks with President Reagan about his approach, he went home without a U.S. commitment. To compound Mubarak's undoubted but unspoken frustration, his lunch with President Reagan coincided with the U.S. veto of a Security Council resolution condemning Israel for raiding villages in southern Lebanon.

Despite these setbacks, the "encouraging developments" of the past few months led President Reagan to send Ambassador Murphy to the Middle East to stimulate further thinking, to assess the situation, and to "explore how the various ideas that have been put forward" could advance the peace process. American thinking was flexible: "We are prepared to respond creatively to practical suggestions . . . , but it is important to set forth on a clear path to direct negotiations" as the "only way a peaceful settlement can be achieved." Although Ambassador Murphy's 16-day trip in April was described as "useful" by the administration, press accounts labeled it a failure. More likely it was something in between: diplomatic alchemy turns "useful" into a euphemism for "stalemate." It seemed at least to have been an attempt to substitute travel for policy, or, more charitably, a futile effort to find someone willing to talk to Israel.[22]

In a recent major address on the Middle East, Secretary Shultz highlighted the familiar theme that the United States is committed to promoting an Arab-Israeli peace through direct negotiations:

> Negotiations work. We have tangible evidence of this today in the peace treaty between Israel and Egypt. This relationship is the cornerstone of the peace process. We must build upon it. The Egyptian-Israeli relationship itself must grow and be strengthened. And others must learn from the example that Egypt and Israel have set. President Mubarak is committed to peace. Others must join him. We are glad that King Hussein has re-established Jordan's diplomatic relations with Egypt. The process of building peace must continue, and the United States is committed to helping the parties move forward.

On the Palestinian dimension of the conflict, the toughest issue and the one that U.S. administrations have skillfully avoided, Secretary Shultz reiterated the basic principles articulated by the Carter and Reagan administrations:

> We have . . . made clear our concern for the Palestinian people. Lasting peace and security for Israel will require a just settlement for the Palestinians that assures their dignity and legitimate rights. How ironic and tragic it is, therefore, that those who claim to act on behalf of the Palestinians have continued to *block* negotiations—the only course that can achieve a just settlement for the Palestinians.

Furthermore, he said, "Now is the time for the Arabs to let negotiations proceed. Now is the time for the Arabs to let King Hussein come forward. There is no alternative to direct negotiations; the longer this truth is evaded, the longer the Palestinian people are the victims." The theme is obvious: the Arab states, not Israel, in effect are responsible for the failure of the Palestinians to achieve a just settlement.

Describing the Reagan initiative as the "most promising route to a solution," the secretary listed six principles that will guide U.S. policy.

> First, we will continue to seek a lasting peace that respects the legitimate concerns of all the parties.

22. Mary Curtius, "Despite Failure of Envoy's Trip, U.S. Sticks to Search for Team to Talk with Israel," *Christian Science Monitor*, 1 May 1985.

Second, the United States will oppose violent and radical challenges to peace and security. We will oppose governments or terrorist organizations of whatever stripe in their efforts to undermine the State of Israel and our Arab friends in the region.

Third, United States policy toward the PLO is unchanged: We will never recognize or negotiate with any group that espouses violent solutions or refuses to accept Resolutions 242 and 338 or recognize Israel's right to exist.

Fourth, the only way to achieve a genuine, lasting peace is through direct negotiations between the Arab states and Israel. No other procedures can substitute. No other approach will get anywhere. No further plans or preliminaries are needed. There is one and only one place to negotiate—at the table, face to face.

Fifth, we will support a negotiated settlement by which the Palestinian people can achieve their legitimate rights and just requirements. We will not support the establishment of an independent Palestinian state in the West Bank and Gaza, nor will we support annexation or permanent control by Israel.

Sixth, and finally, we will always insist on Israel's right to exist in peace behind secure and recognized borders.[23]

What does this speech making add up to? Positive developments certainly, as well as a commitment to what Secretary Shultz called an "indispensable" U.S. role. So far, despite Ambassador Murphy's "useful" trip to the Middle East and the brief visits to Amman and Cairo by Secretary Shultz in May 1985—his first to an Arab country in two years—there seem to be no sense of urgency and no answer to the question of what kind of role the United States should play and when it should act. Perhaps the administration, like Dickens's Mr. Micawber, is confident that something good will turn up if it waits long enough.

U.S. insistence on finding a formula whereby Israelis and Arabs can directly negotiate imposes a particularly difficult precondition for resumption of the peace process. As a result, this effort is likely to collapse unless there is a series of intermediate steps. The fallacy of this approach was pointed out by former Ambassador L. Dean Brown, president of the Middle East Institute, on 24 April 1985. On the occasion of an Arab League conference in Washington on Israeli settlements in the West Bank, Ambassador Brown called upon the administration to begin its efforts to revive the Arab-Israeli peace process with three sets of prior direct negotiations before the United States urged Arabs and Israelis to talk face to face. The first negotiations would take place between the United States and Israel to see what the two governments have in common. "The U.S. and Israel have to have a better understanding of where they are going in the long run," he said. "Without that, there is no hope of an effective U.S. role." In the second set of negotiations Arab governments and the Palestinians would discuss their positions on various peace initiatives. Otherwise, Ambassador Brown observed, the various Arab proposals will share the same "historic grave" as President Reagan's initiative of September 1982.[24] The third set of direct talks would take place among the Palestinians. The Palestinians need to determine where they are going and who can speak for them in the negotiating phase.

23. George Shultz, "The United States and Israel: Partners for Peace and Freedom," *Current Policy,* no. 690, p. 3 (Apr. 1985).

24. David B. Ottaway, "Arab League Conferees Vexed at U.S. Indifference," *Washington Post,* 25 Apr. 1985.

PUSHING THE STONE UPHILL

The case for active U.S. involvement in the peace process—to take advantage of the second Reagan term's small window of opportunity—has frequently been made by moderate Arab leaders during their pilgrimages to Washington. The list includes Saudi Arabia's King Fahd, President Mubarak, Jordanian Foreign Minister Taher al-Masri and, in late May, King Hussein, all of whom probably felt that in time the United States would take the initiative. These leaders have been joined by European and American critics of U.S. policy. For several reasons, it is a much more difficult case to make today than it was a decade ago in the wake of the October 1973 war.

First, the Arab-Israeli conflict is not seen by the administration as putting important U.S. interests at risk. No war clouds are hovering over this conflict. Without a significant threat to U.S. interests and a real risk of war, there is no crisis to manage, no sense of urgency, and thus no need for risky initiatives by the United States. Warnings of the high cost of inaction continue to fall on deaf ears.

Second, the United States has been able to manage bilateral relations with key Arab states and Israel without a peace process. This reason for not establishing a peace process will mean bruising battles over economic aid and military sales, but the administration is used to struggles on Capitol Hill and can bring up economic and military aid to Jordan if the peace process looks promising. Many Arab countries are looking to the United States, not to the Soviet Union, for assistance, moral support, and leadership.

Third, oil no longer weighs heavily on U.S. policy toward the Arab-Israeli conflict. Thanks to the oil glut, concern about U.S access to Middle Eastern oil does not galvanize the policy process. Few persons now can argue convincingly that a significant increase in tension between Arabs and Israelis will lead to a major disruption of oil supplies or politically motivated price hikes.

Fourth, the Soviets, despite their strong ties with Syria, the People's Democratic Republic of Yemen, Iraq, and Libya, have not experienced major successes in the Middle East. Moreover, in the absence of an imminent threat of hostilities between Israel and Soviet so-called clients, concern in Washington about a superpower confrontation has lessened.

Fifth, the Arab-Israeli conflict is not at the top of the Reagan administration's agenda.[25] It remains worrisome but not sufficiently dangerous to generate activism by the United States.

The administration resists involvement in the peace process also because it seems to have no clear idea of what to do about the Palestinian-West Bank issue, which it recognizes as being at the heart of the Arab-Israeli problem. Moreover, it may wonder whether Israel considers the future of the West Bank to be negotiable and thus whether the two sides will have anything to talk about. Nevertheless, a U.S. focus on the quality of life in the West Bank is no substitute for confronting major issues of contention.

Finally, the administration was badly burned by the failure of its policy in Lebanon and by the negative Israeli reaction to the Reagan initiative of 1982.

25. For example, Butros Ghali, the Egyptian minister of state for foreign affairs, glumly told an interviewer in Jan. 1985 that the conflict ranked fifth on Reagan's list of priorities, even though he thought that the president would like to do something to leave his mark on history. See *Christian Science Monitor,* 10 Jan. 1985.

These unhappy lessons have led to wariness toward mediating problems that Arabs and Israelis are not ready to solve themselves. Caution thus looks like smart policy to the United States, while to the Arabs it looks like giving up. The administration is allergic to embarking on a new grand strategy for a comprehensive settlement, and it expects no Sadat-style dramatic gesture from any Arab leader. Besides, it has its own plan.

Still, the task Washington faces is not one of formulating a peace plan but of precipitating a decision by Arabs and Israelis to negotiate. This big step, in turn, will require major decisions and political debate on both sides. These major decisions have not yet occurred, and the debate has just started. Neither is likely to get under way in earnest until talks involving Jordanians, Palestinians, and Israelis seem a real possibility. Short of that, viable interlocutors on either side are hard to find. Meanwhile, skepticism is likely to reign in Washington, even as the administration tries, through soothing rhetoric, to avoid giving Arab leaders the impression that they will never be able to do enough to persuade Washington to play a catalytic role.

These complex considerations have led the administration to fall back on a shopworn Washington metaphor. The ball, the administration reiterates, remains in the Arab court. The actions of Hussein and Mubarak are welcome, but they have not been enough.

In fact, of course, the ball is in no one's court; it is merely up in the air. This means that, although the various parties want peace, none of them is yet ready to take the steps that might eventually lead to negotiations and ultimately to a settlement. Without the United States in the game, moreover, they cannot be assured that an eventual settlement is more likely than a stalemate, for which they will have expended scarce political capital.

TOWARD NEGOTIATIONS

Many arguments in Washington and elsewhere seem to turn on the tactics for moving the two sides closer together. A minority advocates pressure on Israel. The United States, in this view, should push Peres to halt the establishment of settlements on the West Bank and to give renewed assurances about Israel's continued willingness to exchange West Bank territory for peace before granting Israel the economic aid it desperately wants. This argument has fallen flat. The administration, which was on the verge of being preempted by congressional action, rather readily agreed to give Israel $1.8 billion in military aid and $1.2 billion in economic aid for fiscal year 1986. An additional $1.5 billion is to go to Israel as an emergency grant that will be divided between fiscal years 1985 and 1986. When added to the military and economic aid package of fiscal 1985, the two-year total is a massive $7.1 billion.[26]

The administration's Middle East specialists have rejected the pressure-on-Peres argument on grounds that it ignores the difficulty Peres has in taking any significant steps at all without bringing down the government and forcing new elections that he might lose. The administration apparently is not prepared to try to modify Israel's position in connection with the peace process, while it endeavors—without notable success—to use economic leverage on Peres

26. Charlotte Saikowski, "U.S. Proceeds on Emergency Aid to Israel," *Christian Science Monitor,* 3 May 1985.

to bring about painful economic reforms. Pressure on Israel has long been regarded in Washington as counter productive. Agreements obtained in this way, the reasoning goes, will not hold up; instead, they must come through direct negotiations. In addition, from the administration's vantage point, why put pressure on Israel before the Arabs have produced an interesting proposal to which Israel can react favorably?

Another line of thought advocates that the United States take a vigorous role soon. The administration should take advantage of Reagan's second term's window of opportunity when it is still relatively unconstrained in dealing with the Middle East. Proponents of this approach argue that by September 1986, when Shamir is supposed to succeed Peres as prime minister, and certainly by the end of that year, the administration's effectiveness will be greatly diminished. It will be a lame duck concerned with its historic contribution to the Republic. The momentum is there now, but it needs to be increased by U.S. action; such action would strengthen the entire peace process. This argument focuses on what could happen if the United States sits tight, particularly if time is working against the forces of reason and moderation.

In the view of many analysts, without an active U.S. role coherence and coalition building will not necessarily occur in Israel, Jordan, and the West Bank with the passage of time, nor will the other changes take place in the political environment that will be needed to make negotiations possible. Quoting a gloomy French diplomat, John Newhouse observed that time, "if ignored, will lead to war, devastation and possibly some sort of realignment of the sort that followed the First World War. The peace process has become a tactic. No one believes in it."[27]

Overstated as this pessimistic view may be, these specialists make a strong case for the argument that Arabs and Israelis will never be ready for negotiations unless the United States plays a catalytic role, as it did at Camp David and in the negotiations that led to the disengagement agreements following the 1973 war. The miraculous window of opportunity is never open very wide or for very long. It tends to close when overtaken by other priorities. This is just as true of Israelis, Jordanians, and Egyptians as it is of Americans. All of them have different timetables and agendas, and all suffer from pressures from constituents. Other factors will have to be added to the Arab-Israeli equation to overcome the administration's inertia.

The Middle East, we know from experience, is a dangerous place. Hopeful trends are fragile and ephemeral, while "the tinder in the region is becoming drier."[28] Syria opposes what Hussein, Arafat, and Mubarak are doing, and Syria is important. Its president, Hafez al-Assad, is a key player. Despite heavy engagement in Lebanon, he thrives on ambiguity. But ambiguities, in a peace process, eventually will have to be cleared up. Assad probably figures that when they are, the emptiness of current diplomacy will be clear to all. Astute and purposeful, he has tried to maintain the isolation of Egypt, Syria's chief rival for regional influence. Syria also wants to undercut Arafat and dominate the Palestinian movement, and it is a major threat to Jordan. Moreover, many Middle East specialists worry about a war

27. John Newhouse, "A Small Window," *New Yorker,* 11 Mar. 1985, p. 117.

28. Ibid., p. 134.

between Syria and Israel. A war could stem from miscalculations by Israel or Syria over the situation in Israel's security zone in southern Lebanon and attacks on Israel from that area. Neither Israel nor Syria wants a war, but each regards the other as principal adversary and each may regard time as working against its position vis-à-vis the other.

Furthermore, many moderate Arab leaders are feeling vulnerable to Islamic extremism. This sense of vulnerability will increase their reluctance to make the unpopular compromises necessary for launching a peace process. It may also incline them gradually to distance themselves from the United States because of its perceived inability and unwillingness to promote a just solution to the Palestinian problem and its identification with Israel.

On the Israeli side, Abba Eban, for example, has advocated an active U.S. role to head off a blowup. "American passivity," he has written, "would condemn the Middle East to a volcanic status quo leading to possible explosion."[29] When Middle Eastern affairs are allowed to drift, Eban warns, extremists take charge and create the conditions for the next war. Eban worries that Arab moderates will be discredited if their reliance on the United States fails to produce any returns. He fears that the arguments of the rejectionists and fundamentalists will prevail. They reason that only a serious threat to U.S. interests will oblige the United States to come to its senses and abandon Israel.

Although Islamic extremism is not necessarily a tidal wave that will engulf all the friends of the United States in the Middle East, it thrives on frustration and alienation and especially on the failure of Arab governments to meet popular aspirations. The inability of Arab leaders, particularly those closely aligned with the United States, to obtain justice for the Palestinians fuels extremism, especially in Egypt, Jordan, and the West Bank. If this argument has merit, it means that the U.S. position in the Middle East gradually will erode, reversing the progress that has been made in the past decade in bolstering U.S. influence in Middle East calculations.

Finally, the United States has a big investment in the Egyptian-Israeli relationship. The relationship is not healthy; indeed, it is a ragged and cold peace. Without a peace process, however, it will deteriorate despite the likelihood of a summit meeting between Peres and Mubarak and their interest in improved relations. If the United States is serious about wanting to nurture its network of bilateral relationships in the Middle East, and if in the next few months it wants to bolster moderate Arab regimes, it must face the fact that a lack of apparent headway in the peace process will tend to undercut the positions of the moderates and boost those of the hardliners.

Unfortunately for those who make these arguments, the administration lacks both a concern about the course of events in the Middle East over the longer term and a sense that an ongoing peace process is needed to avoid another lost opportunity to capture the initiative. Although the administration is moving hesitantly toward doing something to encourage the peace process, there is as yet no indication in administration pronouncements that the United States has a clear idea of the nature and scope of the role it will have to play to promote direct negotiations.

29. Abba Eban, "No Choice but Activism," *Foreign Policy,* no. 57, pp. 3-7 (Winter 1984-85).

Alas, those responsible for deciding to take action often are oblivious to the need for it until it is too late. But when is the time ripe? How will anyone know while Arabs and Israelis try to clarify positions, guard their flanks, and determine for themselves when the time has come for their own involvement? The difficult choice is not whether to do something but to make the proper decision at the right time based on sound analysis. This is precisely the area of the policy process in which doubt and inertia tend to reign supreme. And doubt produces both passivity and the conviction that the burden of decision making rests on other actors.

In this case, the delicate task is one of determining how the United States should position itself vis-à-vis the peace process. Standing too far back could exert a negative influence. Too much involvement, in the absence of changes in the political environment, could be premature. At a minimum, the United States might say to its Arab friends that Washington wants to be part of the peace process. It wants to keep the diplomatic activity alive, and it is thinking about new ways of doing what it wants to do. This is a long way from a major effort to broker a settlement of all outstanding political and territorial questions, but it goes considerably beyond the perusal of lists of acceptable Palestinians to whom the United States might agree to talk as part of the joint Palestinian-Jordanian delegation.

Is this passive stance sensible, or does it run the risk of losing an opportunity to make progress toward negotiations? Is it true that the policy of tiptoeing back into Middle East diplomacy is working because it is pressuring Arab leaders to take diplomatic action? Making the Arabs come to the United States may not be a bad tactic, but the constant U.S. effort to throw the ball back to Arab leaders may lead our friends to conclude that no matter what they do, the United States will not urge the Israelis to budge. In short, will this posture pressure the two sides to do more, or will our Arab interlocutors give up in dismay and frustation? Perhaps there will be no negotiations unless the political costs of no settlement exceed those of making concessions.

On the other hand, as John Newhouse has observed, there is always the temptation in the Middle East to treat all initiatives with skepticism. Pessimism about peace tends to prevail in the absence of dramatic breakthroughs. It is the norm in the Middle East. But, "just as the prospect of hanging concentrates the mind, the despair of Arab moderates is pushing them hard to make something happen—to create a gleam of hope."[30] That is what momentum is all about, and that is where the United States comes in.

30. Newhouse, "Small Window," p. 134.

* * *

QUESTIONS AND ANSWERS

Q (Dario Scuka, Library of Congress, Washington, D.C.): Your description of U.S. policy toward the Arab-Israeli conflict suggests substantial improvisation without any long-term goals in sight. Do we have to wait for a crisis in order to have a policy in place, especially under currently developing circumstances in which the Israeli economy has become a virtual ward of the United States government?

A: In the absence of a crisis, or a dramatic initiative taken by someone else, administrations are very reluctant to take initiatives. Rather than seize opportunities that may be only dimly perceived, they tend to sit back until they have to do something; that has been the record in the past. If we do not see a crisis or a dramatic initiative, persuading the administration to take the risks of involvement becomes much more difficult, especially if the issue is of low priority. I think that we are likely to see this pattern of reluctance continue over the next several months, although that is not to say the Reagan administration does not want to do anything.

I think there are people in the administration who think something ought to be done. They are not quite sure how to do it; they do not seem to have a very clear concept of what is involved. The focus on direct negotiations as an end in itself, without paying any attention to what is needed in order to begin those negotiations, is symbolic or indicative of the very limited perspective of this administration on what is happening, what the opportunities and risks are, and where we want to be over the next two or three years.

Q (Thomas Harlick, Orange County Community College, Middletown, New York): I have two questions. First, we are trying to start negotiations among Israel, Jordan, and the Palestine Liberation Organization (PLO). After Lebanon, the catastrophes that befell the PLO in Lebanon and the PLO's fragmentation, which segment of the PLO, in fact, would we talk with? And even if we talked with one segment, is there any way in which we can ensure that other segments of the PLO would not reject those talks or even possibly assassinate those who do talk with us?

Second, I can see why we might motivate the PLO to negotiate on the West Bank: time is running out and it is running out very quickly. But given the fact that Israel has built such a massive infrastructure, economically, socially, and politically, on the West Bank, what motivation is there for Israel to negotiate the West Bank issue?

A: I think that it is a cop-out on the part of many people in Washington to say we canot talk to anybody in the PLO because we do not know what they represent or because it is a rump group and what about the others, and so forth. The problem, however, is the one I referred to before. The PLO—including Arafat and the so-called moderates—is not very interested in talking to us unless it thinks we are serious. And are we serious enough to begin to deal with the Israelis in terms of the kinds of compromises the PLO people think are worthwhile? Of course, they—including many moderates—do not think there is any time left. They do not think the Americans are serious about any peace initiative or that we are prepared to put a fair amount of our relationship with Israel on the line. Therefore, why should they get into something that will have no results? Making their concessions up front and then finding nothing in return is the basic dilemma that has haunted policymakers on the Palestinian issue for years.

How do we get around that dilemma? The administration says, in effect, that if the Arabs and the Palestinians—principally those Palestinians living on the

West Bank—want to live the way they are, their lives only getting worse for the foreseeable future and even beyond, then that is their problem. If they want to do something about it, they will have to deal with the Israelis, the Jordanians, and the Egyptians. If the Jordanians, the Egyptians, and the West Bankers can come up with some useful position that will have a beneficial effect on the Israeli position, it will cause a tremendous debate in Israel. The Israelis will then have to decide whether or not they want to make some sort of an arrangement principally with the West Bankers themselves and their Arab allies that will enable the Israelis to resolve future demographic issues, moral issues, and many other problems. The administration would say that when the Arabs come up with something good, it then can go to the Israelis, who will already be in a turmoil over the whole package, and play a useful role. That is what it boils down to in the administration's view; but this scenario has not yet come to pass.

Now as to whether the Benvenisti clock in effect says 11:55, 11:59, or 12:02, I would guess that the process is not irreversible, not yet. I think Benvenisti himself was a little surprised that everybody concluded it was, on the basis of his study—even though the study showed about twice as many Israeli settlers on the West Bank as everybody thought, some 42,000, as I remember.

I think he would say that it is not hopeless, principally, in his view, because of what will happen in Israel in the absence of some kind of an arrangement. The challenge facing not the U.S. govenment but the Israeli government and the Palestinian leadership is coming up with positions, on the one hand, and forming the kinds of political coalitions that would be needed in order to move into negotiations, on the other. This challenge is a tremendous burden on both sides.

I think Shimon Peres probably recognizes that if the Arabs do come up with a good proposal, the coalition in Israel will collapse and there will be new elections in Israel as a result. I think he wants to be sure he comes out on top. From the shuffling that would occur when a real alternative from the Arab side is confronted, Peres sees himself, I think, as the one who will emerge to lead Israel into the new era.

Public opinion in Israel is very much divided on the West Bank issue. I think Peres knows that. I think the administration in Washington knows it, too, but it does not find that the time is opportune yet to do anything about it. Some people would argue—and I would probably be among them—that opportune times do not necessarily just come down the road; opportunities have to be made or enhanced. One cannot just sit back and hope that something will turn up; one cannot use the word "hopefully" all the time, the way the Reagan administration does.

Q (David Brook, Jersey City State College, New Jersey): There is the possibility that the passage of time might in itself lessen dangers and create a better atmosphere for peace. We know from other historical and political situations that when controversial governments and states have been created, after a while even their strongest opponents begin to accept them. For example, the Soviet Union was not recognized for a number of years and the same thing was true of the People's Republic of China.

Could not the same type of evolution be occurring with the Arab-Israeli issue? Would it not be wiser for us to wait until the passage of time makes practical issues more important than the basic issue—at least in the Arab mind—of destroying Israel?

A: Time can work both ways. The passage of time has been one of the things that put pressure on moderate Arabs to begin to think about forming their own coalition around some kind of a useful position because they think that their position, from various points of view, will worsen in the future.

On the Israeli side, some seem to think that they are in such good shape that it is not worth taking risks to change anything, because compromises are dangerous. But many Israelis feel that time is not helping the problem of what Israel wants to be. I think the sense, on both sides, that time is detrimental to the peace process is one of the things that is leading to a flurry of initiatives and signs of flexibility here and there—although this activity is a long way from any kind of negotiating process.

It is certainly the Reagan administration's view that a prolonged passage of time will motivate both sides to develop better proposals, and that in the meantime U.S. interests are not suffering too much. Others would say that the United States cannot be complacent about its position in the Middle East and that it has to decide whether it is just going to sit back and let time pass or whether there are benefits to be gained from doing something more. That is the debate that is taking place, not yet inside the administration, it seems, but outside the administration among its supporters and adversaries alike.

I have mixed views about this, but my basic view is that the passage of time will not initiate a solution to the Arab-Israeli problem. Moreover, a useful role can be played by outsiders. It may not be exactly the right time for the United States to assume such a role, but it might be the right time for the United States to begin to think about how it will position itself vis-à-vis this problem over the longer term. Longer-term planning, however, is the U.S. government's weak suit; it never gets taken seriously. The people who do long-range planning end up working in a crisis working group because crises are fun and planning is dull. And nobody ever got promoted by being skilled at long-range planning. As a result, the passage of time in the policy process tends to produce a certain amount of knuckle gnawing about what bad things appear for the immediate future; nobody is interested in the catastrophes that may lurk a few months beyond that.

Q (George Gruen, Institute of Human Relations, New York City): First, it was mentioned that in the Arafat-Hussein agreement there was a reference to U.N. Security Council Resolution 242. I believe that at best it was an allusion, not a reference, because the agreement declares acceptance of all U.N. and Security Council resolutions relevant to the Palestine question. King Hussein has been very clear in asserting that it is now time to accept 242 as a basis for negotiations. Other elements are also required for negotiations, including Palestinian self-determination, and negotiations would have to occur in a context of a Jordanian-Palestinian federation.

The second question is, To what extent is there really a meeting of the minds on the Arab side? There still seems to be a debate between King Hussein and the PLO about the return of the Israeli-occupied territories and the confederation of those territories.

The third question concerns the country that will be next to the Palestinian state, namely, Israel. The Palestinians will say that their position toward Israel has evolved from total rejection, no negotiation, no recognition, and no peace to acceptance and peace. But they envision an Israel with at most pre-1967 borders, and they anticipate a Palestinian state that includes the West Bank and has East Jerusalem as its capital.

A recent public opinion poll from Hanoch Smith in Israel sought to measure Israeli public reaction to the Mubarak-Hussein idea of a meeting in Cairo with a joint Palestinian-Jordanian delegation. Close to 60 percent—possibly slightly more—of the Israeli public welcomed Peres's favorable response to the idea. Israeli public opinion is volatile; it will change if there is a real offer on the table. For example, Moshe Dayan used to say that if he had a choice between physical control of Sharm el Sheikh and a piece of paper signed by the Egyptians, he would hold onto Sharm el Sheikh. But when Sadat proposed that Israel relinquish all of Sinai, including Sharm el Sheikh, in exchange for real peace, Dayan reversed his position and became one of the strongest advocates of Sadat's proposal.

The last point is that it is crucial to see what is said by the Arabs at Fez, what is said by the Hussein-Arafat agreement. The issue is, What are the intentions? Sadat was outspoken, it was clear where he was coming from. The fear from the Israeli view is that there is a split in the Palestinian camp between the West Bankers, who might be willing to negotiate because they want to get rid of the Israeli occupation, and the major constituency of the PLO, namely the refugees who came from the pre-1948 Israel, not from the West Bank. For the latter Palestinians, a solution of a mini-Palestinian state does not bring about what they would like or have historically sought: a return to their homes. A return to their homes in their view has historically meant a return to a nonexistent Israel. In other words, it has meant the destruction of Israel, not a willingness to live in peace as citizens of Israel. So the ultimate question is, Is this offer that now seems to be on the table for peace with Israel a final, permanent, peaceful arrangement, or is it a first stage in a series in which at first an independent Palestinian state is established in any area from which Israel withdraws but finally Israeli is destroyed? What troubles the Israelis is that there is no reference to Israel or the word "Israel" in the Fez declaration, nor a reference to 242 in the Hussein-Arafat agreement. I would like to see the Israelis move forward. For such movement to occur, I think it is crucial that the United States convince the Arabs that clarity in the Arab position is important.

A: If all the so-called Arab plans were combined there still would be no course of action. But having a course of action at this stage of the game would be unusual. What we are beginning to see is a process among some Arabs with some support of the West Bankers to develop a plan. The Reagan administration emphasizes how much more work the Arabs have to do before achieving some comprehensive peace proposals. Israel, too, sees that there is much work to do, but Peres is trying to encourage the Arabs to do more. In fact in some ways he is ahead of the Reagan administration in this process.

On the Israeli side, there is plenty of hope among a substantial number of Israelis. Their hope depends on what plan is offered. If something looks halfway decent or it seems to be moving in a decent direction I think favorable Israeli opinion would be a lot stronger, and Israelis would accept the plan as a way out of their painful dilemma concerning the future.

For now, however, we do not want to spend much time analyzing the various existing plans because they are so underdeveloped. The shortcomings of the plans reflect the internal difficulties of the various Arab parties. Now the question for the United States is, Is there something useful we can do at this prenegotiation stage? Lack of U.S. action will be taken by the Arabs as a lack of U.S. support. The Arabs will feel that any plan they develop is unfairly criticized by the Americans and the Israelis. The Arabs may well conclude that there is absolutely no way they can come up with any plan that anybody would be interested in. There already are those in the Arab world who say that nothing is going to work. These people perceive the Israelis as too tough, too stuck on their own view of things, and the Americans as too close to the Israelis. On the whole, however, I do not think the Arab side—at least not Jordan, Arafat and some of his people, or the Egyptians—perceives the situation as hopeless. We would be mistaken to expect the Saudis to play a useful role in this. On the other hand, we would be mistaken to label the Syrians as permanent hard-liners or Soviet stooges and not deal with them. The difficult thing for the United States is to formulate something beneficial and useful in this very early phase, something that will not throw cold water on current attempts at peace proposals and that will not make us too prominent or make us come up a failure. That is the challenge.

COMMENT (Freedman): I think there are a couple of things we might want to consider in looking at the peace process. At the same time that the Reagan plan was immediately denounced by Prime Minister Begin, Shimon Peres, then in the opposition party, said a number of very positive things about it. And Peres has been ahead of the Reagan administration in encouraging the peace process. The bottom line seems to be that Peres must be able to go to the Israeli population in an election and present them something that is more than either the Hussein-Arafat agreement or Fez 2, let alone the Fahd plan or Fez 1.

The second factor concerns the settlements on the West Bank. There are really three kinds of settlements there. First, there are the suburbs of Jerusalem and some immediate areas around Tel Aviv. The majority of the population is there. There there are some security settlements along the Jordan River that are part of the old Allon plan. The idea was that an Arab invasion could be prevented by means of these military settlements. The bulk of the West Bank could be returned to Jordan. The third level of the settlements were brought in or inspired by or reinforced by the Begin group when it was in power from 1977 to 1984. The Begin strategy was to increase the number of these settlements around heavily populated Arab areas. This type of settlement has the smallest percentage of Jewish settlers. As of April 1985 there do not seem tobe either so many of these settlements or, more important, so many Israelis living in them that the settlements could not be ultimately given up or some other arrangement worked out for them.

Q (Clark Mueller, University of North Alabama, Florence): The observation has been made that a lack of perceived headway in the peace process will undercut the position of the moderates. First, what kind of headway is necessary? Second, if headway is not made—and I think there is good reason to suspect it will not be—is it necessarily the case that the position of the moderates will be undercut?

A: Headway is a perceptual concept, not a fact. Arab governments consider that the unresolved Palestinian dimension of the Arab-Israeli conflict has an effect on their populations. It worsens the leaders' failure quotient, you might say.

Not all of the Arab populations are so desperate about doing something for the Palestinians, and that desire varies, obviously, from one country to another. It is much more important, for example, to act on behalf of the Palestinians in Jordan, which has a big Palestinian majority. Nevertheless, the failure of Arab governments to deal effectively with this issue is perceived by Arab leaders as undercutting their position.

Headway does not mean very much necessarily. I was trying to suggest that it gives some cause for optimism in Arab countries that the situation is getting better, that somebody is engaged in an interesting process that may offer some hope for the future, that people are dealing at last with the Palestinian issue.

The United States needs to be serious in its efforts; the Israelis need to be flexible. At the moment there is a little optimism that what is happening now may lead to something better. That optimism might be enough for some of the Arab governments, but it will not last for long. I think this short life is what the governments fear. It is what lies behind the urgent pleas by Arab visitors to the United States to get the United States to come to its senses. Arab leaders talk to the United States about its responsibility as a superpower. What they mean is that the United States has a responsibility to help its friends who feel threatened by the absence of any optimism about this problem. In fact some of them said it very bluntly.

When Arab leaders look at trends, they tend to be pessimists. Hussein has been a pessimist all his life; he is the master of gloom and doom. Mubarak is more optimistic. It is hard to make such a sweeping statement, but I think Egyptians in general feel better about themselves and the future than do Jordanians. They are more buoyant, although not quite as buoyant as Sadat, who got way out of step with his own people—but there are differences in how Arab governments see that situation. But even the Egyptians have begun to feel certain pressures, which are noticeable in Cairo's television coverage of Egyptian leaders. Some of the wives are now wearing Islamic dress. Two years ago this would not have been the case, but now Islamic dress is commonplace even at the universities.

The leadership is beginning to feel the need to pander to these sentiments. They have the feeling that they must do something right, and that the only way they can do it is to persuade the Americans to become deeply involved in the peace process. The Reagan administration, however, is unwilling to be involved unless the Arab governments are willing to do more for themselves. I think that the dynamics of the situation itself are leading the Arab governments to form coalitions and alliances internally and with each other that will enable them, with U.S. assistance, to make the kind of headway that will show their own people and the Palestinians that something good is happening. In that sense making headway is both psychologically and politically important.

ANNALS, *AAPSS*, **482**, November 1985

Patterns of Soviet Policy toward the Middle East

By ROBERT O. FREEDMAN

ABSTRACT: Soviet policy toward the Middle East since the 1973 Arab-Israeli war has been essentially reactive in nature, as Moscow has reacted to events in the region that it neither caused nor had much ability to control. Moscow has benefited from some events, such as the fall of the shah, the formation of an Arab anti-Camp David alignment, and U.S. policy errors in Lebanon. Just as frequently, however, Moscow's position in the Middle East has suffered from regional events, such as the movement of Egypt into the American camp, the outbreak and continuation of the Iran-Iraq war, and the numerous internecine splits in the Arab world. The arms that Moscow has poured into the Middle East have not given Moscow much influence in the region. Thus Moscow could not prevent Egypt's exit from the Soviet camp, the signing of the Camp David agreements, or the reestablishment of relations between Egypt and Jordan. Despite continued efforts, the USSR has been unable to bring about an end to the Iran-Iraq war or the rift between Assad and Arafat, nor has it gained solid support for the various versions of its Arab-Israeli peace plan.

Dr. Robert O. Freedman is Peggy Meyerhoff Pearlstone Professor of Political Science and dean of graduate studies at the Baltimore Hebrew College. He is author of Economic Warfare in the Communist Bloc *(1970) and* Soviet Policy toward the Middle East since 1970 *(1982), now in its third edition. He is also the editor of* World Politics and the Arab-Israeli Conflict *(1979),* Israel in the Begin Era *(1982),* Soviet Jewry in the Decisive Decade 1971-1980 *(1984), and* The Middle East since Camp David *(1984).*

ANYONE seeking to understand the nature of Soviet policy in the Middle East must immediately come to grips with two central questions. First, are Moscow's primary goals in the region offensive or defensive in nature? Second, do the Soviet leaders follow one underlying strategy as they pursue their goals in the Middle East or is their policy determined on a country-by-country basis? Different analysts have answered these two questions in different ways and their answers often contain, whether openly or not, policy prescriptions as to how the United States should deal with Soviet activity in the Middle East.

Concerning Soviet goals in the Middle East, there are two major schools of thought.[1] While both agree that the Soviet Union wants to be considered as a major factor in Middle Eastern affairs, if only because of the USSR's propinquity to the region, they differ on the ultimate Soviet goal in the Middle East. One school sees Soviet Middle Eastern policy as being primarily defensive in nature, directed toward preventing the region from being used as a base for military attack or political subversion against the USSR. The other school regards Soviet policy as primarily offensive, aimed at the limitation and ultimate exclusion of Western influence from the region and its replacement by Soviet influence.

The policy implications of this debate are clear. If Moscow is basically defensively oriented in the Middle East, then it is not only possible but actually desirable for the United States to work with the USSR to bring about settlements of such conflicts as those between the Arab states and Israel and between Iran and Iraq. Conversely, if Moscow's goals are offensive, then it is undesirable to try to bring Moscow into the peace process because the Soviet leaders would only exploit the opportunity to weaken the position of the United States. It is my opinion that Soviet goals in the Middle East, at least since the mid-1960s, have been primarily offensive in nature and in the Arab areas of the Middle East, the Soviet Union appears to have been engaged in a zero-sum competition for influence with the United States.

Whether Moscow follows one underlying strategy or functions on a country-by-country, or subregional, basis is also hotly debated. Those analysts who see the Soviet leadership as following a single strategy usually base their viewpoint on the belief that Marxist-Leninist ideology still holds some meaning for the decision makers in Moscow, while those who believe the USSR is acting on a more locally tailored basis in the region treat Moscow as just another great power, not unlike czarist Russia in the nineteenth century. I believe Moscow does in fact pursue one underlying strategy in the Middle East, which is influenced, at least in part, by Marxist-

1. For recent studies of Soviet policy in the Middle East, see Robert O. Freedman, *Soviet Policy toward the Middle East since 1970,* 3rd ed. (New York: Praeger, 1982); Jon D. Glassman, *Arms for the Arabs: The Soviet Union and War in the Middle East* (Baltimore, MD: Johns Hopkins University Press, 1975); Galia Golan, *Yom Kippur and After: The Soviet Union and the Middle East Crisis* (London: Cambridge University Press, 1977); Yaacov Ro'i, *From Encroachment to Involvement: A Documentary Study of Soviet Policy in the Middle East* (Jerusalem: Israel Universities Press, 1974); and Adeed Dawisha and Karen Dawisha, eds., *The Soviet Union in the Middle East: Policies and Perspectives* (New York: Holmes & Meier, 1982); see also Yaacov Ro'i, ed., *The Limits to Power* (London: Croom Helm, 1979). For an Arab viewpoint, see Mohamed Heikal, *The Sphinx and the Commissar* (New York: Harper & Row, 1978); for a Soviet view, see E.M. Primakov, *Anatomy of the Middle East Conflict* (Moscow: Mysl, 1978).

Leninist ideology. Prior to examining overall Soviet strategy toward the region, however, it is necessary to analyze the tactics Moscow uses to expand its influence in the Middle East and the obstacles it faces.

In its efforts to promote Soviet influence while weakening and ultimately eliminating Western influence from the Middle East, particularly from the Arab world, the Soviet leadership has employed a number of tactics. Most important has been the provision of military aid to its clients in the region.[2] Next comes economic aid. The Aswan Dam in Egypt and the Euphrates Dam in Syria are prominent examples of Soviet economic assistance, although each project has had serious problems. In recent years, Moscow has also sought to solidify its influence through concluding long-term friendship-and-cooperation treaties such as those with Egypt in 1971, Iraq in 1972, Somalia in 1974, Ethiopia in 1978, Afghanistan in 1978, South Yemen in 1979, Syria in 1980, and North Yemen in 1984. Repudiations of the treaties by Egypt in 1976 and Somalia in 1977 indicate that this has not always been a successful tactic.

Moscow has attempted to exploit both the lingering memories of Western colonialism and the Western threats against Arab oil producers, and it has, as in the assassination of Indira Gandhi, deliberately used disinformation to discredit American policy.[3] The USSR has also sought influence through the establishment of ties between the Communist Party of the Soviet Union and such Arab ruling political parties as the Syrian Baath and the Algerian National Liberation Front. Yet another tactic aimed at gaining influence has been the provision of security infrastructure assistance to countries such as South Yemen and Ethiopia. Finally, Moscow has offered the Arabs military and diplomatic aid against Israel, although that assistance has been limited in scope because the USSR continues to support Israel's right to exist. The Russians fear alienating the United States, with which they desire additional stategic arms agreements and improved trade relations and they also regard Israel as a convenient rallying point for potentially anti-Western forces in the Arab world.[4]

While the USSR has used all these tactics, with varying degrees of success over the last two decades, it has also run into serious problems in its quest for influence in the Middle East. First there are numerous inter-Arab and regional conflicts—such as that between Syria and Iraq, or between Algeria and Morocco—and when the USSR has favored one party, it has alienated the other, often driving it over to the West.

Second, the existence of Middle Eastern Communist parties has proven to be a handicap for the USSR, as Communist activities have, on occasion, caused a sharp deterioration in relations between Moscow and the country in which the Communist party has operated. The Communist-supported coup d'etat in the Sudan in 1971, Communist efforts to organize cells in the Iraqi army in the

2. For studies of Soviet military aid, see Glassman, *Arms for the Arabs;* and George Lenczowski, *Soviet Advances in the Middle East* (Washington, DC: American Enterprise Institute, 1972); see also Amnon Sella, *Soviet Political and Military Conduct in the Middle East* (New York: St. Martin's Press, 1981); and Bruce D. Porter, *The USSR in Third World Conflicts* (New York: Cambridge University Press, 1984).

3. See Richard H. Shultz and Roy Godson, *Dezinformatsia: Active Measures in Soviet Strategy* (New York: Pergamon-Brassey's, 1984).

4. For a view of the role of Israel in Soviet Middle East strategy, see Freedman, *Soviet Policy toward the Middle East since 1970,* chap. 8.

mid- and late 1970s, and the activities of the Tudeh Party in Khomeini's Iran are recent examples of this problem.[5]

Third, the wealth that flowed to the Arab world—or at least to its major oil producers—since the quadrupling of oil prices in late 1973 has enabled the Arabs to buy quality technology from the West and Japan, which has weakened the economic bond between the USSR and such Arab states as Iraq.

Fourth, since 1967 and particularly after the 1973 Arab-Israeli war, Islam has been resurgent throughout the Arab world. Identified in the Arab world with atheism, the USSR has been hampered as a result, espeically since invading Afghanistan in 1979, where it has been fighting against an essentially Islamic resistance force.

Fifth, in the diplomacy surrounding the Arab-Israeli conflict, Moscow is limited by its lack of diplomatic ties with Israel, a factor that enables the United States alone to talk to both sides in the conflict.

Finally, the United States, and to a lesser extent, France and China, have actively opposed Soviet efforts to achieve predominant influence in the region. Middle Eastern states, therefore, are frequently able to play the extraregional powers off against each other, preventing any one of them from securing predominant influence.

5. For studies of Soviet policy toward the Communist parties of the Arab world, see Robert O. Freedman, "The Soviet Union and the Communist Parties of the Arab World: An Uncertain Relationship," in *Soviet Economic and Political Relations with the Developing World,* ed. Roger E. Kanet and Donna Bahry (New York: Praeger, 1975), pp. 100-134; John K. Cooley, "The Shifting Sands of Arab Communism," *Problems of Communism,* 24(2):22-42 (1975); and Arnold Huttinger, "Arab Communism at a Low Ebb," *Problems of Communism,* 30(3):17-32 (July-Aug. 1981).

To overcome these difficulties, Moscow has evolved one overall strategy: the development of what it terms an anti-imperialist bloc of states in the Arab world. Moscow wants these states to bury their internecine rivalries and, along with such political organizations as the Arab Communist parties and the Palestine Liberation Organization (PLO), form a united front against what the USSR has called the linchpin of Western imperialism in the Middle East: Israel. The Russians hope that the Arab states will then use their collective pressure against Israel's supporters, especially the United States.

The ideal scenario for Moscow, one to which Soviet commentators have frequently referred, occurred during the 1973 Arab-Israeli war—the Yom Kippur War—when virtually all the Arab states supported the war effort against Israel, while also imposing an oil embargo against the United States. Not only did the oil embargo create domestic difficulties for the United States; it also caused serious problems in the North Atlantic Treaty Organization (NATO), a development that was warmly welcomed by Moscow. Unfortunately for the USSR, however, this anti-imperialist Arab unity was created not by Soviet efforts, but by the diplomacy of Egyptian President Anwar el-Sadat. When Sadat changed his policies and turned toward the United States, the anti-imperialist Arab unity sought by the USSR fell apart. Nonetheless, so long as Soviet leaders think in terms of such Leninist categories as united fronts—"anti-imperialist" Arab unity, in Soviet parlance, is merely another way of describing a united front of Arab governmental and nongovernmental forces—and so long as there is a deep underlying psychological drive for unity in the Arab world, Moscow can be expected to continue to pursue this overall strategy as a long-term goal.

SOVIET POLICY 1973-85: AN OVERVIEW

In the aftermath of the Yom Kippur War, Moscow increasingly found itself on the sidelines of Middle Eastern diplomacy. Having intervened on the side of Egypt and Syria during the war and having encouraged the Arab oil embargo against the United States during and after the conflict, the Soviet leadership subsequently saw its fortunes decline. First Egypt and then Syria restored diplomatic relations with the United States; the oil embargo was lifted; U.S. Secretary of State Henry Kissinger mediated two Israeli withdrawals in the Sinai, in January 1974 and August 1975, and one on the Golan Heights, in May 1974. Egypt gradually moved into the American camp, despite billions of rubles in military and economic aid and the considerable risks Moscow had incurred on Egypt's behalf both during the War of Attrition in 1970 and the Yom Kippur War. While Syria did not follow Egypt into the American camp, it became increasingly embroiled in a conflict with Iraq, with which Moscow was also seeking close ties, and with the PLO as well, by 1976.

The problem of internecine conflict among the Soviet Union's Arab friends came to a head in 1976 during the Lebanese civil war. Syria, Moscow's primary Middle Eastern ally, sided with the Christian Lebanese against the PLO and its Muslim allies and subsequently found itself isolated. Soviet fortunes were to improve, however, following the election of Jimmy Carter as the new American president. Jettisoning Kissinger's step-by-step approach, Carter embarked on an effort to achieve a comprehensive Middle East peace settlement and decided that Moscow could be a suitable partner in this endeavor. The end result of this process was the joint Soviet-American statement on the Middle East of 1 October 1977, which called, among other things, for the reconvening of the Geneva conference by December 1977.[6]

Yet in bringing Moscow back into the center of Middle East peacemaking—a major gain for Moscow—Carter made a serious error because the Soviet concept of a Middle East peace settlement was very different from that held by the United States. As it has evolved since 1973, the Soviet peace plan has consisted of three major components: (1) Israeli withdrawal from all territory captured in the 1967 war; (2) the establishment of a Palestinian state on the West Bank and Gaza; and (3) the acknowledgment of the right to exist of all states in the region, including Israel. According to Soviet leaders, the main vehicle for reaching such a peace settlement would be an international conference—preferably a reconvened Geneva conference that would be chaired by the USSR along with the United States—attended by all parties to the conflict, including the PLO.

The Soviet peace plan is clearly to Moscow's advantage. First, it would preserve the state of Israel, the existence of which has become an important part of Soviet strategy in the Middle East. As stated earlier, the Soviet Union has sought to consolidate anti-imperialist Arab unity around Arab enmity toward

6. For a discussion of the events leading up to the 1 October 1977 joint statement, and for an evaluation of it, see Freedman, *Soviet Policy toward the Middle East since 1970,* pp. 307-11.

Israel. An Israeli withdrawal to the prewar 1967 lines would not remove the potential threat of a future Israeli attack on the Arabs, or vice versa, or the memories of the generations-long Arab-Israeli conflict. Indeed, by supporting the concept of a limited peace, while opposing a more extensive solution in which Israel would have trade, cultural, and diplomatic relations with its neighbors,[7] the Soviet Union would hope to keep some latent hostility alive in the Arab-Israeli relationship. This would force the Arabs to retain at least a modicum of unity against the putative Israeli threat. The Soviet leaders evidently hope they could then exploit that unity to enhance their own influence in the Middle East and weaken that of the United States. In any case, continuing tension in the Arab-Israeli relationship would reinforce Moscow's importance as an arms supplier to the Arabs.

A second benefit of the plan would be the termination of the American role as mediator in the Arab-Israeli peace process. This role has been a key to American influence in the Arab world since the 1973 war, for it demonstrated to the Arabs that it was the United States, and not the Soviet Union, that was able to secure Israeli territorial withdrawals. Once a limited but final agreement—as opposed to another partial one—were reached, the necessity for American mediation would be ended. The Soviet leaders may reason that this would lead to a drop in U.S. prestige and influence in the Arab world, as well as to an end to the quarrels among the Arab states over making peace with Israel, quarrels that have impeded the Soviet drive to help create anti-imperialist Arab unity.

Yet another benefit would be that by preserving Israel, the plan would not alienate the United States. Given the strong emotional and political ties between the United States and Israel, the Soviet Union would jeopardize the remnants of détente and the chances for a Senate ratification of another strategic arms agreement if it sought to destroy Israel. For this reason, if for no other, the Soviet leadership, in speeches to Arab leaders as well as in peace plans, has endorsed Israel's right to exist as an independent state. Concomitantly, the establishment of a limited Arab-Israeli peace would also lessen the possibility of a superpower conflict erupting from an Arab-Israeli war.

The establishment of an independent Palestinian state, which Moscow began to advocate in late 1973, might well benefit the Soviet Union. The Soviet leadership obviously hoped in 1977—and still seems to hope today—that such a state would be an ally of Soviet policy in the Arab world and would help combat American influence. Given that Moscow's closest Arab allies—South Yemen, Syria, and Libya—are mistrusted by their fellow Arab nations, the Soviet Union would clearly gain from having another ally in the very center of the Middle East. In addition, the Soviet leadership appears to believe that a Palestinian state on the West Bank and Gaza would be dependent on Soviet support because of its location between a hostile Israel and a suspicious Jordan that is mindful of past PLO attempts to overthrow its government.

7. In an editorial in 1977 in the Soviet foreign policy weekly *New Times* it was asserted that "it is no secret that by 'real peace' the Tel Aviv expansionists mean the notorious 'open borders' between Israel and its Arab neighbors, the 'free movement of peoples and goods', and even 'cooperation in respect of security'—all of which would make Tel Aviv the center of a huge neo-colonialist 'empire' in the Middle East." *New Times,* no. 36, p. 1 (1977).

Gains and losses

While Moscow may have hoped that convening the Geneva conference in December 1977 would have created momentum in favor of its peace plan, these expectations were not realized. Indeed, the joint Soviet-American peace statement became moot because the surprise visit of Sadat to Jerusalem in November 1977 and the subsequent Camp David agreements changed the face of Middle Eastern diplomacy. Moscow was again thrown on the defensive and quickly expressed its concern that other Arab states would follow Egypt's example by signing what the Soviet media decried as "a separate deal" with Israel. Indeed, since September 1978, Moscow has been constantly preoccupied with the dangers of an expanded Camp David process. Consequently, one of the central thrusts of its Middle Eastern policy has been to try to isolate Egypt in the Arab world and thereby prevent any expansion of Camp David.

Fortunately for Moscow, there was almost universal Arab antipathy toward the Camp David agreements and the subsequent Egyptian-Israeli peace treaty of March 1979. Indeed, Moscow had hopes that the large Arab coalition that had come together at Baghdad in November 1978 to denounce Camp David—a coalition highlighted by the rapprochement between Syria and Iraq—might form the anti-imperialist Arab bloc the USSR had sought for so long.

At the same time that Moscow was taking satisfaction from the formation of the anti-Camp David bloc in the Arab world, it received another bonus—the fall of the Shah of Iran. Under the Nixon Doctrine the shah had become the U.S. policeman of the oil-rich Persian Gulf and had been liberally supplied with U.S. weaponry as a result. In addition, because of the shah's close ties with Egypt and his positive relations with both Saudi Arabia and Israel, Iran served as the pivot of what might be termed a U.S.-aligned Middle Eastern grouping of those states that, by combining military and petrodollar power, effectively limited Soviet influence in the region. This tacit alignment suffered its first blow after Camp David when ties between Egypt and Saudi Arabia were severely strained; diplomatic relations were to be broken after the signing of the Egyptian-Israeli peace treaty. Subsequently, the shah fell and the successor Khomeini regime adopted a very hostile attitude both to Israel and to Egypt. U.S. policy appeared to be left in shambles.

Moscow then moved to try to prevent any rapprochement of Iran with the United States by quickly coming out in support of the terrorists who seized the U.S. embassy in Iran in November 1979 and spreading disinformation that the U.S. was about to attack Iran during the final stages of the hostage-release talks in January 1981.[8]

While these developments were clearly bonuses for Moscow in its zero-sum competition with the United States for influence in the Middle East, the USSR subsequently ran into serious difficulties because of two major events that were to have a very negative effect on its position: its invasion of Afghanistan and the outbreak of the Iran-Iraq war.

There appear to be two overriding causes of the Soviet invasion of Afghanistan in December 1979.[9] First, the Com-

8. These incidents are discussed in Freedman, *Soviet Policy toward the Middle East since 1970,* pp. 370-71, 399.

9. For very competent studies of the invasion, see Henry S. Bradsher, *Afghanistan and the*

munist regime that had seized power in an April 1978 coup had quickly alienated the Afghan people, and even the steadily increasing numbers of Soviet advisers could not prevent the regime from nearing the point of collapse. In this respect, Soviet policy from April 1978 to December 1979 was not unlike U.S. policy in Vietnam from 1962 until the major U.S. troop commitment in 1965. Second, Moscow probably thought it was a low-risk operation. The United States had done virtually nothing in Iran, where it had major interests, either when the shah fell or when the hostages were seized. How much more unlikely must it have seemed to Moscow that the United States would take action in Afghanistan, where there were almost no American interests.

Whatever the cause of the Soviet invasion, that action was to have a very negative effect on the Soviet position in the Middle East. The Gulf Arabs again turned to the United States as a counterbalance, despite Camp David. Then the anti-Camp David coalition, already weakened by renewed hostility between Iraq and Syria, fell apart. By January 1980 three major groupings had emerged in the Arab world. On the one hand there was the pro-Western camp, led by Egypt and including the Sudan, Oman, and Somalia. This grouping supported Camp David, opposed the Soviet invasion of Afghanistan, and cooperated with the United States in joint military exercises. On the other side of the Arab spectrum there was the so-called Front of Steadfastness and Confrontation, led by Syria and including Libya, South Yemen, the PLO, and Algeria.[10] This grouping opposed Camp David and, with the exception of Algeria, supported Soviet activity in Afghanistan. In between was a centrist group composed of Saudi Arabia, Jordan, Kuwait, the United Arab Emirates, Morocco, Iraq, North Yemen, Tunisia, Bahrein, and Qatar. These centrists opposed both Camp David and the Soviet invasion of Afghanistan.

From the Soviet viewpoint, the diplomatic goal was now to move the centrist Arab grouping back to the Steadfastness Front, where they had been at the Baghdad conference, thus isolating Egypt and the other members of the pro-Western Arab bloc. Unfortunately for Moscow, however, the outbreak of the Iran-Iraq war eight months later made this task far more difficult. Indeed, from the Soviet viewpoint the Iran-Iraq war was the wrong war at the wrong time at the wrong place, and it has caused Moscow major problems.[11]

When border skirmishing erupted into a full-scale war in mid-September 1980, the Soviet Union was in a very awkward position because a good argument could have been made in the Kremlin to aid either side. On the one hand, Moscow was linked to Baghdad by a treaty of friendship and cooperation and had long been Iraq's main supplier of weaponry. In addition, Iraq had been a leading foe of the Camp David agreements and, as a nation with pretensions to leadership in the Arab world, could one day become the focus of the anti-imperialist Arab unity that Moscow had

Soviet Union (Durham, NC: Duke University Press, 1983); and Thomas T. Hammond, *Red Flag over Afghanistan* (Boulder, CO: Westview Press, 1984).

10. The Steadfastness Front, which initially included Iraq, had come into existence in response to Sadat's visit to Jerusalem in 1977.

11. The origins of the war are discussed in Stephen R. Grumman, *The Iran-Iraq War*, Washington Paper no. 92 (New York: Praeger, 1982).

sought for so long. Indeed, by its leadership at the Baghdad conference, Iraq demonstrated a potential for just such a role. Yet another argument for aiding Iraq was that such aid would demonstrate to the Arab world that Moscow was indeed a reliable ally; some Arab states had questioned this, despite Soviet aid to the Arab cause in the 1973 war. With respect to the Soviet economy, aid to Iraq would help ensure the continued flow of Iraqi oil to the USSR and its East European allies.

Soviet opponents of aid to Iraq could point to the continued persecution of Iraqi Communists and to Iraq's clear move away from the USSR since its treaty with the Soviet Union was signed in 1972. This disharmony was typified by Iraq's condemnation of Moscow after the invasion of Afghanistan, its February 1980 pan-Arab charter, which called for the elimination of both superpowers from the Arab world, and the growth of its economic and even military ties with France and other West European nations. On balance, however, since the Russians saw Iraq as objectively a major anti-Western force, a very good argument could have been made to aid the Iraqis.

On the other hand, a very good case could also have been made for aiding Iran. First and foremost, the Khomeini revolution had detached Iran from its close alignment with the United States, thereby striking a major blow to the U.S. position in the Persian Gulf in particular and the Middle East as a whole. In addition, by holding onto the American hostages, the Khomeini regime carried on a daily humiliation of the United States, which further lowered American prestige in the region. Consequently, any major Soviet effort to aid Iraq contained the possibility of ending the hostage impasse, or of even moving Iran back toward the American camp because of Iranian dependence on U.S. military equipment. Given Iran's large population—three times that of Iraq—and its strategic position along the Persian Gulf and at the Strait of Hormuz, such a development would clearly not be in Moscow's interest. Another strategic factor that the Soviet leadership had to take into consideration was that Iran, unlike Iraq, had a common border with the USSR as well as with Soviet-occupied Afghanistan. While Iranian efforts on behalf of the Afghan rebels had thus far been limited, one could rule out neither a major increase, should Moscow side with Iraq, nor a more pronounced effort on the part of Khomeini to infect the USSR's own Muslims with his brand of Islamic fundamentalism. Finally, as in the case of Iraq, there was an important economic argument. While Iran had cut off gas exports to the USSR, the signing of a major transit agreement between the two countries just before the war erupted may well have seemed to Moscow to be the first step toward their resumption. Given Iran's plentiful reserves of this fuel, Moscow may have wished to encourage the supply relationship as a hedge against its own natural gas and oil reserves.

Soviet opponents of aid to Iran could have pointed to the Islamic fundamentalists' treatment of the Tudeh—although Tudeh members were not yet as brutally treated as were Iraq's Communists—as well as to their treatment of Iranian minorities with whom the USSR hoped to cultivate a good relationship. Here again, however, Iran's treatment of its Kurds seemed no worse than Iraq's. Finally, opponents of aid to Iran could have pointed to Iran's leading anti-Soviet role in Islamic conferences, although again there may not have been too much difference between Iran's anti-Sovietism and Iraq's. The main factor in the Soviet evaluation of both countries was that they seemed far more anti-American than anti-Soviet, and both contributed to the weakening of the American position in the Middle East. For this reason, Moscow needed a good relationship with both and could not afford to alienate either.

Yet as Moscow remained neutral during the first two years of the conflict, the fallout from the war negatively affected its Middle East position. First, while Syria and Libya backed Iran, the centrists and the Egyptian bloc of Arab states backed Iraq, with Egypt selling it large quantities of weapons. Under the circumstances, and as the Iraqi invasion first bogged down and then reversed into a retreat, some rapprochement between the centrist Arabs, who feared Iran, and Egypt became almost inevitable. This momentum accelerated after the formation of the Gulf Corporation Council in 1981, a group of five centrist Arab states—Saudi Arabia, Kuwait, Bahrein, Qatar, and the United Arab Emirates—plus one Arab state in the Egyptian camp, Oman.

A second negative result was the strengthening of the U.S. position in the Gulf. The stationing—and eventual sale—of U.S. Airborne Warning and Control System (AWACS) aircraft to Saudi Arabia and the positioning of ground radar personnel there following Iranian threats to close the Strait of Hormuz seemed to demonstrate American willingness to help defend Saudi Arabia and other Arab states in time of need. That show of good will made the American military buildup in the Indian Ocean more diplomatically acceptable to the Arabs, thereby refuting Moscow's charge that the U.S. buildup was a threat to seize the oil of the Arab world. Indeed, the AWACS move appeared to reverse the decline in Saudi-American relations caused by Camp David and U.S inactivity during the fall of the shah, and Moscow became concerned that Saudi Arabia might even be enticed to join the Camp David process.

Moscow's response to these negative trends was threefold. First, on a December 1980 visit to India, Brezhnev issued a declaration advocating the neutralization of the Persian Gulf, a proposal he repeated at the Twenty-sixth Soviet Communist Party Congress in February 1981.[12] Second, Brezhnev also stated at the congress that the USSR was taking steps to promote a rapid end to the war, a goal Moscow repeatedly urged. Finally, Moscow began to woo two key centrist nations, Kuwait and Jordan, in an effort to slow the rapprochement between the centrist Arab states and Egypt. Moscow had some success with Kuwait, the most neutralist of the states of the Gulf Cooperation Council. The Kuwaiti foreign minister, Shaykh Sabah al-Ahmad al-Jabir Al Sabah, was willing to give lip service to some Soviet policy positions, including the neutralization of the Gulf, in return for at least the appearance of Soviet support against a possible Iranian invasion. In the case of Jordan, King Hussein also drew somewhat closer to Moscow out of concern over Ariel Sharon's growing influence on the Israeli government—Sharon had repeatedly said that Jordan should be the Palestinian state.[13]

12. For the text of Brezhnev's statement, see Freedman, *Soviet Policy toward the Middle East since 1970,* p. 398.

13. Soviet policy toward Kuwait and Jordan in 1981 is discussed in ibid., pp 403-5.

Nonetheless, despite small gains with Kuwait and Jordan, Middle Eastern trends continued to move against the USSR. The freeing of the U.S. hostages by Iran in January 1981 and the regime's increasing pressure on the Tudeh Party apparently led the USSR to lose hope that Soviet efforts to improve relations would be reciprocated. Consequently, Moscow, which had embargoed arms shipments to Iraq at the onset of the war, resumed small-scale shipments in late 1981.

At the same time things appeared to be going from bad to worse in Egypt, where Anwar el-Sadat expelled the Soviet ambassador and a number of other officials in early September of 1981. Three weeks later Sadat was assassinated, but any Soviet hope that Egypt would rapidly reorient its foreign policy seemed dashed as Sadat's successor, Hosni Mubarak, affirmed the continuity of his regime's policies with those of Sadat's, albeit with a somewhat more neutralist tone. Mubarak's Egypt, like Sadat's, remained a major recipient of American military and economic aid and regularly carried on joint military exercises with the United States. Indeed, several consequences of the assassination were to have negative implications for Moscow. With Sadat gone, the heavy propaganda carried on by Egypt against its anti-Camp David Arab neighbors ceased, and Mubarak sought to accelerate the reintegration of Egypt into the Arab world while at the same time maintaining Egypt's peace treaty with Israel. Yet another negative result was that Britain and France agreed to provide troops for the multinational force in the Sinai, thus supplying the first example of multinational NATO cooperation on a Middle East issue since the Suez crisis of 1956.

In sum, on the eve of the 1982 Israeli invasion of Lebanon, the major Middle Eastern trends seemed to be going against Moscow: the Iran-Iraq war continued unabated, the United States improved ties with the Gulf Arabs, and the centrist Arab states were slowly moving toward a reconciliation with Egypt.

The Israeli invasion was to cause further problems for Moscow, at least initially.[14] In the first place, Soviet credibility suffered a major blow because its frequent warnings to the United States and Israel during the course of the war proved to be ineffectual. Second, the quality of Soviet military equipment and, to a lesser degree, the quality of Soviet training were called into question by the overwhelming victory of U.S.-supplied Israeli weaponry over the military equipment supplied by Moscow to Syria. Finally, the Soviet leadership had to deal with a situation in which the United States, having mediated the PLO withdrawal from Beirut, had the clear diplomatic initiative.

The Reagan and Fez plans

On 1 September—the eve of a long-delayed Arab summit conference—President Reagan announced his plan for a Middle East peace settlement. In a clear effort to gain centrist Arab support, Reagan called for a stop to Israeli settlement activity on the West Bank and announced U.S. refusal to accept any Israeli claim to sovereignty over the West Bank. In his most controversial statement, he also called for a fully autonomous Pales-

14. For a detailed discussion of the Soviet reaction to the Israeli invasion, see Robert O. Freedman, "The Soviet Union and the Middle East," in *Middle East Contemporary Survey 1981-82,* ed. Colin Legum, Haim Shaked, and Daniel Dishon (New York: Holmes & Meier, 1984), pp. 40-49.

tinian entity linked to Jordan. To satisfy the Israelis, Reagan emphasized U.S. concern for Israel's security, asserted that Israel's final borders should not be the boundaries that existed before the 1967 war, called for the unity of Jerusalem and direct Arab-Israeli negotiations, and reaffirmed U.S. opposition to a Palestinian state on the West Bank.[15] Although it denounced the Reagan plan and denigrated Israeli Prime Minister Menachem Begin's rapid rejection of it, Moscow was concerned that the plan might prove attractive in the Arab world. Indeed, *Izvestiya* correspondent Vladimir Kudravtzev noted that "judging from press reports 'moderate' and 'pro-Western' Arab regimes find positive elements in the American initiative."[16]

Given this situation, Moscow seemed pleased by the outcome of the Arab summit at Fez, Morocco, which not only indicated that the Arab world had regained a semblance of unity but which also brought forth a peace plan that, except for its lack of explicit clarity as to Israel's right to exist, was quite close to the long-standing Soviet peace plan in that it called for an Israeli withdrawal to the 1967 boundaries but no normalization of relations.[17] Moscow also was pleased that the Sudanese proposal to readmit Egypt formally to the Arab League was rejected. Nonetheless, the Fez conference did not reject the Reagan plan, thereby leaving it, along with the Fez plan, as one of the solutions that the Arabs would consider to resolve the post-Beirut diplomatic situation in the Middle East.

With both the Reagan and Fez plans now being discussed, Moscow evidently felt that it too had to enter the diplomatic competition, and in a speech on 15 September, Brezhnev announced the Soviet Union's own peace plan.[18] While a number of its points repeated previous Soviet proposals, new elements seem to have been added to emphasize the similarity between the Fez and Soviet plans. Thus Moscow called for the Palestinian refugees to be given the right to return to their homes or receive compensation for their abandoned property; for the return of East Jerusalem to the Arabs and its incorporation into the Palestinian state, with freedom of access for believers to the sacred places throughout Jerusalem; and for Security Council guarantees for the final settlement—all provisions taken, almost word for word, from the Fez declaration. Brezhnev also used the opportunity to repeat the long-standing Soviet call for an international conference on the Middle East with all interested parties participating, including the PLO, which the Soviet leader again characterized as "the sole legitimate representative of the Arab people of Palestine."

In modeling the Soviet peace plan on Fez, Brezhnev evidently sought to prevent the Arabs from moving to embrace the Reagan plan. Nonetheless, with the United States clearly possessing the diplomatic initiative in the Middle East and Arab leaders, including Jordan's King Hussein and PLO leader Arafat, expressing interest in the Reagan plan, Moscow was on the diplomatic defensive. It was at this point, in mid-November, that Brezhnev passed from the scene. His successor, Yuri Andropov, had the task of rebuilding the Soviet position in the Middle East.

15. The Reagan plan is discussed in Barry Rubin, "The United States and the Middle East," in *Middle East Contemporary Survey*, ed. Legum, Shaked, and Dishon, pp. 30-33.

16. *Izvestiya*, 10 Sept. 1982.

17. For the text of the Fez plan, see *Middle East Journal*, 37(1):71 (Winter 1983).

18. *Pravda*, 16 Sept. 1982.

Under Andropov, Moscow's Middle East fortunes began to rise again, due less to Soviet successes than to mistakes by the United States. To be sure, Andropov moved to restore Soviet credibility in January 1983 by sending to Syria SAM-5 antiaircraft missiles, weapons that had never before been deployed outside the Soviet bloc. He also shipped SS-21 ground-to-ground missiles in September, following the first U.S.-Syrian confrontation in Lebanon. The Soviet position was also aided by two major developments that severely weakened U.S. diplomatic efforts in the Middle East: the challenge to Arafat's position in the PLO and the virtual collapse of the U.S. position in Lebanon.

Arafat had publicly stated in November 1982 that he was resigned to dealing with the United States as the dominant superpower in the Middle East,[19] thereby indicating his willingness to negotiate on the Reagan plan. During a visit to Moscow in January 1983 he had clashed with Andropov by calling for a Palestinian-Jordanian confederation. While Moscow was in favor of an independent Palestinian state, linking it to Jordan, a centrist state, not only seemed to associate the PLO partially with the Reagan plan but also appeared to signal its defection from the Steadfastness Front, which had already been badly weakened by the Israeli invasion. Consequently, the USSR only expressed its "understanding" of the PLO position—a diplomatic way of demonstrating its opposition.[20]

Fortunately for Moscow, Arafat's position soon weakened. Syria and Libya, which shared the Soviet interest in preventing a PLO turn to the United States, actively moved to undermine Arafat's position. The efforts of the anti-Arafat forces proved successful at the meeting of the Palestine National Council (PNC), which finally convened in mid-February 1983 in Algiers after a number of postponements. There, the PNC formally stated its refusal to consider the Reagan plan "as a sound basis for a just and lasting solution to the Palestine problem and the Arab-Israeli conflict."[21] Needless to say, Moscow was pleased with this development; *Pravda* correspondent Yuri Vladimirov praised the council's policy document as a reaffirmation of the PNC's determination to continue the struggle against imperialism and Zionism.[22]

On 10 January—before the PNC meeting—King Hussein declared he would decide by 1 March whether or not to join Israel in peace talks. As sentiment within the PLO hardened against the Reagan plan, King Hussein began to back away from the talks. On 10 April, claiming that Arafat had reneged on an earlier agreement, Hussein said that Jordan would not enter into the peace negotiations after all.[23] Hussein's statement was greeted with great relief by Moscow, which had long feared that Jordan would be attracted to the Reagan plan, considered by the Soviet leadership as an extension of Camp David.[24]

One month later, despite Arafat's public renunciation of the Reagan plan, Syrian President Hafez al-Assad moved to undercut the PLO leader's position within Fatah, his power base, by engineering a split in the organization. Sub-

19. Cited in the report by Loren Jenkins, *Washington Post,* 13 Nov. 1982.

20. *Pravda,* 13 Jan. 1983.

21. Cited in the report by Thomas L. Friedman, *New York Times,* 23 Feb. 1983.

22. *Pravda,* 25 Feb. 1983.

23. Cf. report by Herbert H. Denton, *Washington Post,* 11 Apr. 1983.

24. Cf. *Pravda,* 13 Apr. 1983.

sequently, Arafat was expelled from Syria, and his loyalists in the Bekaa Valley came under increasing pressure. Ultimately, most of his troops were forced to move overland to Tripoli, Lebanon, where Arafat joined them in the early fall. He and his men were to suffer another humiliating forced withdrawal in December, this time under heavy Syrian pressure. Moscow, which sought to maintain good ties with both Arafat and Assad, found itself once again in the quandry of being caught between two Arab forces that it was seeking to influence.[25]

Meanwhile, the United States had successfully mediated a troop-withdrawal agreement between Israel and Lebanon, which was signed on 17 May 1983. However, this agreement was doomed by Syrian opposition; the inability of the United States to mobilize the support of other Arab states, such as Saudi Arabia, on behalf of the accord; and major political mistakes by Lebanese President Amin Gemayel, who alienated both the Lebanese Shiites and the Druze and drove them into the arms of Syria. By coming out strongly in support of Gemayel, the United States became a party to the renewed Lebanese civil war and by September found itself in a military confrontation not only with the Druze and Shiites, but with Syria as well. The September crisis, precipitated by the Israeli withdrawal from the Chouf Mountains, ended in a cease-fire without a direct military conflict between Syria and the United States. Nonetheless, the attack on the U.S. Marine headquarters in October increased Syrian-American tension, which, in early December, led to a military confrontation as two American Navy planes were shot down by Syrian antiaircraft fire.[26]

Interestingly enough, during this entire period Moscow kept a very low profile, indicating that it wished to avoid a superpower conflict over Lebanon, which, by itself, was only tertiary in Soviet interests. Nonetheless Moscow sought to exploit the Syrian-American confrontation by tying the U.S. attack on the Syrian positions in Lebanon to the strategic cooperation agreement concluded between Reagan and Israeli Prime Minister Yitzhak Shamir a week earlier, and by claiming that this action disqualified the United States as an "honest broker" in the Middle East. Moscow also again appealed for Arab unity on an anti-imperialist basis in an evident attempt to exploit the Syrian-American clash in order to slow the rapprochement between the centrist Arabs and the pro-American Egyptian camp in the Arab world.[27]

U.S. downfall in Lebanon

Two months after the Syrian-American confrontation came the collapse of the U.S. position in Lebanon, a development highlighted by the redeployment of U.S. Marines to their ships in the Mediterranean. This was perceived throughout the Middle East as a major victory for Syria, Moscow's principal Arab client, and a major defeat for the United States and for the Reagan plan as well. The U.S. redeployment, which the other members of the multinational force soon copied, was accompanied by

25. Moscow's quandry in dealing with the Assad-Arafat conflict is discussed in Robert O. Freedman, "The Soviet Union, Syria and the Crisis in Lebanon: A Preliminary Analysis," in *The Middle East Annual—1983,* ed. David H. Partington (Boston: G. K. Hall, 1984), pp. 103-57.

26. These incidents are discussed in detail in ibid.

27. Ibid.

American naval shelling of antigovernment positions in the vicinity of Beirut. The rationale for the shelling was never clearly explained by the Reagan administration; indeed, the general course of U.S. policy during this period seemed confused at best. Whatever mistakes the United States had made in backing the Gemayel government up to this point, the hurried exodus of the Marines from Beirut, coupled with what appeared to be indiscriminate artillery fire into the Lebanese mountains, hurt the U.S. image not only in Lebanon, but in the Middle East as a whole. Moscow clearly welcomed and sought to exploit these problems, despite the death of Andropov in February.[28]

Moscow was to achieve another success when Gemayel, now virtually bereft of U.S. military support, could turn only to Syrian President Assad for help in staying in power. Assad, at least in the short term, proved willing to help—for a price. The price was the abrogation of the Israeli-Lebanese agreement of 17 May; Gemayel announced its abrogation on 5 March. Moscow hailed this development; Soviet commentators called it a major blow to the entire Camp David process.

Despite the collapse of the U.S. position in Lebanon, there were a number of problems that the new Soviet leader, Konstantin Chernenko, had to face. First, a power struggle had erupted in Damascus over a successor to President Assad, who apparently had not fully recovered from his November 1983 heart attack. Second, despite its victory in Lebanon, which the Syrian media were hailing as equivalent to Nasser's nationalization of the Suez Canal, Syria remained in diplomatic isolation in the Arab world, whereas Egypt continued to improve its ties to centrist Arab states. Egypt's rapprochement with the centrist Arabs was reinforced by the surprise visit of Arafat to Cairo after his expulsion from Lebanon in December 1983. The next month Egypt was readmitted to the Islamic Conference, a development attributed by Moscow to the "pressure of conservative Moslem regimes."[29] That Libya, Syria, and South Yemen walked out of the conference indicated the continuing isolation of Moscow's closest Arab allies. The USSR also had to be concerned about the possible formation of a new Arab front that would move to reincorporate Egypt into the Arab League and possibly revive the Reagan plan. Soviet concern with such a development could only have increased with Mubarak's visit to King Hassan of Morocco—the first official visit to an Arab country by the head of the Egyptian state since the 1979 peace treaty as Moscow television unhappily noted.[30] Mubarak's meeting with King Hussein in Washington in mid-February, as the two Arab leaders prepared for talks with President Reagan, gave the Soviets no comfort either.

U.S. aid in the Gulf

Meanwhile, as Egypt's relations with centrist Arab nations improved, Syria appeared to remain isolated, despite its victory in Lebanon. Thus not only was

28. Cf. reports by E. J. Dionne, *New York Times,* 12 Feb. 1984; David Hoffman, *Washington Post,* 12 Feb. 1984; and idem, *Washington Post,* 15 Feb. 1984.

29. TASS, 20 Jan. 1984, in *Foreign Broadcast Information Service Daily Report: Soviet Union,* 23 Jan. 1984, p. H-5.

30. Moscow Television Service, 8 Feb. 1984, in *Foreign Broadcast Information Service Daily Report: Soviet Union,* 9 Feb. 1984, p. H-6.

its influence insufficient to prevent the Islamic Conference from readmitting Egypt; it was again in isolation when the Arab League foreign ministers, in a meeting in mid-March that Syria and Libya boycotted, took a strongly anti-Iranian position. The meeting condemned Iran for its continuing "aggression against Iraq" and warned Iran that the continuation of the war would force the Arab states to reconsider their relations with it.[31] Indeed, as this episode showed, the war in the Gulf was again causing problems for Moscow. Iran had undertaken a major new offensive against Iraq and was threatening the key southern Iraqi city of Basra while at the same time repeating its threats to close the Strait of Hormuz if Iraq interfered with Iranian oil exports. Moscow was clearly concerned that the United States, which had again pledged to keep the strait open and had increased the size of its fleet near the Gulf, would exploit the Iranian threats in order to reinforce its position with the Arab states of the Gulf, thereby diverting attention from its failure in Lebanon.

Unfortunately for Moscow, this was exactly what happened. When Iraq, using its Exocet-equipped Super Etendard bombers, began to attack oil tankers near the main Iranian oil-export terminal at Kharg Island, Iran responded by attacking Kuwaiti and Saudi tankers. This attack brought urgent requests from both Gulf Arab states for U.S. protection. The United States moved to supply Saudi Arabia with short-range Stinger antiaircraft missiles and another KC-10 tanker to help keep its air defense system of U.S. AWACS aircraft and Saudi F-15s in the air for longer periods. Saudi Arabia responded by shooting down an Iranian fighter bomber, with the help of information provided by AWACS aircraft. Another instance of U.S.-Saudi defense cooperation came several months later when, after the mining of the Red Sea, Saudi Arabia sought U.S. help in sweeping the mines near its port and thus protecting the *hajj,* the pilgrimage to Mecca. Kuwait, whose relations with the United States had long been strained, also turned to the United States for support and asked for Stinger missiles. After the United States offered improved Hawk antiaircraft missiles instead, the Kuwaiti minister of defense went to Moscow—the trip had been planned in advance of the Stinger request—and signed a military agreement with the USSR. Kuwait did later sign a military-training agreement with the United States also, as Kuwaiti-American relations improved.[32]

The Soviet peace plan of 29 July 1984

While the American buildup in the Gulf was of concern to Moscow, the possibility of a revived Reagan peace plan continued to trouble the Soviet leadership as well. To be sure, King Hussein of Jordan announced in mid-March 1984 that he would not enter into talks with Israel, even if the Israelis halted the construction of settlements in occupied territories. The reason given was that the United States had lost its credibility and was no longer a "trusted mediator"—just the message that Moscow was trying to convey to the Arab world.[33] Nonetheless, two weeks later Hussein

31. Baghdad INA (in Arabic), 14 Mar. 1984, in *Foreign Broadcast Information Service Daily Report: Middle East,* 15 Mar. 1984, p. A-2.

32. See the report by David Ottaway, *Washington Post,* 1 Dec. 1984.

33. The text of King Hussein's interview is in *New York Times,* 15 Mar. 1984.

made clear in a statement about the just-announced Israeli election scheduled for 23 July that he was keeping his options open. He indicated that a healthy change would result from a victory by the Labor Party, which opposed annexation of the West Bank, advocated territorial compromise with Jordan, and whose leader, Shimon Peres, had spoken favorably of the Reagan plan.[34]

During the spring and summer of 1984, therefore, Soviet diplomacy had a special Jordanian focus. Thus Moscow assiduously wooed King Hussein, hoping to keep Jordan from embracing the Reagan plan in the event that, as the polls predicted, the Labor Party scored a major victory in the Israeli elections.[35] The Soviet leadership prepared a new variant of its Middle East peace plan, one that might prove more amenable to King Hussein. While the Jordanian monarch had long shared the Soviet goal of an international conference to settle the Arab-Israeli conflict, he also had long desired a link between any Palestinian entity or state on the West Bank and Jordan, whose population was more than 60 percent Palestinian. Therefore, the Soviet peace plan of 29 July, which mentioned such a link, can be considered a major gesture to Hussein.[36]

Modeled on the Brezhnev peace plan of 15 September 1982, which had combined the basic three-point Soviet peace plan with the major components of the Arab program announced at Fez, the new Soviet plan had one additional key element: the acknowledgment that the new Palestinian state could form a confederation with a neighboring country. Given the previous clash with Arafat over this issue during his visit to Moscow in January 1983, the Soviet leadership's inclusion of this element in its peace plan may also be seen as a gesture to the PLO leader. Arafat was then engaged in a prolonged political battle to win over the Marxist elements of the PLO—the so-called democratic alliance of the Popular Front for the Liberation of Palestine, the Democratic Front for the Liberation of Palestine, and the Palestine Communist Party—while struggling to isolate the so-called National Alliance of Palestinian factions controlled by Syria.

The timing of the Soviet peace plan is also significant in that it was apparently prepared to coincide with the Israeli elections on 23 July. Contrary to expectations, the Labor victory was so narrow that it did not appear as if Peres would be able to make the concessions that the Reagan plan would require, even if he could manage to form a narrow parliamentary majority. This was a bonus for the USSR, which now sought to use the plan as a rallying point for centrist and Steadfastness Front Arabs to draw them together and away from the United States and its Egyptian-camp allies.

Not unexpectedly, Israel quickly rejected the Soviet peace initiative. In addition to refusing to participate in an international conference at which the PLO would be present, Israel also opposed the conference out of fear that it would reduce the Arabs to their lowest common denominator—opposition to Israel's right to exist. The United States, whose administration was deeply suspi-

34. Cited in *Foreign Broadcast Information Service Daily Report: Middle East*, 2 Apr. 1984, p. ii.

35. Numerous Jordanian delegations visited Moscow, and many Soviet delegations visited Jordan, and the Soviet press was full of praise for Jordan's "independent" position.

36. For the text of the peace plan, see *Pravda*, 30 July 1984; an English translation of the plan may be found in *Current Digest of the Soviet Press*, 36(30):9-10 (1984).

cious of Soviet motivations in the Middle East, also rejected the Soviet proposal.

Much to Moscow's satisfaction, however, its peace initiative was warmly received in the Arab world, especially by such centrist Arab states as Jordan and Kuwait. Arafat's wing of the PLO also accepted the plan, as did Lebanon, and it received favorable comment from North and South Yemen, Syria, and Saudi Arabia. Buoyed by the positive Arab reaction for the plan—although the Arab states tended to be more supportive of the international conference than of the specific elements of the Soviet proposal—Moscow moved ahead during the summer of 1984 to garner increased backing for it. It appears doubtful that the Soviet leadership really thought a Middle East conference was obtainable in the near future, given the opposition of both Israel and the United States. Indeed, it seems as if Moscow was capitalizing on their opposition as it put forth a basic framework on which both the Steadfastness Front and centrist groupings in the Arab world could agree. While this might not reunite the two Arab camps, it would at least slow the rapprochement between Egypt, which was at best lukewarm about the Soviet plan, and the centrist Arab states, while at the same time highlighting the United States as the opponent of the Arab consensus on the peace program.

The Palestine National Council in Amman

Despite Moscow's tactical success in garnering at least verbal support from most of the Arab world for its peace plan, the pattern of Middle Eastern events once again seemed to confound Soviet strategy. Thus in late September, soon after President Reagan, from the rostrum of the United Nations, had again emphasized the Reagan plan as U.S. policy in the Middle East, and after a Peres-led national unity government had taken office in Israel, King Hussein suddenly reestablished full diplomatic relations with Egypt. This move, which was the final stage of a steady improvement of Jordanian-Egyptian relations since December 1983, appeared to be a major step in the rapprochement between the centrist Arab camp and Egypt. To be sure, Moscow may have hoped that given the continuing tension in U.S.-Jordanian ties and the steady development of Soviet-Jordanian relations, Jordan might pull Egypt away from its close ties to the United States instead of being pulled by Egypt toward the Reagan plan. Nonetheless, despite resuming relations at the ambassadorial level with the USSR in August, Egypt continued its close military and economic relationship with the United States, as exemplified by the joint military exercise Sea Wind, carried on by the two nations in early November.

The low-level treatment given in the Soviet press to the resumption of Egyptian-Jordanian diplomatic relations seemed to indicate that Moscow was trying to play down the development while continuing to cultivate Jordan. Yet the resumption of diplomatic relations with Egypt was not the only action taken by King Hussein that was to discomfit the Soviet Union, not to mention Moscow's chief ally, Syria, which bitterly attacked Hussein for reestablishing ties with Egypt. In November 1984, King Hussein agreed to the convening of the PNC meeting in Jordan's capital. Arafat was eager to convene this meeting in friendly territory—he had been turned down by Algeria and South Yemen—and managed to achieve a quorum in Amman despite the boycott of the session by the Syrian-backed Palestinian National Alliance and by the Marxist Democratic Alliance, which included the pro-Soviet Palestinian Communist Party.

Moscow's displeasure with the PNC meeting was exemplified not only by the failure of the Palestine Communist Party to attend, but also by the failure of the Soviet ambassador to Jordan to attend the session and by the pro-Soviet Israeli Communist Party's opposition to it.[37] In addition, both George Habash, leader of the Popular Front for the Liberation of Palestine, and Naef Hawatmeh, leader of the Democratic Front for the Liberation of Palestine, announced their opposition to the meeting after hurried visits to Moscow.

The PNC meeting was orchestrated by Arafat to demonstrate his control over the PLO while also offering a renewed tie to both the Democratic and National Alliances. Because it was shaped by these purposes, the meeting did not make any dramatic moves toward peace. The very fact that the meeting took place when and where it did held out the possibility of a final split in the PLO between Arafat's backers and those of Syria. Indeed, Assad's speech at the Syrian Baath Congress in January 1985, in which he implied that Syria would take command of the Palestinian movement, and the December 1984 assassination of PLO Executive Committee member Fahad Kawasmeh, which Arafat blamed on Assad, seemed to hasten such a split.

As the relationship between Arafat and King Hussein deepened, the two Arab leaders signed a major cooperation agreement on 11 February that was warmly endorsed by Egypt and bitterly attacked by both Syria and the USSR, which saw in it an extension of Camp David.[38] At this point, the United States again became actively involved in the peace process. Following visits to the United States by King Fahd of Saudi Arabia and Mubarak and a warming of relations between Israel and Egypt, Assistant Secretary of State Richard W. Murphy journeyed to the Middle East in an effort to bridge the remaining gap between the Hussein-Arafat position on peace and the Israeli position. Whatever the final results of the Murphy mission, or the subsequent visit of his boss, Secretary of State George Shultz, to the Middle East a month later, it seemed clear by May 1985 that, despite the U.S. debacle in Lebanon, the diplomatic momentum had swung back to the United States. In any case, the Murphy visit provides a useful point of departure for analyzing the thrust of Soviet Middle East policy since the 1973 war.

CONCLUSION

In looking back at the course of Soviet policy in the Middle East since the 1973 Arab-Israeli war, there are two central conclusions that may be drawn. First, Soviet policy toward the Middle East has been essentially reactive in nature: Moscow has responded to events in the region that it neither caused nor had much ability to control. Sometimes events have occurred from which Moscow benefited. The fall of the shah, the formation of an anti-Camp David Arab alignment, and U.S. policy errors in Lebanon are prime examples of this. Just as frequently, however, Moscow has been

37. *Jerusalem Post,* 20 Nov. 1984.

38. Cf. report by Konstantin Geyvandov, *Izvestiya,* 28 Mar. 1985.

reacting to regional events that had negative consequences for its Middle Eastern position. Examples of this are the activities of Henry Kissinger from 1973 to 1976 that kept Moscow on the diplomatic sidelines while they moved Egypt from the Soviet to the American camp; the Iran-Iraq war, which contributed to the strengthening of the U.S. position in the Gulf region; and the numerous internecine splits in the Arab world, such as the ones between Assad and Arafat, which made the Soviet hope of creating a lasting anti-imperialist Arab alignment so difficult to achieve.

A second conclusion is that Soviet influence in the region remains very limited despite all the arms that Moscow has poured into it. Thus Moscow was unable to prevent Egypt's move to the American camp, the signing of the Camp David agreements, and the reestablishment of relations between Jordan and Egypt. At the same time, despite continued efforts, the USSR has been unable to bring about an end to the Iran-Iraq war or the rift between Assad and Arafat. In addition, Moscow has been unable to gain solid support for the various versions of its Arab-Israeli plan, and Soviet diplomacy continues to suffer from the fact that as long as Moscow can only talk to one side of the Arab-Israeli conflict and remains unwilling to use military force to coerce Israel, the United States will necessarily remain the primary external diplomatic force in the Arab world.

In sum, despite its control over Afghanistan and the billions of rubles in arms it has sent to the Middle East, the USSR remains as far from exerting dominant influence over the region in 1985 as it was in 1973. Nonetheless, given the oil and strategic communication routes in the Middle East, and the emergence of a young and vigorous new leader in the Kremlin, it is unlikely that Moscow will end its competition with the United States for influence in the region in the near future.

* * *

QUESTIONS AND ANSWERS

Q (Dario Scuka, Library of Congress, Washington, D.C.): Why would the Soviets wish to settle the Iran-Iraq war?

A: I feel that the Iran-Iraq war is the wrong war, at the wrong place, at the wrong time for Moscow. First, as a result of the Soviet invasion of Afghanistan, the Arab world was divided into three groups: the pro-Soviets, which comprise Syria, Libya, the Palestine Liberation Organization (PLO), Algeria, and South Yemen; the Egyptian Camp David group, with Egypt explicitly and with Sudan, Oman, and Somalia implicitly in support of Camp David; and the other Arabs, who are centrist. By "centrist" I mean that, on the one hand, they are opposed to Camp David but, on the other hand, they oppose the Soviet invasion of Afghanistan.

What, then, is the impact on the Arab scene, as viewed by the Soviets, of the outbreak of the Iran-Iraq war? Two of the Steadfastness Front nations, Syria and Libya, back Iran and initially the PLO, until Arafat switches sides and backs Iraq.

The centrist Arabs unanimously back Iraq, as does Egypt, by supplying it with many millions of dollars in military equipment. From the Soviet perspective, support of Iraq is one element pushing the centrists and the Egyptian camp together.

For U.S. diplomacy, moving the centrists toward Egypt first and then toward the Camp David process is very desirable, if Camp David is ever to be expanded. It is in the interests of Soviet diplomacy, however, to restore the Baghdad situation of November 1978, when Egypt was isolated.

So, first, the outbreak of the Iran-Iraq war moved some of these centrist Arabs toward Egypt. Second came the formation of the Gulf Cooperation Council. The council consists of five centrist Arabs states plus Oman. Oman constantly agitates from within for a closer military relationship with the United States. The Soviets actively cultivate Kuwait to serve as a break on this movement.

The third element is a greater legitimation of the U.S. military presence in the Indian Ocean. When the war broke out initially, the Iranians threatened to close the Strait of Hormuz. The United States then moved to keep it open. Providing AWACS to the Saudis reinforced U.S. ties to centrist Arabs. It slowed, if not turned around, the gradual deterioration of ties between the United States and a lot of the Gulf countries that occurred as a result of the fall of the shah and the decreasing credibility on the part of the United States in the area.

The fourth element is a more recent need for U.S. aid. This occurred when the Iraqis escalated the war and declared the exclusion zone around Kharg Island. The Iranians responded by bombing Kuwaiti and Saudi tankers, and all of a sudden the United States was needed again. Reagan bucked congressional opposition by sending Stingers and also a KC-10 tanker, and the Saudi planes then succeeded in shooting down one Phantom, but again this was a symbolic gesture. The Kuwaitis, who try to be neutralist toward the United States, want Stingers as much, I think, as a symbolic gesture of support from the United States as for their military security. After all, the improved Hawks that the United States had suggested selling to them probably would be more useful than the Stingers.

In any case, constant escalation of the war in the Gulf, let alone its mere continuation, is one element the Soviets see pushing the centrist Arabs toward the Egyptian camp and legitimating and promoting an active role for the United States in the Gulf. I will just mention briefly that it took only three months after the war broke out for Brezhnev himself, during a trip to India in December 1980, to call for the neutralization of the Gulf to prevent exactly this kind of establishment of military ties. So for all of these reasons, I think, the Soviets would very much like to end the war. Brezhnev himself said at the party congress in February 1981, "We are actively moving to end this senseless war which only benefits the imperialists."

Q (Marvin Weinbaum, University of Illinois, Urbana): As you describe them, both superpowers have had problems dictating to their friends or clients in the area. Is it therefore a corollary that the United States and the Soviet Union have something very much in common in assuring that clients do not commit the patrons to positions, to actions—indeed, to a confrontation—of which the superpowers disapprove? That is, do not both superpowers need a higher degree of predictability in the area than they currently have? Are there some bases for negotiation that are beyond the current implicit understandings between the superpowers and their friends or clients? Is there some basis for negotiation or more explicit understandings?

A: I think the answer is clear from the Soviet point of view, and most recently from Soviet behavior during the escalation of the crisis in Lebanon. The USSR constantly refrained from spreading its umbrella of support over Syrian activities in Lebanon, and Syria was constantly trying to get that support as its conflict with the United States escalated. The Soviets were very careful to keep their support low key. For example, they sent SAM-5 missiles to Syria in January 1983 with Soviet advisors to install them. However, they did not mention publicly that there were Soviet advisors present. Thus, if the Israelis took out the SAM-5 missiles, the Soviets would not then have to respond because their prestige was at stake.

In the crisis of September 1984, where a U.S. battleship sailed up at the very first stages of the fighting after the Israelis pulled out of the Chouf Mountains, the Soviets were the first ones to applaud the cease-fire that was worked out on 25 September and very happy that no escalation had occurred.

In December, the Soviets similarly played down the shooting down of two U.S. planes by a Soviet client, Syria. The Soviets did not want this kind of confrontation to get out of hand. I think that as much as they would like to expand their influence in the Middle East, and as rapidly as possible, they will not pay the cost of a superpower confrontation that might escalate into a nuclear war. In general, then, in situations in which the United States is actively involved, the Soviets will in fact be quite cautious.

On the other hand, in the absence of active U.S. opposition, the Soviets have shown no hesitation to exploit crises. In two recent examples, Angola and Ethiopia, the United States was hamstrung from moving in to block Soviet-Cuban activity. In the case of Angola, Congress stopped U.S. action. In the case of Ethiopia and Somalia, on the one hand the Soviets were intervening on the side of the angels essentially because Somalia broke the Organization of African Unity rule about crossing colonial borders; on the other hand, the Carter administration wavered back and forth about the proper response.

I think that the Soviets invaded Afghanistan as quickly as they did and the way they did was due in part because of the U.S. response to Iran. The United States had a major interest in Iran, yet when the shah fell and when the hostages were taken, the U.S. response was miniscule. How much less likely would a U.S. response be to events in Afghanistan, in which there is almost no U.S. interest? I think this lowering of the threshold of any risks for the Soviets if they intervened was one of the things that brought them in.

Another example is the civil war in Yemen in 1967. Nasser pulled out his troops after the Six Day War to bring them back to Egypt. A civil war then heated up and the Soviets sent in planes, advisors, troops, and other forms of assistance to aid the Yemeni republicans against the royalists. The Soviet support broke the siege of Sana and enabled the republicans to win. The United States stayed out of this situation.

In those cases where the Soviets think they can get away with something without an active American response, they will move. That Soviet tendency brings me to the final point. I think the Soviets, much as we might not like to look at it this way, tend to view the Middle East as a zero-sum competition with the United States for influence. They never want to push it to the point where nuclear confrontation might break out, however, and that is why the 1973 war in the Middle East was very dangerous. Nonetheless, they will push it to some degree, because what they see as a victory for themselves is an equivalent loss for the West.

The United States has tried to tell the Soviet Union on any number of occasions that the Middle East is not a zero-sum game. In the case of the Iran-Iraq war, at least on a short-term tactical basis both countries are tilting, at this stage of the game, toward Iraq. I would not say, however, that this is an area for any long-term U.S.-Soviet cooperation.

The Soviets will play a zero-sum game to the greatest degree possible if there is no risk of superpower confrontation. If there is, the Soviets will tend to be cautious.

Q (George Fox Mott, Washington, D.C.): Neither the United States nor any other nation has cared to express unhappiness about the Afghanistan situation. Even though the Soviet Union has used methods outlawed in conventional warfare, it is still not in control of Afghanistan. Would you comment on this issue and on why it may be a cause of other problems?

A: One of the problems the Soviets now face in the Middle East is a direct result of their invasion of Afghanistan, their supression of an essentially Islamic rebellion against their control. That is causing any number of problems: it reinforces hostility between the Soviet Union and Iran, and it reinforces the suspicion of Soviet motives in the conservative Islamic areas of the Middle East, not only in Iran but in Saudi Arabia as well.

Second, the invasion has had a very negative effect on what I call the Arab balance. In many ways the invasion served to split the Baghdad unity against Egypt. Now the centrist Arabs oppose Camp David but they also oppose the Soviet invasion of Afghanistan. The Soviets have been trying to recoup the political costs of their invasion ever since; the invasion has had a very poor effect on their overall policy toward the Middle East by again helping to legitimate the American presence in the Middle East, however much certain Arab states might not like the United States for its policy on the Arab-Israeli conflict. In addition, the American military presence is seen as a necessary counterbalance to any future Soviet moves. In a purely diplomatic view of the Middle East, I would say the Soviet invasion of Afghanistan has indeed had a number of very negative effects.

I do not know if the Afghan rebellion can succeed. I hope that it will, but the war is becoming very costly and the Soviets thought it could be a one-shot deal. I have studied the various reasons why the Soviets invaded and all the various theories that explain the invasion. One theory holds that the Soviet Union feared that the Islamic sea on its southern border would affect Soviet Muslims by spilling over into the USSR.

Another theory holds that after the Communist seizure of power in Afghanistan in April 1978, the regime that took power put through immediately any number of so-called reforms that alienated the vast majority of the Afghan people. Soviet advisors were needed in increasing numbers; they came in and the United States protested rather ineffectually. By December 1979 the situation had really gotten out of hand. I think the Soviets faced a situation not unlike that faced by the United States in 1965. I was an infantry officer at that time. I remember talking to my colleagues just back from serving as military advisors in Vietnam in March and April 1965. They were saying that the Vietnamese by themselves could not put down the rebellion, but some good American troops could. Two decades later, I had the feeling while I was talking to some Soviet scholars that they had some of the very same feelings: they seemed to feel that Soviet troops could end the insurgency. They had other problems, too, such as splits in the Afghan Communist Party, but I think it was a miscalculation clearly as to the invasion's cost in the Arab world, as to how quickly the rebellion would be suppressed, and as to the very serious cost to U.S.-Soviet relations. So the Soviets did not get home scot-free from their invasion of Afghanistan, and it continues to cause them, I think, very serious problems both vis-à-vis the United States and especially in the Middle East.

Q (Joseph Ostroy, Long Beach, New York): Would you comment on two points? First, there were many references made to our friends the moderate Arabs, but the U.N. vote by Arab states was heavily against the United States on almost every issue. Second, almost 61 percent of the population of Israel comprises Sephardic Jews who came from Arab countries. Many Jews have suffered in the Arab countries. They have been hanged, their rights have been taken away, and so forth. The Sephardic population in Israel is strongly opposed to any rapprochement with the Arab states.

A: As far as U.N. votes are concerned, I think we have to take a look at which U.N. votes are under discussion. The Arab states were overwhelmingly opposed to Soviet activity in Afghanistan, for example. On the question of Israel's right to exist, Arab votes go the other way.

I think a lot of misinformation is being spread that the so-called Sephardic Jews are the hotheads. Those who joined Meir Kahane's groups are not Sephardic primarily; they are mostly American-born Ashkenazic Jews, who settled on the West Bank.

You are quite right in indicating that the Jews who left the Arab world lost a lot of their property in the process and there is clearly unhappiness about that. On the other hand, they also bring with them a good bit of Middle Eastern and Arab culture. I do not see them as being the obstacle to rapprochement with the Arab nations.

It is frequently mentioned that the Sephardim supported Begin, and here I am going to set up a logical error. The Sephardim supported Begin. Begin was strong hard-liner against the Arabs particularly regarding the West Bank, with the exception of the Israeli-Egyptian peace treaty, of course. Therefore, the Sephardim are hard-liners against the Arabs.

That is the logic that is usually set up, and I think it is false. The Sephardim supported Begin primarily because the leadership of the Mapai—of the Labor Party—in Israel, which was primarily Ashkenazic, neglected them and did not bring them actively into the political system. It was Begin with whom they identified. Like him, they were in the opposition: he was in the political opposition, and they were in the opposition with respect to social class. He sympathized with them. Although he was an Ashkenazic Jew, he nonetheless met their needs religiously, whereas the Labor leadership was far more secular. The Sephardim supported him because he understood them and because he symbolized their opposition to the Ashkenazic power structure. The public opinion surveys that I have seen and the people who run Sephardic research institutes in Israel with whom I have spoken indicate that Sephardic Jews voted for Begin not for his hard-liner stance but because he was moving to raise their status in Israel.

It is interesting to note that in this last election in 1984, there was a clear drop in Sephardic support for the Likud government because it lacked Begin and because of the war in Lebanon, which was not really supported by the Sephardic Jews because it diverted money that could otherwise have been used for developing the Sephardic communities in development towns on the periphery of Israel.

ANNALS, *AAPSS,* **482,** November 1985

Water: An Emerging Issue in the Middle East?

By FREDERICK W. FREY *and* THOMAS NAFF

ABSTRACT: A potentially severe problem is emerging in the Middle East—the threat of major water shortages. This developing issue is likely to exacerbate already strained relations between states in the region. A number of aspects of this crisis can be illustrated through an examination of one river system, the Jordan. Proceeding from this example, the first steps can be taken toward an effective theory of issues and water conflicts. Application of this theoretical framework reveals that the water issue means different things to different actors. Water is a highly complex, fragmented issue, which possesses special qualities that distinguish it from other foreign relations determinants. While water is not usually an issue to some actors, under conditions of severe shortage it is highly conflict-prone. Yet the water issue paradoxically is also a possibly unique vehicle for cooperation if the parties view that as the only possible solution.

Frederick W. Frey is professor of political science at the University of Pennsylvania. Dr. Frey specializes in the analysis of power. He has spent several years in the Middle East and wrote a major study of Turkish politics.

Thomas Naff, the director of the Middle East Research Institute of the University of Pennsylvania, is a specialist in the politics and diplomacy of the modern Middle East. He is author of a number of works, including Water in the Middle East: Conflict or Cooperation?

PROBABLY the outstanding physical characteristic of the Middle East is aridity. With few exceptions, water is scarce and precious—a fact that has conditioned life in the region for millennia. Local populations, heavily clustered on coasts, riverbanks, and oases, have learned over time to live with meager water resources, adapting their cultures and even their conflicts to this basic parameter of regional existence.

Had nothing else changed, one's paramount reaction might be merely to admire the adaptation. At least we could continue to ignore water issues for more pressing problems such as oil, superpower rivalry, and religious and international strife. However, increased population, immigration, irrigation, industrialization, and other thirsty changes of modernization have been superimposed upon the fragile hydropolitical economy of the area. From both policy and theoretical perspectives, the resulting situation demands attention.

A few examples illustrate the point. According to many analyses, Israel and Jordan are currently using virtually all of their renewable water resources. If Turkey carries out the large-scale irrigation projects proposed for its southeastern region, unaccustomed shortages of Euphrates River water may begin to plague the downstream countries, especially Syria. Even the Nile, thus far a comparative success story, may pose problems if development or regime changes transform Egypt's southern neighbors.[1]

What will happen when Israel, Jordan, and then other Middle Eastern nations hit what might be called "the water barrier"—100 percent use of renewable water supplies? Is it realistic or alarmist to be apprehensive about the possibility of severe water crises exacerbating the strained situations in much of the Middle East? How valid is the "hydraulic-imperative" interpretation of Israel's Middle Eastern moves, which sees them as primarily motivated by water needs?[2] If water does surface as a leading issue in the near future, what consequences might plausibly be anticipated? What kind of issue is water likely to be, especially politically?

Such is the subject of our analysis. We will first examine the issue with reference to one water system, the Jordan River. From that example, we will turn to a general and theoretical approach, trying to get an analytic handle on the problem.

EMPIRICAL CONSIDERATIONS

One useful framework for examining the empirical dimensions of our analysis is water as a vital issue in international relations. This framework encompasses the interest-position-power matrix that will be developed in the theoretical section of this article. As a basic determinant of relations between sets of nations, the water factor is peculiar unto itself, exhibiting characteristics that distinguish it from other foreign affairs issues:

1. Because water is essential not only to existence but also to the quality of life, no issue is so crosscutting as water.

1. For a fuller exposition, see Thomas Naff and Ruth C. Matson, eds., *Water in the Middle East: Conflict or Cooperation?* (Boulder, CO: Westview Press, 1984).

2. See, e.g., John K. Cooley, "The War over Water," *Foreign Policy*, 54:3-26 (Spring 1984); Joe Stork, "Water and Israel's Occupation Strategy," *MERIP Reports*, 13(6):19-24 (1983); and Thomas Stauffer, "The Price of Peace, the Spoils of War," *American-Arab Affairs*, 1:43-54 (1982).

2. Scarcity of water is always a zero-sum security issue and thus creates a constant potential for conflict.

3. Because of its sheer complexity in practical, ideological, and symbolic terms, the issue of water is more difficult for policymakers and scholars to grasp in its entirety and tends to be dealt with piecemeal both domestically and internationally; it is thus more fragmented than other issues.

4. Law as a means of settling and regulating water issues remains rudimentary and relatively ineffectual. There are no agreed-upon legal structures in place for settling international water disputes. Therefore, law lacks the capacity at present of being an effective instrument for regulation.[3]

5. Finally, precisely because it is essential to life and so highly charged, water, unlike most other volatile issues of international relations, can—perhaps even tends to—produce cooperation even in the absence of trust between the concerned actors. The operation of "superordinate goals" appears to have had considerable influence in retarding water-based conflict in the Middle East. When hostile groups are compelled, for whatever reasons, to share essential common goals—superordinate goals that are by nature overriding—and when cooperation clearly benefits all concerned, the hostile groups tend to cooperate rather than fight. Furthermore, this cooperation produces positive changes in how the actors perceive one another.[4] Nowhere has this corollary of water-based conflict been demonstrated more dramatically than in the modern Middle East; even in the bitterest strife between Middle Eastern riparians, remarkably few military attacks have been targeted against waterworks.

The Jordan River system as a model

The Jordan River system, where the problems of water use are at an advanced stage, illustrates a cross section of the water issue. A few basic facts will suffice to frame this issue between Israel and Jordan. The total annual flow of the Jordan system, without loss to evaporation or extraction for irrigation, is 1850 million cubic meters (MCM); the actual usable amount is 1400 MCM. This volume is double the amount of water available from all other sources in Israel and three times all other sources in Jordan. The total area of the Jordan River basin is 18,300 square kilometers, of which only 3 percent lies in pre-1967 Israel.

Israel's total annual needs are about 1750 MCM. Of Israel's current renewable supply from both surface and underground water sources, 95 percent to 99 percent is presently being used. Water from the Jordan River system fills 30 percent of Israel's water needs; up to 40 percent comes from the West Bank aquifer; the remainder, in varying amounts, comes from catchments, reclamation, underground sources, and various applications of technology. Israel is likely to fall into a water deficit within two years, and by the year 2000 its annual needs are projected to be about 2500 MCM.

Jordan's total annual needs are 870 MCM, of which 46 percent comes from the Jordan River and 54 percent from

3. Naff and Matson, eds., *Water in the Middle East*, pp. 1-15, 158-80.

4. Muzafer Sherif, "Superordinate Goals in the Reduction of Intergroup Conflict," *American Journal of Sociology*, 63(4):349-56 (Jan. 1958).

rain catchment, reclamation, underground, and out-of-basin transfers. Jordan gets no water from the West Bank. Jordan is presently in a state of water shortage requiring more than 100 percent of available renewable supply. By the beginning of the new century Jordan's needs are estimated to be 1000 MCM, exceeding the supply by 20 percent.[5]

For the past few years Israel and Jordan have been experiencing the worst drought in some 20 years. In 1983 more than 200 artificial reservoirs in Israel dried up and in 1984 the Israeli Water Commission cut allocation to farmers by 10 to 25 percent. In Jordan, where 78 percent of the country normally receives less than 200 millimeters of annual rainfall and where only 5.7 percent of the land is cultivable, agriculture is sustained by irrigation from the Jordan River system. In 1984, water supplies for irrigation dropped by 20 percent, and as much as a 50 percent loss was predicted for 1985 unless conditions improved. The Jordan Valley Authority rationed water to farmers, reduced the irrigation periods, and stopped pumping from the east stations of the King Talal Dam.[6]

In water-scarce regions where margins of tolerance are so narrow, even mild changes in the supply of water can have repercussions quickly and widely in an economy and can also have a significant impact on relations between states sharing a common water resource. The present state of water supply and quality in Israel and Jordan has produced a variety of conditions that demonstrate some of the ways water issues complicate and shape relations between riparian powers, for the most part in conformity with the interest-position-power matrix.

By the mid-1990s, unless consumption patterns change, there is a high probability that Israel, Jordan, and the West Bank will face acute and progressively worsening perennial water shortages. In this circumstance, the Jordan River system holds the greatest potential for conflict. Israel enjoys an upper riparian position and overpowering military advantage in relation to Jordan. Furthermore, as Israel's and Jordan's water needs grow in the face of diminishing resources, water will assume increasing primacy as a strategic factor in their regional policies. However, being in a much weaker riparian and military posture, Jordan can bolster its position only through a network of linkages to other states within and outside the region, thus increasing the chances that any ensuing conflict could overflow the region. The obvious way to avoid conflict would be to restructure the economies of the adversaries so as to alter present patterns of consumption, but deeply entrenched and interrelated ideological, security, and symbolic considerations make the necessary political

5. See Naff and Matson, eds., *Water in the Middle East*, pp. 17-61; J. Schwarz, "Water Resources in Jordan, Samaria, and the Gaza Strip," in *Judea, Samaria, and Gaza: Views on the Present and Future*, ed. Daniel J. Elazar (Washington, DC: American Enterprise Institute, 1982), pp. 81-100; Uri Davis, E. I. Antonia, and John Richardson, "Israel's Water Policies," *Journal of Palestine Studies*, 9(2):1-27 (Winter 1980); Itzhak Galnoor, "Water Policymaking in Israel," *Policy Analysis*, 4:339-44, 354 (1978); and Leslie Schmida, "Israel's Drive for Water," *Link*, 17(4):1-2 (Nov. 1984).

6. *Haaretz*, 10 Nov. 1983; ibid., 19 Feb. 1984; *Maariv*, 21 Dec. 1983; *Davar*, 15 Dec. 1983; *Al-dustur*, 6 Mar. 1984; ibid., 8 Mar. 1984; ibid., 17 June 1984; *Jerusalem Post*, 1 Mar. 1984.

decisions virtually impossible in both Israel and Jordan at present.[7]

Israel's application of internal power over West Bank Palestinians in regard to water-related behavior exemplifies another aspect of our model. By controlling the use of water, Israel reinforces its de facto exercise of sovereignty over the occupied territory. Palestinians are forbidden to dig new wells or repair old ones. Palestinian wells have an average depth of 70 meters while wells drilled by the Israeli settlements average 300 meters to 400 meters in depth, resulting in about one-third the level of salinity and a much greater productive capacity. In the presence of a deep proximate Israeli well, the shallow Palestinian well dries up and is not permitted to be replaced or improved. The net result of this policy, according to a 1981 statement by Meir Ben Meir, Israel's water commissioner, is that the per capita use of water by Israeli settlers is at least five times greater than West Bank Arab use. Other water-related controls such as prohibiting Palestinians from farming after 4:00 p.m. and forbidding the cultivation of certain crops while extending various advantages—including water subsidies—to the Israeli settlers enables Israel to use water as an instrument for establishing and maintaining control over a majority population in the interests of a minority group.[8]

The Jordan River system provides instructive illumination of the limits of cooperation and legal solutions. During the 1950s, American negotiators made intensive efforts to formulate among the riparian parties a comprehensive, multilateral approach for the regional development of the Jordan. While the final plan—the Johnston plan—failed to win full ratification, both Israel and Jordan undertook unilaterally to proceed with their own development within the allocations that the plan laid down. One of the features of the Johnston plan that never won approval, let alone ratification, provided for an international administrator who could settle differences. In consequence, subsequent unilateral implementation of the unratified agreement has been fragmented, fraught with controversy and misunderstanding that, in years of critical shortage, have had to be mediated on an ad hoc basis by outside—usually American—intervention.[9]

The developing danger of serious water shortages, as illustrated by the

7. Michael Brecher, *Decisions in Israel's Foreign Policy* (New Haven, CT: Yale University Press, 1975), pp. 173-224; Mark A. Heller, *A Palestinian State: The Implications for Israel* (Cambridge, MA: Harvard University Press, 1983), 126-31; Kanier Buren, "Permanent Sovereignty over National Resources in the Occupied Palestinian and Other Arab Territories," *Report of the United Nations Secretary General*, 1982. According to a 1983 report by the Middle East Institute, Washington, DC, Jordan is critically dependent on so few water facilities that "four successful Israeli air raids would cripple its economy." *Christian Science Monitor*, 25 May 1983.

8. Meron Benvenisti, *The West Bank and Gaza Project: A Survey of Israel's Policies* (Washington, DC: American Enterprise Institute, 1984), passim; Nafiz Nazzal, "Policies of the Israeli Occupation in the West Bank" (Wilson Center Working Papers, no. 46, International Security Studies Program, Princeton University, Sept. 1983); D. Epstein and Sharon Goulds, "West Bank in Troubled Water," *Middle East International*, 11 Aug. 1981; *Al-Quds*, 9 Dec. 1983; *Jordan Times*, 29 Aug. 1984; *Arab Report*, 14 Mar. 1979. The Israeli government's view of these policies is illustrated in Ministry of Foreign Affairs, *Briefing* (Jerusalem: Government of Israel, 14 Feb. 1982).

9. Naff and Matson, eds., *Water in the Middle East*, pp. 30-53, contains a fuller examination of the various plans for the Jordan River system and the policies of the riparian states.

example of the Jordan River system, will have far-reaching consequences for relations between states in the area. For an analysis of this complex issue, a general theoretical framework will be useful. It is to this task that we now turn.

ISSUES AND ISSUE ANALYSIS

The emergence of a major new issue tends to distort and disrupt established relations. Domestic and international politics take new turns, priorities and perspectives alter, new actors appear and old ones realign. Lipset, for example, argues that the emergence of "postmaterialist" or "quality of life" issues, has produced a momentous split in the Left of many Western nations, sundering its blue-collar and white-collar components. The result has been the rise of conservatism and the political ascendancy of the Right.[10] Vietnam, Watergate, the oil crisis, and the Iranian hostage crisis are other examples of largely unanticipated issues that tumbled regimes and recast politics.

Obviously, we should like to be able to predict the issues that will challenge political systems and, even more, foresee their important features and consequences. We might thus obtain enough leverage to mitigate conflicts, reduce costs, and shape outcomes. However, this task is far easier said than done. The essential requirement is to have some established theory to guide us. Having it, we might be able to diagnose a severe water crisis as an instance of a specific type, presenting particular dangers, treatable in particular ways, having particular costs, side effects, timetables, and so forth. Without it, we are doomed to myopia no matter how insightful the occasional analysis. The difference is similar to that between scientific navigation and flight by the seat of one's pants.

A typology of issues

A first theoretical tool for analyzing the significance of water as an emerging national and international issue in the Middle East seems to be a typology of issues. If patterns of power vary from one issue to another, what basic kinds of issues are there and where does a serious national shortage of water fit in under such a scheme? A general classification of issues might indicate other important features of the particular issue of concern and fruitful hypotheses about how these features are related. It would suggest ideas about what actors are likely to be involved, how severe a conflict is likely to be, what tactics will probably be employed, how likely a conflict is to spread, and so on.[11]

10. Seymour Martin Lipset, "Whatever Happened to the Proletariat?" *Encounter,* 56:18-34, esp. 24-30 (June 1981).

11. That issues both differ and matter beyond their immediate, specific content is one of the fairly recent discoveries of political science. First community power studies and then international relations observed that patterns of power frequently vary from issue to issue. Hence, to speak of a single power structure of a political system is usually seriously misleading. What type of system one is dealing with depends in part on what issue one examines. For landmark community power studies that developed the significance of issues, see Ernest A. T. Barth and Stuart D. Johnson, "Community Power and a Typology of Social Issues," *Social Forces,* 38:29-32 (Oct. 1959); Robert A. Dahl, *Who Governs?* (New Haven, CT: Yale University Press, 1961); Nelson W. Polsby, *Community Power and Political Theory* (New Haven, CT: Yale University Press, 1963); Andrew S. McFarland, *Power and Leadership in Pluralist Systems* (Stanford, CA: Stanford University Press, 1969); and Roy Forward, "Issue Analysis in Community Power Studies," *Australian Journal of Politics and History,* 15:26-44 (Dec. 1969).

Alas, political science has not yet developed such a general typology of issues, and deeper contemplation of the problem suggests that the very idea of one is misleading. Interesting attempts have been made, however, and several of them are useful despite their basic failure.[12] Perhaps the most famous is Lowi's distinction of distributive, regulatory, and redistributive issues, based essentially on the degree to which issues can be disaggregated. Distributive issues can be most minutely parceled, involve relatively small actors such as individual firms, invoke limited tactics such as logrolling, and provoke only very low intensity and noncontagious conflict. Redistributive issues, on the other hand, are maximally aggregated, involve large actors such as classes and movements represented by "peak associations," lead to clashes of elites and counter-elites, and generate intense, often violent and contagious conflict. Regulatory issues are intermediate in disaggregation and involve groups and interactions in the generally understood "pluralistic" pattern.[13]

Other well-known classifications of issues have emphasized their representativeness and importance, whether they tend toward the "pole of power," involving national security, or the "pole of indifference," involving minor values; whether they are "symmetrical," affecting all members of the system similarly, or "nonsymmetrical"; whether they are "tangible," involving visible resources, or "intangible"; whether they are "zero-sum"—if I win, you lose—or not; whether they involve crisis, with threat, short time span, and surprise, or are routine; whether they are foreign or domestic; and so forth.

The problems with these typologies are several and severe. First, it is often very difficult to determine the analytic category into which a particular issue fits. Some seem to fall between categories while others overlap categories. The categories are neither exhaustive nor exclusive, or the so-called issues are not homogeneous. Second, it is often quite unclear whether the asserted concomitants of an issue—actors, processes, and so forth—are empirically valid propositions or merely added definitional features; little evidence is adduced. Third, each of the various typologies seems to offer valuable insights into at least some situations while not capturing all-important elements of others.

These problems suggest that it is illusory to think that any single typology can do justice to the enormous number and variety of issues. What these ty-

12. Landmark international relations studies include, *inter alia*, Arnold Wolfers, *Discord and Collaboration* (Baltimore, MD: Johns Hopkins University Press, 1962); James N. Rosenau, "Pre-theories and Theories of Foreign Policy," in *Approaches to Comparative and International Politics*, ed. R. Barry Farrell (Evanston, IL: Northwestern University Press, 1966), pp. 27-92, esp. 71-88; idem, "Foreign Policy as an Issue-Area," in *Domestic Sources of Foreign Policy*, ed. James N. Rosenau (New York: Free Press, 1967), pp. 11-51; Thomas L. Brewer, "Issue and Context Variations in Foreign Policy: Effects on American Elite Behavior," *Journal of Conflict Resolution*, 17: 89-114 (Mar. 1973); William Zimmerman, "Issue Area and Foreign Policy Process: A Research Note in Search of a General Theory," *American Political Science Review*, 67:1204-12 (Dec. 1973); and William C. Potter and Joel King, "Issue Area and the Comparative Study of Foreign Policy: An Empirical Approach" (Paper presented at the Annual Meeting of the International Studies Association, San Francisco, CA, 18-20 Mar. 1976).

13. Theodore J. Lowi, "American Business, Public Policy, Case Studies and Political Theory," *World Politics*, 16: 677-715 (July 1964); idem, "Making Democracy Safe for the World: National Politics," in *Domestic Sources of Foreign Policy*, ed. Rosenau, pp. 285-331.

TABLE 1
ISSUE PROFILE: A CURRENT, COMMON, INFORMED ISRAELI VIEW OF THE JORDAN WATER ISSUE

	1	2	3	4	5	6	7	
Routine					✓			Crisis
Symbolic	✓							Pragmatic
Domestic				✓				Foreign
Unique					✓			Recurrent
Contagious		✓						Isolated
Aggregate		✓						Disaggregate
Secret					✓			Open
Short-run					✓			Long-run
Intense			✓					Relaxed
Public			✓					Private
Technical		✓						Nontechnical
Power		✓						Nonpower
Simple					✓			Complex
Prestige			✓					Nonprestige
Legitimate			✓					Illegitimate
Costly		✓						Cheap
Tangible			✓					Intangible
Many-actor			✓					Few-actor
Narrow					✓			Broad
Zero-sum			✓					Non-zero-sum
Survival		✓						Nonsurvival
Intrinsic		✓						Instrumental
Old				✓				New
Symmetric					✓			Nonsymmetric
Salient			✓					Background

pologies do is to take one or a few of the many important features of issues and erect a typology in those terms. A better strategy, perhaps, is not to think of typologies in the usual sense but rather to think in terms of what we shall call issue profiles. In other words, we might concentrate on elucidating what seem to be the main or most critical general features of issues, assuming that these will be more than a few. Issues would thus be characterized in more complex fashion by an indication of their relative positions along a number of defined dimensions, not merely in terms of one or a very few features. A schematic representation of such an issue profile in a form borrowed from the semantic differential is presented in Table 1.[14]

14. On the semantic differential, see Charles E. Osgood, George J. Suci, and Percy H. Tannenbaum, *The Measurement of Meaning* (Urbana: University of Illinois Press, 1957). The adjectival scales—e.g., routine to crisis—presented here are mixed in directionality, as presented to respondents. Factor analysis might reveal more basic groupings of scales, such as the well-established factors of evaluation, power, and activity. However, for issue analysis, particular dimensions—or scales—will probably also retain their individual significance.

The "to whom?" problem

We would be happy to report that the problems of issue analysis end here, but they do not. Another formidable difficulty that has been sadly neglected can be called the "to whom?" problem: to whom is a given situation an issue? By this we refer to the fact that what an issue is and what its main features or concomitants are depend very much on the eye of the beholder—they are matters of perception. Nevertheless, most analysts most of the time have acted as if issues were a matter of automatic consensus. Some have even argued explicitly that the substance or content of an issue is a clear, objective matter and that issues can therefore be effectively classified by the analyst—for example, as military, political, economic, or cultural—without regard to the participants.[15]

Although such a view would greatly simplify analysis and should thus be welcomed if otherwise acceptable, it appears naive. If an issue is defined as a situation in which one or more actors perceive that their interests are blocked or frustrated by one or more other actors, then it is inescapably a perceptual phenomenon. For sane actors, perceptions and objective reality are linked; but we well know that such linkage is loose enough to permit wide variations. These occur as a result of cognitive differences and differences in felt interest.

Hence, in analyzing issues, one must ascertain the issue profiles of all essential actors in the political system of concern. One cannot get away with the more-than-heroic assumption that all the issue profiles are identical. Water shortage, for example, means different things to different actors. It is usually not an issue for some even in Israel or Jordan; for others to whom it is an issue, its dimensions may vary greatly. This means that our analysis becomes highly iterative—or incorporates much trial and error—as we try to determine who are the critical actors involved in water politics in each country, how each one views the shortage situation, what their likely interactions will be, and so on. Situations—sets of circumstances—can be relatively objectively defined, as in a decrease in river flow or water table, although objective definition is far from easy. But issues—whether participants will see their interests frustrated by others—are always subjective, perceptual data for the analyst. The extent to which a specific situation produces uniform issue perceptions is an empirical question not to be begged.[16]

15. See Michael Brecher, Blema Steinberg, and Janice Stein, "A Framework for Research on Foreign Policy Behavior," *Journal of Conflict Resolution,* 13:75-101 (Mar. 1969); and Potter and King, "Issue Area and the Comparative Study of Foreign Policy," pp. 15ff.

16. The critical distinction here is that between an issue and a situation, a distinction generally and unfortunately confused in most analyses. The former is, by definition, a psychological variable; the latter is any set of circumstances that an actor may perceive. A situation becomes an issue for an actor if and only if that actor perceives it to involve blockage of felt interests by another actor. Situations may sometimes have the inherent properties that certain analysts mistakenly suggest for issues, although the idea raises difficult philosophic questions. Issues, however, are always determined by the perceiver, and the same situation may generate quite different perceptions—and therefore different likelihoods of being an issue—for various actors. The general relationships between situations and issues are a crucial concern of cognitive political psychology. When we say that patterns of power vary from issue to issue we actually mean from situation to situation and assume—often wrongly—that issues vary correspondingly.

FIGURE 1
COGNITIVE MAP OF THE GENERAL ISRAELI PERSPECTIVE OF THE JORDAN WATER ISSUE

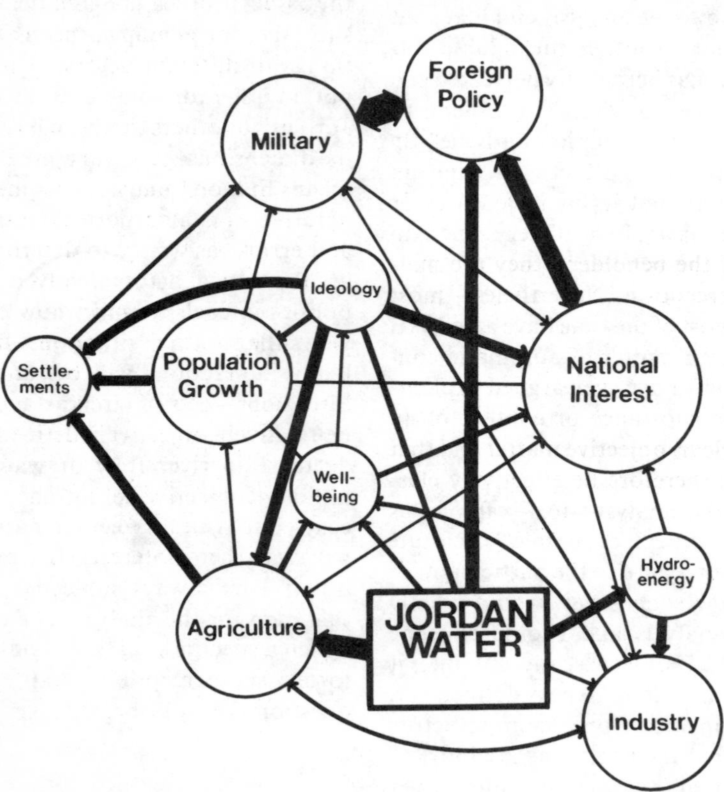

SOURCE: Thomas Naff and Ruth C. Matson, eds., *Water in the Middle East: Conflict or Cooperation?* (Boulder, CO: Westview Press, 1984), p. 186.

Cognitive mapping

One approach to this problem that we have found helpful is Robert Axelrod's "cognitive mapping."[17] This involves ascertaining the cognitive elements in an actor's perception of an issue as well as the perceived linkages among those elements. One thus obtains a kind of mental map or cognitive structure of the issue as seen by the relevant actor. Composite cognitive maps for what seem to be a fairly typical Israeli view of the Jordan water situation and a fairly typical Turkish view of the Orontes water situation are presented in Figures 1 and 2, respectively.

The comparison of the cognitive maps of an issue held by each major actor is instructive for locating critical differences that may be determining policy and behavior, and for ascertaining whether the issues are real—that is, whether the perceptions are similar and the problems lie in conflicting inter-

17. Robert Axelrod, *Structure of Decision: The Cognitive Maps of Political Elites* (Princeton, NJ: Princeton University Press, 1976).

FIGURE 2
COGNITIVE MAP OF THE GENERAL TURKISH PERSPECTIVE OF THE ORONTES WATER ISSUE

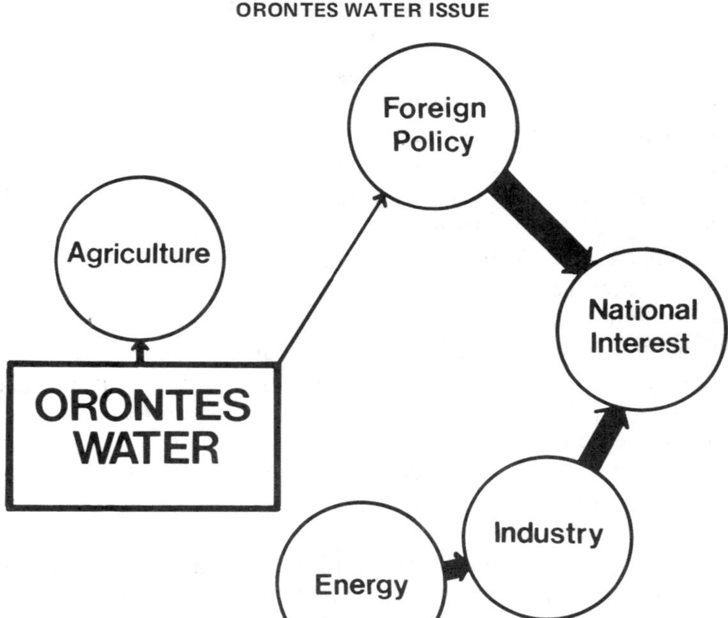

SOURCE: Naff and Matson, eds., *Water in the Middle East,* p. 188.

ests—or whether at least a significant part of the conflict is due to the utilization of discrepant cognitive maps that might be resolved by negotiation, information, or other means. Of course, as currently developed, these cognitive maps capture only a part of the major dimensions of issue perception, as a comparison of Table 1 with Figures 1 and 2 will reveal. They are, however, very useful in depicting the complexity and critical components of the way in which actors view situations.

Several fundamental observations emerge from an examination of Figure 1, which depicts a presumably common Israeli view of the water situation. Even at this condensed level, the interconnectedness of the water factor with other key factors is revealed. Aggregation is high. From the Israeli perspective, water is strongly linked to agriculture. This is ideally—and very often actually—irrigated agriculture; dry farming is not the prevailing image. A fuller map would interpolate an irrigation cognition between water and agriculture. Agriculture, in turn, is strongly linked to ideology. The Israeli and Zionist aspiration to "make the desert bloom," as David Ben-Gurion said, makes water, according to the Israelis' own change of metaphor, the "lifeblood" of the system—"a prerequisite for a new society," and a "nation rooted in its land." As Galnoor stresses, "Water carries ideological weight" because of its association with agriculture; it is never, for

Zionists, "merely another economic resource."[18]

Nor is Israeli agriculture merely an ordinary economic sector or even a model life-style. It is linked to the crucial matter of settlements, and settlements are linked to defense and national security. Settlements are seen as strategic outposts used as a first step in the consolidation of territory, providing frontier resistance and thus time in case of attack. Agricultural settlements each consisting of 60 to 80 specially trained families accomplish this much more effectively than urban-industrial communities.

Water in Israel is also linked to energy. Roughly a quarter of Israel's energy resources is used for the National Water Carrier, irrigation, and other water purposes. Water is also seen to relate in many ways to population growth and national well-being through potation, sanitation, recreation, aesthetics, and the like. In the minds of many important Israelis, as one prime minister, Moshe Sharett, put it, "water to us is life itself."[19] It is linked strongly to many major beliefs and values. Indeed, it is regarded as a primary need, overriding lesser concerns and justifying even the most drastic actions if its supply is threatened. Although water may not have been the prime impetus behind the Israeli acquisition of territory, as the "hydraulic imperative" alleges, it seems to be perhaps the main factor determining its retention of that territory.

The Israeli cognitive map of the Jordan water situation is in sharp contrast to the Turkish map of the Orontes. (See Figure 2.) Here one finds a map with fewer cognitive elements, which are much less well connected. Settlements, security, and agriculture are not so keenly affected, and ideology is less involved. Not surprisingly, perceived Turkish interests in this water source and associated issues display small potential for conflict. Unless the issue becomes highly symbolic, serious contention seems unlikely.

Putting all this together, water appears to be a highly complicated set of issues rather than a single focus. It is, of course, a basic human need; but it is not ordinarily a political issue and water conflict is not an everyday occurrence—at least not yet. The main reason for this is Maslovian.[20] At the individual level, the demand for water is highly inelastic, although fairly readily satiable. Personally, we do not need much, but we need that small amount urgently and reliably. Once the basic needs are satisfied, the salience of water as an issue disappears. The sinister corollary of this, however, is that if such basic needs are not met, they override more sophisticated interests and become absolute and obsessive. Water tends to be taken for granted and to be less salient than other resources under normal conditions. But, under extreme conditions, it is clearly a fighting matter, as many a range war in the United States has demonstrated. If sudden and extremely threatening changes in a nation's water

18. Itzhak Galnoor, "Water Policymaking in Israel," pp. 339-65.

19. Brecher, *Decisions in Israeli Foreign Policy*, p. 184, quoting from *Divrei Ha-knesset* [Official records of the Knesset], 17: 495 (3 Jan. 1955).

20. A. H. Maslow, *Motivation and Personality* (New York: Harper & Brothers, 1954), pp. 80-122. Maslow's classic work distinguishes concentric levels of motivation. From inner to outer these are: physiological needs, safety needs, belongingness and love, esteem, and self-actualization. If the inner needs are satisfied, the outer needs dominate behavior; if the inner needs are not satisfied, they dominate.

situation occur, surprisingly swift eruption of conflict may well follow.

Under conditions of severe shortage, water becomes for many key actors a highly symbolic, legitimate, zero-sum, survival, aggregated, crisis, contagious, intense, salient, prestige- and power-packed, complicated, technical, tangible, and public issue. As such, it seems to have a strong potential for violence unless conflicts are mediated by a strong authority, which is patently lacking in the region. Furthermore, under the chronic tension of severe shortage, other features of the water situation become dangerous. For example, water supply is markedly affected by climate; annual and seasonal variations are often striking. Should there be a drought when tensions are already high from increasing water shortage, a bad situation may become perilously worse. For all these reasons, if a pessimistic scenario appears at all plausible, early attention to the possibility and likely consequences of water crises in the Middle East would appear essential.

MODELING WATER CONFLICTS

There are, obviously, many actions that nations of the Middle East that are nearing the "water barrier" could take to delay or avoid that prospect.[21] Technology has long been seen as the certain panacea. It may yet be; technological breakthroughs are notoriously difficult to predict. At present, however, although one or two hopeful flames still flicker, most of the anticipated answers—such as desalination through nuclear power and replacing spray irrigation with drip methods—have proven highly uneconomical and/or prohibitively expensive on the scale required. As shortages develop, ideas of what cost levels are prohibitive can be expected to change. For now, however, the economic obstacles to technological change on a scale that would make a difference are dominant.[22] One reaction to the economic problem might clearly be to ask for foreign financial aid to make up the difference. If the alternative were seen as violent international conflict in the region, the nations asked might even perceive the expenditure as the lesser of two evils.

Remedies other than technology might also solve the problem. Israel, for example, uses about 80 percent of its water supply for agricultural purposes. Hence, one evident response would be to downgrade agriculture in favor of light industry, which is nearly a third more productive of income per unit of water. Probably some movement in this direction is inevitable, but it looks as if it will not come easily. We have already mentioned the heavy symbolic and ideological weight of water and agriculture in Zionism and Israel. To this must be added the heavy political weight of the agricultural lobby in Israeli politics. A de-emphasis of agriculture would presumably be seriously resisted and cause difficult domestic strife.

If all else fails, severe water shortages might well provoke armed conflict among riparians in the main river basins affected. Part of any analysis must therefore be an attempt to finds ways to assess the likelihood and location of such conflict as much before the fact as possible. The water shortages projected

21. The discussion in this section of this article borrows from, and is somewhat more fully developed in, Naff and Matson, eds., *Water in the Middle East*, pp. 192-95.

22. Ibid., passim; *Jerusalem Post*, 16 Oct. 1982; ibid., 13 Feb. 1983; ibid., 22 July 1984; ibid., 12 Aug. 1984.

would advance upon the countries of the Middle East over time, probably in the course of one or two decades. The typical response, therefore, is most likely to be muddling through—grudging, incremental adjustments in the face of a steadily worsening situation. Then, at some point, one or more actors may find the strain excessive and attempt to alleviate it by military action. Is there any way of anticipating when and where the conflict would likely occur and who would be involved?

At a very elementary level, at least three major factors appear to shape riparian-use water conflicts: (1) interests and issues, or the motivations and perceptions of the actors; (2) riparian position; and (3) projectable power.[23]

Felt interests and perceived issues define the particular motivations and cognitions of the participants, channeling them toward collision or cooperation. If interests are perceived as fostered or complemented by other actors, the pressure will be toward cooperation. Indeed, the water situation brought the Middle East as close as it has ever come to durable peace in 1955 under the Johnston plan. It might conceivably do the same again, even though the prospects now seem worse. With uncommon leadership and luck, water shortage can be the kind of overriding, obvious concern that produces an awareness of common goals.

On the opposite side, if interests are perceived as blocked by others, the pressure will be toward conflict. If the blockage is seen as deliberate, avoidable, and illegitimate, and if it occurs close to goal realization, the threat of conflict is increased. Such factors are cumulative.

Blockage, however, does not always lead to conflict. It is frequently constrained or suppressed by considerations of power. In the simplest cases, either the aroused actor does not see itself as possessing the power to reduce or eliminate the blockage, or, although it has that power, it finds that the costs of using it exceed the benefits anticipated.

In riparian-use water issues, one power factor is sufficiently determinative to justify its separation from the rest for special notice. This is riparian position. In general, upstream position confers marked power advantages. From such a position one can usually take actions that confront downstream competitors with *faits accomplis*, the alteration of which is far more demanding than the original actions. Diversion, overuse, contamination, and flow delay are tactics available in accordance with one's position on the riparian totem pole. The main qualification is an adjustment for flow; being upstream ceases to be such an advantage if one is above significant flow. An example of the significance of upstream position is Israel's forcible alteration of its riparian position from originally being downstream on all important Jordan River tributaries except the Dan to having a controlling upstream position on all except the Yarmuk.

The third factor, projectable power, refers to a nation's ability to threaten its opponents credibly at whatever distance is necessary and thus to shape their behavior regarding water issues. Internal power over water-related actions—especially the ability to control water distribution and the allocation of costs—may also be significant. One aspect of

23. For the notion of projected power, see W. Scott Thompson, *Power Projection: A Net Assessment of U.S. and Soviet Capabilities* (New York: National Strategy Information Center, 1978).

TABLE 2
MODEL MATRICES FOR RIPARIAN-USE WATER ISSUES IN TWO MIDDLE EASTERN RIVER SYSTEMS

River System and Constituent Riparian States	Interest	Riparian Position	Power	Total
Jordan				
Lebanon	2	2	1	5
Syria	2	2	3	7
Jordan	5	3	2	10
Israel	5	4	5	14
Euphrates				
Turkey	3	5	5	13
Syria	4	3	3	10
Iraq	4	1	4	9

SOURCE: Thomas Naff and Ruth C. Matson, eds. *Water in the Middle East: Conflict or Cooperation?* (Boulder, CO: Westview Press, 1984), p. 194.

this analysis that commands particular attention is that of the military and strategic implications of large-scale water projects. We suspect that these may act rather like nuclear weapons in some senses; they may induce caution under most conditions, but, if involved—that is, if attacked—they may seriously escalate conflict.

At present, we are attempting to evaluate the riparians of each of the major water systems in the Middle East in terms of the three basic factors just described. Each nation is rated numerically according to its relative strength along each criterion and given an overall ranking that is the sum of the three, as depicted in Table 2 for the Jordan and the Euphrates. The main hypothesis informing the analysis is that conflict potential is generally highest among riparians with relatively high interest and relatively equal overall ratings, provided there is no higher-ranked actor with strong interest. Thus, Syria and Iraq are in a conflict position regarding the Euphrates under conditions of full use or shortage of the river's water supply. Turkey is in the most advantageous position of all, but its lower degree of interest inhibits its dominance of the situation. For the Jordan system, the data are especially revealing. When Israel was in a relatively poor riparian position, the prospects for trouble were very great and trouble did occur. Israel had high interest, great relative power, but poor riparian position—almost a prescription for strife. Now, as far as the Jordan waters alone are concerned, Israel dominates the scene, strong on all three factors. Major conflict is precluded.

CONCLUSION

We have had two major goals in this article. The first and most immediate has been to alert policymakers and the concerned public to what we regard as a potentially severe crisis gathering in several parts of the Middle East: the danger of increasingly serious water shortages. Various key aspects of such crises were described and illustrated through an examination of the Jordan River situation.

If water shortages do emerge as a critical new issue in the Middle East, we are, of course, deeply interested in projecting their likely consequences for that troubled area. To do so essentially requires having some effective theory to guide us. Our second goal, therefore, has been to contribute to the development of such theory, now largely lacking. We have discussed basic problems of issue analysis, suggesting a reconceptualization of the notion of an issue and outlining some useful approaches to empirical investigation such as issue profiles and cognitive mapping. Using these approaches we were able to indicate that the water issue means different things to different actors under different conditions. Under severe shortage, however, it tends to become a highly symbolic, crisis, contagious, aggregated, intense, salient, complicated, zero-sum, power- and prestige-packed issue, thus highly prone to conflict and difficult to resolve. At the same time, the very severity of the issue makes it a possibly unique vehicle for cooperation if the parties see that as the only feasible solution. The latter is, however, a tantalizingly difficult image to create.

We have also proposed a very simple model of the conditions leading to violent conflict over water. Three factors seem most relevant: interest, riparian position, and projectable power. When interest is high and the overall weights are nearly equal, conflict is most likely.

These are, naturally, but the first steps toward a more comprehensive and effective theory of issues and water conflicts. If they do no more than call attention to the problem and stimulate urgently needed analyses, our paramount objective will have been realized.

* * *

QUESTIONS AND ANSWERS

Q (George Gruen, Institute of Human Relations, New York City): I spent some time studying the Yarmuk Valley development plans in the sixties and then also in the seventies. Now the problem of the West Bank water is obviously a very serious one. It was envisioned in the original plan that there would be a shortage unless the water of the Yarmuk were properly tapped, the Yarmuk being the major tributary of the Jordan.

My understanding is that Jordan did develop the East Ghor Canal. The original plan, which predated the 1967 war, envisioned that a dam on the Yarmuk itself, either at Maqarin or Mukheiba, would provide enough water to extend the East Ghor Canal in East Jordan, as well as bring water—by a siphon—to the West Bank and therefore not compete with the water that Israel was using.

The East Ghor Canal has been built, but the High Dam has not been built. I understand that part of the problem is the Israeli occupation of the Golan Heights, but the Syrians seem to be contributing to the problem, too. Do Syrian-Jordanian relations present an obstacle, and, if they do, how can the obstacle be removed?

A (Naff): Nothing is happening now concerning the plans for the High Dam. The inactivity is due partly to relations between Jordan and Syria but also to the diversion of Syrian attention and resources to Lebanon and the occupation of Lebanon. But the plans still remain. There is expressed intention and, depending on who is asked, determination to go ahead with the High Dam. This example is a good illustration of how highly fragmented the issue of water is. Plans are being made for another project on the tributary of a larger system, and its impact will extend beyond that immediate area. There are three countries involved: Syria, Iraq, and Turkey. The projects are being implemented in southeastern Turkey, and they are going to have a major impact on the use of the Tigris and the Euphrates for three riparian nations; yet the nations are not talking to each other. There is no effort whatsoever, for political reasons; there is no effort to attempt an integrated or comprehensive approach at solving these problems.

Q (David Wishart, Wittenberg University, Springfield, Ohio): Horace Engineering Company, which developed plans for the Maqarin Dam, indicated to me in the summer of 1984 that there was a 15-year hiatus in the dam project as a result of Syrian intransigence on the issue, and not so much because of any objections by Israel on the dam. Since the Johnston negotiations in the 1950s, Israel has pretty much agreed to building the dam.

I am not sure about the meaning of water shortages. It has been said that a water shortage can only exist if the price of water is below that necessary to equate quantity demanded with quantity supplied. This is certainly the case in Israel. Agricultural water users pay about a third of what municipal and industrial water users pay. This cost schedule has two negative side effects. First of all, too much water is devoted to agriculture and agriculture is the most consumptive form of water use; it also has the lowest value of water use in Israel. Second, too little attention is devoted to technological change toward more efficient water-use methods in Israel. Israel has been a pioneer in that area and could go even further if the price of water to agricultural users were allowed to rise.

Current water costs in Israel have an implication for Jordan as well, given that the Maqarin Dam is not going to be built for the next 15 years or so. The best hope for Jordan lies in technological improvement, which was given quite a lot of attention at the Jordan National Water Symposium in 1978.

One thing that was not addressed at the symposium was the efforts made in Israel over the last 12 to 15 years toward more efficient water use. It seems that Jordan could benefit a great deal by the research that has gone on in Israel concerning efficient water-use technologies and also in terms of bureaucratic structure for centralized water management.

There has been some transfer of technologies from Israel to Jordan by way of a black market that has developed on the West Bank. Pipes and systems for drip irrigation are being sold to Jordanian farmers and transferred across the border through the black market. It seems that this is an area in which some effective work might be done toward positive policy. Instead of an underground market, why could there not be an above-ground market? It would be a way of brightening an otherwise hopeless situation.

A (Frey): Most of Israeli water is used for agricultural purposes. One of the things that we are concerned with is technological improvements to produce better use of that water. A considerable portion of Israeli agriculture is now irrigated through spray irrigation, and conversion to drip would reduce the water usage. Conversion, however, is expensive.

Related to achieving efficient water use is the presence in Israeli politics of a very significant agricultural lobby. There will have to be some major internal political battles fought if Israel is to take some of the progressive measures that you described. Also related is Israeli policymaking regarding agriculture. My understanding is that it is quite good in many ways up to a subcabinet level. But many problems about water, as far as we can tell, have not been very effectively discussed at the highest levels of the Israeli political system.

One can consider the possible or likely technological changes and try to calculate the savings and costs that result, but one of the more pessimistic conclusions drawn is that these changes at their best will not be enough if other trends continue.

COMMENT (Naff): The 15-year duration of the hiatus in building the Maqarin Dam is an odd length of time. I do not know how they arrived at it exactly. It is not official policy or even intention. I think it describes the perception of circumstances and the chances of getting things moving.

I think that this setback could turn around very rapidly, provided that the political agreements are in place. That black market in pipes is an interesting development, but that kind of exchange has long existed in the region among adversaries, and the volume of transfers through the black market is not large enough to make any real impact. The bottom line is to establish the required political agreements, and there are a lot of obstacles to doing that.

COMMENT: I would like to underscore that so much of the problem with water in the Middle East, as elsewhere, is not scarcity but management. In Egypt, for example, there is too much water. The pricing of water is too low and has led to deterioration of the soils of Egypt. In Libya we see a decision to utilize pivot irrigation, which uses fossil waters. That decision is wrong because fossil waters are nonrenewable sources. Efficient management of water will require more examination of the internal politics of these countries to determine why such inefficiencies exist. Very often the solutions are political, as you suggest. Some of the solutions—perhaps more than are given credit—are also technological; drip irrigation certainly is one example. Another is the Israeli goal of eliminating orange groves simply because the demand for water in orange groves is so high. I think that the technological side must be built into the model more than it has been.

COMMENT (Frey): One of the fundamental questions is whether the best judgments we can find regarding water management would be enough to counter the tendencies toward inefficient use. My own feeling at this juncture—and it may change as we get more information—is that they probably cannot. Also, water management very often is an international matter, an aspect that raises additional complications.

COMMENT: Saudi Arabia has the ability and, depending on the price, the income to afford the price of providing water that would be economically not feasible.

COMMENT (Frey): You are exactly right. Our technical experts take the proposal of using an iceberg as a water source very seriously. Apparently the biggest problem is hauling that iceberg out of the Antarctic currents because if only a minor mistake is made in navigation, the cargo will end up in the Indian Ocean or the Pacific or some other place than the desired destination. With precise navigation, moving the iceberg is thinkable.

The Saudi case is, however, irrelevant in some respects because the Saudis have energy to burn, to use a literal comment. The technological development that seems most promising at the moment is the reverse osmosis process, by which they are able to develop a giant membrane—of an extent that we have not been able to contemplate before—for use in the purification of water. But all the proposals that we have looked at so far are not economical; they are several times more expensive than current sources of water.

COMMENT (Naff): It must be remembered that the situation is not static. The projections of needs at the turn of the century are obviously relative figures. We do not know precisely what will be needed because we do not know precisely what will be happening between now and the end of the century or what kind of political situation will exist.

The price factor as a controlling element in the management of water is extremely important but also very complicated. In the final analysis it is not likely to be the only determinant; it will be one important determinant among many. All kinds of variables must be taken into account in any given model, but we are looking at a moving target. Essentially need and consumption are moving in one direction at the moment, and change in order to mitigate the problem is moving in another. The gap between the two presents the problem that we are looking at now and about which we are trying to make projections.

With regard to the iceberg, some of our people have calculated that even if the navigation were perfect, the vessel and its iceberg, due to the current, would still have to circumnavigate the southern part of the globe four times before they could get to port.

Q (Duygu Sezer, Columbia University, New York City): The irrigation project in southeastern Turkey is still in the initial stages, as far as I know. I think one of the interesting questions that you have raised concerns the prospects for—and at the moment, the apparent impossibility of—cooperation among the regional riparian states, Syria, Iraq, and Turkey. My first question is, Is there any regional cooperation on irrigation projects at the international level among countries reflecting more or less the same socioeconomic and social-plus-political interaction? Second, have you been able to obtain official views on what the countries see the project to be promising for them? For example, does Syria or Iraq see future problems in the Turkish project?

A (Frey): We hope our next step will be sending analysts to the various countries to interview policymakers and other people with regard to these water problems. We have not made a comparative study outside the Middle East. We are comparing the various nations within the Middle East and the various river basins that we are examining. Maybe a comparative study would be a good thing to do in the international legal area.

If Turkey goes ahead with the plans that have been projected, then there may be a considerable change in the water of the Euphrates. These plans involve a major switch from using water essentially for hydroelectric power to using water much more for irrigation and agriculture, and the latter are much more consumptive of water. Some of the plans have been implemented, but many of them have not. If they all were to be realized, the change would be very great. One of the things we are trying to study is whether they will be realized or not.

ANNALS, *AAPSS*, **482**, November 1985

The Rule of the Clerics in the Islamic Republic of Iran

By MARVIN ZONIS

ABSTRACT: Direct rule by Islamic clerics in Iran is an important new phenomenon in Middle Eastern politics. The legitimacy of clerical rule is based on an ideology developed from Shiite thought by Ayatollah Ruhollah Khomeini and his neofundamentalist followers. This ideology is embodied in the Iranian Constitution, which institutionalizes rule by Islamic clerics. Their sense of legitimacy has been reinforced by Khomeini's commitment to maintaining clerical rule, by his claim to leadership on the basis of a divine calling, and by a monopolization of the interpretation of the sacred law. The principal themes of clerical rule include grandiosity, an insistence on unity, ascription of hostile motives to the actions of other states, a preference for military solutions to political problems, and a belief in ultimate victory. Replication of the Iranian pattern of clerical rule elsewhere in the Middle East will be problematic without the emergence of a figure like Khomeini or the assistance of Iran.

Marvin Zonis is professor of behavioral sciences in the Committee on Human Development at the University of Chicago, where he teaches psychology of politics and Middle Eastern politics. Since 1983 he has been international editor at WBBM-TV, Chicago. From 1976 to 1979 he was the director of the University of Chicago's Center for Middle Eastern Studies. His publications include The Political Elite of Iran.

AMONG the most startling recent phenomena in the politics of the Middle East has been the direct rule of Islamic clerics in Iran. Shiite theologians fill major political offices in an Islamic republic whose supreme power is, by its constitutional principle of *velayat-e faqih* ("the rule of the jurist") concentrated in Ayatollah Ruhollah Khomeini.

While clerics have frequently been influential in the politics of Middle Eastern states in the past—and they have been influential qua clerics—they have only infrequently held formal political power. The clerical political activism now so evident throughout the region, furthermore, is distinguished by the breadth of its geographical scope. Virtually the entire Middle East—including, given certain fascinating parallels, Israel—is witnessing an intense struggle for political power by religious clerics.

Were Ayatollah Khomeini to realize his deepest wish, that struggle would be decided in favor of the clerics. That is certainly the end to which Iran's foreign policy is directed. In that sense, Iran's experience of rule by the clerics may be instructive for the future of the Middle East.

Four components of clerical rule in Iran are examined here. One component is the ideology drawn from Shiite thought that is used to legitimate clerical rule. This ideology has been largely formulated by Ayatollah Khomeini and his fellow neofundamentalists. Second, the articles of the Constitution of the Islamic Republic of Iran that specify clerical rule are identified. Third, I speculate on the consequences of the ideology and the constitutional provisions for the world view of the clerics in their political roles. Finally, key themes of clerical rule in Iran are outlined. These themes, it is suggested, are not unique to clerics as political leaders, but they nonetheless are fostered by the interplay of religion and politics.

THE IDEOLOGY OF CLERICAL RULE

The first and most significant split in the history of Islam, between Sunnis and Shiites, occurred over the issue of political leadership—specifically, who would succeed the Prophet Muhammad. The partisans, or Shiat, of Ali, who was the cousin and nephew of the Prophet, argued that the meaning of the Quran could be divined only by those in the Prophet's family. This esoteric view of the Quran's meaning, which held that the Prophet and his descendants were blessed with divine power or knowledge, was upheld against the prevalent exoteric understanding of the Quran adhered to by the majority Sunnis. The Sunnis argued that any man who could demonstrate he had the moral, ethical, and intellectual qualities to implement the evident—as opposed to the hidden—exigencies of the Quran could claim the caliphate. This claim, in turn, had to be subject to the consensus of the community. Given this fundamental difference in attitude toward the Quran—toward the word of God—there was no way for the Sunnis and the Shiites to agree on the basis for leadership of the community. The result was the development of the sharp schism that has persisted to the present.

Out of that schism and the subsequent competition for leadership of the Islamic community and—most importantly—out of the martyrdom of Hussein, Ali's second son, in the desert of Karbala in southern Iraq, several key themes in Shiite thought emerged. Among these, as Hamid Enayat observed, "the most astounding feature . . . is an attitude of mind which refuses to admit that the majority opinion is necessarily true or right."[1] The Shiites developed the belief that their community, by its lineage to the Prophet as passed through the 12 *imams*, has a kind of monopoly over the comprehension of Islam. This belief, in turn, engendered an attitude of self-righteous indignation or even contempt for those who claim—as do the Sunnis—that because they represent the majority, their interpretation of Islam and, hence, their leadership of the Islamic community, are legitimate.[2]

Thus the sense of moral superiority in Shiite thought is closely tied to a strong sense of political elitism. The belief that the 12 *imams*—the Shiite line of successors to the Prophet—were infallible, in contrast to the inherent weakness of most men, produced an elitist theory of governance according to which the *imams* would make all decisions and rulings for the community.

In time, it was argued that until the return of the twelfth *imam*, still in occultation, the *mujtahids*, the most learned of the *ulama*, or the Islamic clerics, would fulfill the rule of the *imams*. The basis of their authority was not held to be any possession of divinity or infallibility. Rather, that claim was based on their knowledge of the Quran, the example (*sunna*) of the Prophet, and the traditions (*hadith*) of the Prophet and the other *imams*.[3]

But to the extent that the masses were willing to accord the *mujtahids* the quality of infallibility, the latter could derive great power and authority. This became particularly true during the middle of the nineteenth century in Iran, when the concept of the leading *mujtahid* (*marja-i taqlid*) arose. According to this concept, Shiites were to choose a living *mujtahid* after whom they would pattern their lives, and thus the *mujta-*

1. Hamid Enayat, *Modern Islamic Political Thought* (Austin: University of Texas Press, 1982), p. 19.

2. Because Iran was eventually to become the center of Shiism while the Sunni sect came to predominate in the Arab world, an ideological basis was created for Iranian-Arab hostility. Many subsequent historical events, most recently the Iran-Iraq war, have fortified that division and the mutual contempt between Arabs and Iranians. The Islamic Republic of Iran has found that its efforts to lead the Islamic world have been impeded by that mutual hostility. Consequently, it has devoted considerable effort to downplaying the significance of differences with the Arab world. For example, Iran's Majlis Speaker, Hojatolislam Ali Akbar Hashemi Rafsanjani recently addressed a Tehran conference attended by theologians from Arab countries. He assured his largely Sunni audience that "we consider the Arabic language as one of the noblest in the world and believe that Arab literature is a divine blessing bestowed upon humanity by the almighty. It is the language of the Quran, the Prophet, the Imams, as well as our religion and our history. Our glosses in the libraries are all in Arabic. Our Ulema are now writing in Arabic. . . . So you can see that we are not prejudiced towards the Arabs. On the contrary, we feel sentimental towards them." *Kayhan International*, 5 May 1985, p. 1.

3. Some scholars hold that the tradition by which the *mujtahids* assumed the role of representing the *imams* is rooted in the story according to which the sixth *imam*, Jafar al-Sadiq, delegated this authority to the *ulama*. See Leonard Binder, "The Proof of Islam: Religion and Politics in Islam," in *Arabic and Islamic Studies in Honor of Hamilton Gibb* (Leiden: E. J. Brill, 1965). Still others, notably Eliash, argue that the story of Sadiq's delegation of authority does not adequately explain how the *mujtahids* came to be powerful. He argues that their leadership was not the result of any action taken by Imam Jafar but rather that it was the result of a historical process during which the *mujtahids* gradually assumed more responsibilities in the community. See Eliash, "The Ithna'ashari Shi'i Juristic Theory of Political and Legal Authority," *Studia Islamica*, vol. 29 (1960).

hid would be known as the "source of imitation" (*taqlid*).[4] From the group of leading *mujtahids* could then be chosen one grand, leading *mujtahid*—the *marjai mutlaqi taqlid*—whose position suggested a strong parallel with that of the *imams*.

The possibility that the authority of the leading *ulama*, the *mujtahids*, will be seen as rooted in their characteristic or divine qualities has been tempered by the Shiite emphasis on the right of the *mujtahids* to use their powers of reason to interpret (*ijtihad*) the sources of Islamic law. In contrast to the orthodox Sunni position, according to which the process of deducing Islamic law from the Quran and the *sunna* of the Prophet ended in the tenth century, the Shiites argue that this process of *ijtihad* continues, given that the complete meaning of the word of God is still to be fully divined.[5]

Although Shiite thought holds that the *mujtahids* are to play a role as the ethical guides of the community, this does not resolve the question of their role vis-à-vis temporal political power. Since Ali was the last legitimate leader, or caliph, of the Muslim community and since there will be no truly legitimate ruler until the return of the twelfth *imam*, Shiite doctrine assumes that "all states are inalienably usurpatory, even those of formal Shi'i affiliation."[6] In practice, however, the *ulama* were willing to accord a certain degree of legitimacy to governments depending on the extent to which they respected Shiite laws and cultural traditions.

Under the Safavids—from 1503 to 1722—such a close relationship developed between the *ulama* and the secular leaders that the shah was considered, for a time, to have divine powers. However, during the Qajar period, from 1785 to 1925, when the secular leaders paid no heed to Shiite norms, ignored the wishes of the *ulama*, and abused the rights of their subjects, the state was accorded little or no legitimacy. The *ulama* refused to be co-opted into the institutions of the state—unlike the official *ulama* in the Sunni world—and thus emerged as a kind of opposition force representing the interests of the people against those of the state.

The Pahlavi period, from 1925 to 1979, witnessed a repeat of the pattern established under the Qajars. As Reza Shah and later his son, Mohammad Reza Shah, increased their control over the state apparatus and, in turn, enhanced the power of that apparatus over the society, the *ulama* took an increasingly oppositional stance. Their opposition mounted throughout the 1970s until, in concert with a variety of secular forces from all positions of the political spectrum, they ousted the shah, his dynasty, and the entire Pahlavi political system.[7]

4. Subsequently there developed the tradition of each of the leading sources of imitation publishing a treatise of his interpretations of proper conduct for his imitators in each area of life, including nearly all aspects of personal conduct. This genre of religious works became highly stylized and there are few differences among the works of the current Shiite sources of imitation. Ayatollah Khomeini's version of this genre has recently been published in English translation; see Ruhollah Khomeini, *The Explanation of Problems* (Boulder, CO: Westview Press, 1984).

5. It should be noted that keeping open the gate of *ijtihad* provides the Shiites with the possibility of a progressive, liberal interpretation of Islam reflecting contemporary social conditions.

6. Hamid Algar, "The Role of the Ulema in Twentieth Century Iran," in *Scholars, Saints, and Sufis*, ed. Nikki Keddie (Berkeley: University of California Press, 1972), p. 232.

7. See Marvin Zonis, "Iran: A Theory of

The oppositional stance of the *ulama* to the Pahlavis did not blossom until the death of the leading *mujtahid*, Ayatollah Mohammad Hussein Burujerdi, in the early 1960s. Burujerdi had supported the shah and had argued that Shiism demanded quietism and submission to authority. Reacting against this line of thinking, two schools of thought arose: a neofundamentalist school identified with Ayatollah Khomeini[8] and a reformist-modernist school identified with the leading moderate *ulama* such as Ayatollahs Murtaza Mutahhari and Mahmoud Taleghani, as well as with prominent religiously minded intellectuals such as Mehdi Barzargan and Dr. Ali Shariati.[9]

While both schools argued for man's active participation in restoring justice to the world and opposing tyranny, they differed fundamentally in their definitions of justice and in their approaches to organizing a political community. The reformists rejected a literalist interpretation of the concept of the infallibility of the *imams*; they claimed instead that the "Imam's supernatural qualities . . . are indicative, not of their superiority over other Muslims, but merely their worthiness of a higher station in the Hereafter; in the sensible world, all the faithful are equal."[10] Having rejected elitism, the reformists could then argue against a political system in which the *ulama* would rule over and against the wishes of the people.

Moreover, in the tradition of Ayatollah Mohammad Hussein Naini, the clerical leader of the 1905 Constitutional movement in Iran, the reformers claimed that Shiism demanded constitutional democracy. Shiism required the most efficient political system for securing the rights, welfare, and justice of the community. That system, they assumed, was a democratic one. By arguing in this fashion, the reformists could uphold the legitimacy of a government in which the *ulama* played a limited role, but in which the lay political leadership—by employing an enlightened, forward-looking concept of the doctrine of free interpretation (*ijtihad*)—could pass modern legislation inspired by the values of Shiism. Islam and secular leadership would thus be made compatible.

While the influence of Western ideas is evident in the thinking of the reformist-modernists, it would be incorrect to conclude that they were simply arguing

Revolution from Accounts of the Revolution," *World Politics*, 35: 586-660 (1983).

8. The term "neofundamentalist," as opposed to "fundamentalist," is used here because the concept of a fundamentalist refers, in its accepted usage, to an individual who insists upon a literalist interpretation of the Quran. Since in the Shiite religion, however, the full revelation of the word of God is not accessible through the Quran, and will become evident only upon the return of the twelfth *imam*, Shiism can be seen as intrinsically antithetical to fundamentalism. However, Khomeini's brand of Shiite fundamentalism does share certain major characteristics with Sunni fundamentalism, the most important of which is the urge to reestablish a united, Islamic community founded on authentic rather than foreign values. This emotional impulse toward Islamic unity and authenticity engaged the imagination of both Sunnis and Shiites.

9. Shahrough Akhavi, *Religion and Politics in Contemporary Iran: Clergy-State Relations in the Pahlavi Period* (Albany: State University of New York Press, 1980), pp. 117-58.

10. Enayat, *Modern Islamic Political Thought*, p. 46. It is important to note that this generalization concerning Shiite modernism overemphasizes its unanimity. There were, in fact, differences within the modernist school as well. For example, the modernists included such moderates as Ayatollah Kazem Shariat-Madari, thinkers with more radical inclinations such as Ayatollah Mutahhari, as well as neo-Marxists, the most important of whom was Dr. Ali Shariati.

for the adoption of Western theories of government in the guise of Islam. To the modernists, the basic traits of Western political thought, as found both in socialism and in liberal democracy, were an inherent and authentic part of Islam—properly interpreted. Indeed, they argued that only by rediscovering these traits in Islam could Muslims protect their spiritual heritage from the ethical void of Western materialism.

To the neofundamentalists, however, the position of the reformists appeared to increase the danger of further Western penetration of Iranian society. Reacting to what they saw as Iran's cultural, social, economic, and political surrender to the West, the neofundamentalists argued for a narrow interpretation of Shiism that emphasized Iran's Shiite authenticity and its cultural, economic, and political unity (*tawhid*) in the face of the perceived Western threat.[11] To regain the society's cultural and political independence and unity, Khomeini insisted, it was necessary to build a society in which the best protectors of Islam—the *mujtahid*s—would rule. He thus interpreted the doctrine of the infallibility of the *imam*s and the elitism of the *mujtahid*s in a literal fashion. Moreover, by referring to himself as the "representative" of the *imam*, he invited comparisons between himself and the twelfth *imam* and hence implied that his authority was divinely inspired.

The quasi infallibility of Khomeini called for a political order in which the wise *mujtahid*s would define and protect the interests of the oppressed—and fallible—masses. The participation of the masses in the electoral system, in turn, was in practice limited to electing candidates approved by the *ulama*. Meanwhile, Khomeini forbade any pluralist, fragmenting system of politics, insisting, as the Constitution of the Islamic Republic says, that Islamic government "does not arise from the notion of classes and mediation among persons or groups, but is a crystallization of political idealism based on religious community."[12] This Islamic form of popular authoritarianism was, finally, justified by recourse to a limited interpretation of the principle of *ijtihad*, which was to be understood as the prerogative of the *ulama* rather than that of the people.

It is obvious that Khomeini's vision held far greater sway over the Iranian masses than did the less revolutionary vision of the reformists. With their support and that of a cadre of dedicated and loyal clerics, many of whom had been Ayatollah Khomeini's students decades earlier, the neofundamentalists were able to establish and maintain their dominance over the winning revolutionary coalition that succeeded in forcing the shah from power.[13]

11. For a more detailed discussion of the neofundamentalist school in Iran and its victory in that country, see Marvin Zonis and Daniel Brumberg, "Interpreting Islam: Human Rights in the Islamic Republic of Iran," in *Islam and the Baha'i Faith*, ed. Heshmat Moayyad (forthcoming).

12. "Constitution of the Islamic Republic of Iran," *Foreign Broadcast Information Service Daily Report: Middle East*, FBIS-MEA 29-236, 5(236), supp. 034 (6 Dec. 1979); all excerpts of the Iranian Constitution in this article are from this publication.

13. The significance of the teacher-student relationship in the triumph of the clerics cannot be overemphasized. It made for ties of deep trust and unshakable loyalty. Ayatollah Mutahhari, for example, was one such Khomeini student and played a crucial role in the revolution while Khomeini was in exile. Mutahhari was assassinated in Tehran on 2 May 1979. Ayatollah Khomeini wept openly at his funeral—he did not do so at the public ceremony commemorating the

THE CONSTITUTION OF THE ISLAMIC REPUBLIC OF IRAN

That victory over the shah is enshrined in the Constitution of the Islamic Republic.[14] The document reflects the neofundamentalist view by making Islam central to all aspects of Iranian life and by guaranteeing the rule of the clerics. The constitution repeats again and again that the basis of political life and loyalty shall be Islam and that the goal of political activity shall be the realization of an Islamic vision. Principle 1 of the constitution states that "the Government of Iran is an Islamic Republic." Principle 4 specifies that "all civil, penal, financial, economic, administrative, cultural, military, political, etc. . . . laws and regulations should be based on Islamic rules and standards. This principle shall be absolutely or in general dominant over all the principles of the Constitution, and other laws and regulations as well." Principle 12 states more precisely that "the official religion of Iran is Islam, and the sect followed is Twelver Shiism."

Having established that all laws, regulations, and principles of the government must accord with Shiite Islam, the constitution goes on to state the basis upon which the *ulama* claim their right to rule. Also specified are the mechanisms by which the *ulama* will secure the right to define what is Islamic as well as the means—legislative means, in particular—by which they will enforce this definition. Here the constitution, in its introduction, invokes the Shiite theory of the imamate and the rule of the clergy, stating that "the responsibility for growth and advancement belong to the leadership which will have all the rights to govern the oppressed."[15] Following this, the constitution states:

> So as to assure the permanent security of the Constitution, the rights of clerical leadership [are] under all conditions to be the leadership recognized by the people. (The course of affairs is in the hands of those who know God and who are trustworthy in matters having to do with what He permits and forbids.)
>
> The just jurist is equipped to insure that the various organizations do not deviate from their true Islamic duties.

To support the claim of *ulama* rule, the constitution then cites the following phrases from the Quran and from various *hadith* of the Prophet and the 12 *imams*:

> The Special Qualities of Leadership:
>
> 1. Is not He, then, who shows the way to truth more worthy to be followed than he who does not show the way unless it is shown to him? (Surah 10:35).
> 2. God has chosen him above you and has imbued him abundantly with knowledge and strength (Surah 2:247).
> 3. God has given it to the imams of justice to appoint themselves by the weakness of the people (The Way of Eloquence).
> 4. The courses of affairs are in the hands of the religious scholars, whose office it is to say what is permissible and what is forbidden (The Gift of Intellects).

death of his son—and referred to Mutahhari as "the fruition of my life." "Mutahhari—Martyr for Islam," *Echo of Islam*, p. 1 (June 1979). That Mutahhari was a modernist was not sufficient to overcome the deep ties between him and his former mentor. His death undoubtedly facilitated the victory of the neofundamentalists.

14. The neofundamentalist constitution was won only after considerable political struggle. For a description of the infighting over the formulation and adoption of that document, see Shaul Bakhash, *The Reign of the Ayatollahs* (New York: Basic Books, 1984).

15. "Constitution," p. 4.

Government posts

Of special interest in the foregoing citations, and in others that follow them, is their emphasis upon the weakness of the people in contrast to the inherent virtues of wisdom and strength of the *imams* and, by implication, of the *ulama*. The overall premise at work here is that the *imams* have delegated their authority to the leading scholars, or *mujtahids*, among the *ulama*. Having established this premise, the constitution can then proceed to outline the concepts of *velayat-e faqih* ("the rule of the jurist") and *marja-i taqlid*, the rule of the leading *mujtahid*, who is Ayatollah Khomeini:

Principle 5: During the absence of the Glorious Lord of the Age [the missing twelfth *imam* of the Shiite sect], may God grant him relief, he will be represented in the Islamic Republic of Iran as religious leader and imam of the people by an honest, virtuous, well-informed, courageous, efficient administrator and religious jurist, enjoying the confidence of the majority of the people as a leader. Should there be no jurist endowed with such qualifications, enjoying the confidence of the majority of the people, his role will be undertaken by a leader or council of leaders, consisting of religious jurists meeting the requirements mentioned above, according to Principle 107.

The Leader or The Leadership Council

Principle 107: Whenever one of the jurists who fulfills the conditions mentioned in Principle 5 of the law is recognized by a decisive majority of the people for leadership and has been accepted—as is the case with the Great Ayatollah Imam Khomeini's high calling to the leadership of the revolution—then this leader will have charge of governing and all the responsibilities arising from it. Otherwise, experts elected by the people from all those qualified for leadership will be investigated and evaluated. Whenever a candidate who has outstanding characteristics for leadership is found, he will be introduced to the people as a leader. Otherwise, 3 or 5 candidates who fill the conditions for leadership will be appointed members of the Leadership Council and introduced to the people.

Of the two operating concepts in the preceding principles, *velayat-e faqih* and *marja-i taqlid*, it is the latter concept that is of major interest. For while provision is made for collective leadership among the leading *mujtahids*,[16] power can be concentrated in the hands of one *mujtahid*, making him, in essence, an absolute ruler. This power is not conferred upon the *mujtahid* through elections but rather through a form of popular acclamation, by his "enjoying the confidence of the majority of the people as a leader" or by his being "recognized by a decisive majority of the people for leadership." In short, his power flows through a kind of charismatic authority—a divine election, perhaps—as suggested by the phrase that "in the absence of the Glorious Lord of the Age, he will be represented . . . by a . . . religious jurist," and by the reference to "Imam" Khomeini. Khomeini himself has denied that the delegation of authority to the *mujtahids* implies that they carry divine power or infallibility (*isma*). Yet many Iranians concede such power to him and to the charismatic process implicit in his selection. It seems reasonable to conclude, then, that his

16. While the constitution is not completely clear on this matter, it seems that the members of the Leadership Council, like the leading *mujtahid*, are to be selected by popular acclamation as well. Moreover, it appears in Principle 20 that the Guidance Council is responsible for arranging for their selection; yet half of the members of the Guidance Council are selected by the Leadership Council! Hence the *ulama* appoint each other. See Principle 108.

absolute power over the affairs of the country, as specified in Principle 110, flows from a certain attribution of divine qualities.

Principle 110 specifies the enormous powers of the leading jurist. It gives him the duty of appointing the members of the Council of Guardians, the highest judicial authorities, as well as the commanders of the three armed forces—upon the suggestion of the High Council of National Defense, which he himself is charged with organizing. Most important, he is given the power to sign "the order formalizing the election of the president," to approve "the competence of candidates for the presidency," and to dismiss "the president of the republic in consideration of the good of the country (after an order is issued by the Supreme Court charging him with violating his legal duties)." In short, the leading jurist can negate the process by which the president is elected, with only the most minimal restraints upon his actions.

It remains for the constitution to specify the power of other members of the religious hierarchy and the mechanism by which they enforce conformity to Islamic unity as they themselves define that unity. Principle 91 sets out the answer to this problem, establishing the Council of Guardians, whose responsibility is to "investigate" the legislation of the Majlis, or Parliament, so that it "will conform with the Islamic standards and constitutional laws. And if they find any contradiction, [it] will be returned to the assembly for revision." Moreover, Principle 99 states that "the Council of Guardians is responsible for supervising the presidential election (and) the elections of the [Majlis]." Since the members of this assembly, with the exception of the seats reserved for religious minorities, must, according to Principle 67, "pledge to be the guardian(s) of the inviolability of Islam" and since, according to Principles 115 and 121, the president must be "pious" and a "believer in . . . the official religion of the country" and must dedicate himself to "the propagation of religion," it is evident that the Council of Guardians can enforce its definition of Islamic conformity in both the executive and legislative branches.

The Council of Guardians is made up of 12 men, 6 of whom are selected by the revolutionary leader—namely, Ayatollah Khomeini—or in his absence, the Leadership Council. The other 6 are elected by the Majlis on the suggestion of the High Council of the Judiciary. The constitution specifies in Principle 96 that a "majority of six religious members of the Council of Guardians" can decide whether a piece of legislation contravenes Islam. As these are precisely the members selected by the revolutionary leader, Khomeini or his successors can, in the final analysis, maintain control over legislation.

In short, the Constitution of the Islamic Republic specifies the institutionalization of clerical rule through *velayat-e faqih* ("the rule of the jurist") and through the Council of Guardians. At present, of course, Ayatollah Khomeini occupies the position of revolutionary leader. But much of the politics of the Islamic Republic can be understood as a struggle over the succession to Khomeini. He has already declared that he has made his choice of that member of the *ulama* who should succeed to supreme jurist at his death. He has claimed that he has specified that cleric in his last will and testament, which has been sealed and delivered to the parliament, not to be opened until his death. While Ayatollah Khomeini has refused to reveal his choice, there is near unanimity that Ayatollah Hussein Ali Montazeri is his designated successor. But there still does not appear to be unanimity over the desirability of that choice.

Thus a concerted campaign has been launched to build the reputation for Montazeri that will facilitate his designation. Yet there are periodic indications that there are differences among Iran's leading political figures over the suitability of Montazeri. There are clearly leading *mujtahid*s outside the government who oppose the selection of Montazeri.[17] The succession politics cover an array of activities, from seeking to deny Montazeri the position entirely to trying to ensure that no one individual succeeds Ayatollah Khomeini but that a Leadership Council is designated instead. As the massive propaganda on behalf of Montazeri continues and as he assumes ever more visible responsibilities in lieu of Ayatollah Khomeini—such as receiving important dignitaries—the possibilities of denying him the position of supreme jurist seem to have diminished.

Irrespective of the support that Montazeri can now command and the probability of his succeeding to leadership when—some would say if—Ayatollah Khomeini dies, there is virtual unanimity among the *ulama* of Iran over the need to maintain clerical rule. The policies of the Khomeini regime have made it impossible, however, to determine the solidity of that near unanimity. One of the *marja-i taqlid* ("sources of imitation") among the *ulama* whose theological—but not political—eminence equals, if not surpasses, that of Ayatollah Khomeini is under house arrest. Ayatollah Kazem Shariat-Madari, before his silence was forced by the regime, made his opposition to direct clerical rule widely known. Shariat-Madari asserted, like the Shiite modernists, that nothing in Shiite thought demanded the direct rule of the clerics. To the contrary, he argued, the rightful role of the clerics in an Islamic state is to monitor the adherence of state policy to Islamic law, not to formulate or to execute that law. Given his widespread popularity, and especially his strong base of regional support in his native province of Azerbaijan, Shariat-Madari was viewed as a grave threat to the institutionalization of Ayatollah Khomeini's reign. His subsequent suppression makes it difficult to ascertain the depth of his current support.

But with the exception of Shariat-Madari, the clerics appear united behind the preservation of their rule. Hojatolislam Rafsanjani, the Speaker of the Majlis, for example, frequently reminds his listeners of the benefits of such rule. In speaking recently of the war with Iraq, he declared:

> Those who tread on God's path will never face defeat since the path of God is all but victory—each and every turn of it. With this mental attitude that God is omnipotent and it is He who has destined us to do this job since if He wanted to do it He would have the power beyond any other powers to accomplish the task. Therefore, in such a predestined

17. For example, one of the five Shiite sources of imitation—the most revered of the *ulama*—is reported to have spoken with Ayatollah Khomeini on this point. Ayatollah Mohammad Reza Golpaigani is alleged to have sought an audience to protest the propaganda campaign on behalf of Montazeri and also Montazeri's selection of Friday prayer leaders, who are the senior clerics in Iran's provincial cities and towns. The basis of Golpaigani's argument was that the designation of clerical status should not be controlled from the political system but emanate from the Shiite faithful. See *Keyhan* (London), 6 Sept. 1984, p. 1.

situation, victory is certain and there will be no defeat.[18]

Rafsanjani made it clear that the "us" who were "destined" by God to defeat the Iraqis were the armed forces of the Islamic Republic and their clerical leaders.

This clerical commitment is sustained by a variety of factors. But the rewards of rule and the fear of what would befall the clerics in the event of their overthrow must be considered additional powerful factors facilitating that commitment. Whatever factors sustain the clerics in their belief of the righteousness of their rule, the Iranian experience has demonstrated an impressive ability to wield power. They have been successful in exercising total political power while achieving both the elimination of Iraqi invaders from Iranian territory and the maintenance of a level of oil exports sufficient to meet basic economic needs.

THE WORLD VIEW OF THE RULING CLERICS

Three basic factors appear to account for the clerics' accomplishments. First, the clerics have been sustained by the strength of Ayatollah Khomeini's personal commitment to maintaining clerical rule. Clerical rule is the bedrock of Khomeini's entire value system, for without that rule, he believes, it will be impossible to realize the transformation of Iranian society and, eventually, of Muslims everywhere. The depth of that commitment, coupled with the extraordinary charisma that Ayatollah Khomeini continues to enjoy vis-à-vis the Iranian people, is basic to maintaining clerical rule. By serving as his agents, the clerics contribute to their own sense of self-righteousness and legitimacy. That certitude both provides a sense of self-justification and reinforces the belief of their followers in the justness of the entire enterprise that is the Islamic Republic.

A second factor that contributes to the success of the clerics is their claim to a monopoly on the legitimate interpretation of the Shiite *sharia*, or sacred law. Shiite law is living; that is, it necessitates ongoing, contemporaneous interpretation—at least until the return of the twelfth *imam* from his occultation. Moreover, the regime has successfully institutionalized the right to make definitive interpretations through the principle of *velayat-e faqih* in the person of Ayatollah Khomeini. Thus the regime and, in particular, its clerical members act with the assurance supplied through a firm sense of the sacred appropriateness of their own actions.

Finally, the clerics can rule with the knowledge of yet another factor that supplies them with the sense of their legitimacy. The core of the system is Ayatollah Khomeini, whose role is widely understood, by his followers at least, as a reflection of a divine calling. His claim to leadership and by extension the claim of his clerical followers are based ultimately on a claim of *barakah* ("charisma"), which is a product of the grace of God—divine election. The *barakah* that emanates from the Almighty and operates through the *nayeb-e imam*, the deputy of the twelfth *imam*, as Ayatollah Khomeini has been entitled, is yet a final source of legitimacy for the clerics.

These three factors, then, sustain the rule of the clerics. Serving as the agents for the realization of Ayatollah Kho-

18. *Sobh-i Azadegan*, 1 Mar. 1985, p. 19, trans. in *Joint Publication Research Service*, JPRS-NEA-85-055, 18 Apr. 1985, p. 75.

meini's divinely inspired vision that supplies him and, through him, the clerical community as a whole with a monopoly on legitimate interpretation provides different forms of crucial legitimation. It legitimates the rule of the clerics for many Iranians. More important, it legitimates clerical rule for the clerics themselves. And, ultimately, it is the assurance of that legitimacy that is the single most important factor in sustaining their rule.

Shaykh Muhammad al-Ghazali is known as "one of the pillars of the Society of Muslim Brothers." Although an Egyptian and a Sunni cleric and far from exercising power in his own country, he has clearly articulated the sense of clerical legitimacy that sustains his Iranian Shiite counterparts:

> Religious thinking, in terms of its source, is genuine and true, because it comes from God. It arises from divine infallible inspiration. It is not subject to doubt and it is not encumbered by falsehood from any direction.
>
> The person who retains his right, clings to it, and prevents oppressors from usurping it, is not a fanatic. Islam is innocent of all fanaticism.[19]

THEMES OF THE RULE OF THE CLERICS

To this point, we have examined the ideology of Shiite neofundamentalism that justifies rule by the clerics, the provisions of the Constitution of the Islamic Republic of Iran that institutionalize clerical rule within the political system, and the sources of certitude and righteousness that supply the clerical rulers of Iran and their followers with a sense of profound legitimacy. It remains to specify the principal themes that are the hallmarks of clerical rule.

The *ulama*, ruling with a deep sense of their own legitimacy and with an equally deep commitment to the divinely inspired virtue of their rulings, manifest a sensibility of grandiosity. They see God, rather than ordinary human motivations, as their chief inspiration. By definition, then, their decisions are not merely correct but unassailable. Ruling with God to realize his wishes for man, they project a sense of rightness that constitutes grandiosity.

A second major theme characterizing clerical rule is an insistence on unity. Given that the clerics rule with God's inspiration to realize his will, competing or even alternate interpretations of his will are inadmissable.

The principle of *velayat-e faqih* ensures that there will be no such alternative interpretations. Ayatollah Khomeini has created an ideology based on Shiite thought that serves to legitimate the insistence on unity in support of clerical rule and the decisions of the *faqih*. He has done so by broadening the concept of *tawhid* beyond its narrow theological meanings. Originally, the notion of *tawhid* was a concept that captured God's unity, the monotheism that is the underpinning of Islam. The ayatollah has gradually broadened the concept by insisting that such monotheism encompasses not only the oneness of God but the oneness of the Islamic community and also the one, proper way to realize God's will.

Tawhid has thus become a catchword used to justify the Islamic Republic's elimination of domestic opposition and the imposition of stringent rules for domestic political life. And because the clerics claim legitimacy to realize God's vision in all areas of the life of the

19. Muhammad al-Ghazali, "Interview," *Al-ahram al-iqtisadi* (Cairo), 11 Feb. 1985, pp. 50-53.

community—as befits the claims of Islam—equally stringent rules can be applied by the regime in all aspects of the life of the faithful that contribute to the life of the community.

A third central theme of the clerics is to see the world in terms of allies and enemies. The world is not populated by others who pursue their own understandings and their own policies calculated to advance the well-being of their own peoples, as defined by them. On the contrary, extending the domestic insistence on *tawhid*, the clerics regard understandings and policies that they consider incompatible or inimical to those of the Islamic Republic as the acts of enemies. Thus virtually all other states are counted as the enemies of Islamic Iran. They have all failed in basic ways, either by failing to take steps to realize Ayatollah Khomeini's visions within their own borders or by taking active steps to prevent the realization of that vision. Even those countries that have assisted Iran in attaining certain of its goals are suspect for having failed to accept the entire Islamic vision of the ayatollah. Syria, for example, has helped Iran realize some of its goals in Lebanon, but President Hafez al-Assad refuses to tolerate within Syria those political forces that seek to realize a more complete Islamic vision. As a result, he is suspect in the eyes of the Iranians.

For the clerics of Iran, the United States remains the enemy of God. As the president of the Islamic Republic, Hojatolislam Seyyid Ali Mussawi Khamenei, recently put it:

> The United States, which claims to be democratic and liberal-minded, enforces an extensive dictatorship on nations throughout the world. She has spread her dictatorial domination as far as her material and military powers permit. She appears wherever she thinks she has interests and does whatever she likes regardless of the aspirations, wishes, rights, and interests of the peoples of those regions. In our opinion, it is the ugliest and most difficult form of dictatorship.[20]

Seeing the world as populated by allies and, especially, by many enemies, the clerics manifest yet another theme: that the policies of their enemies are conspiracies meant to disrupt, if not overthrow, the Islamic Republic. The United States, according to this view, is not merely pursuing its own interests, but is also, in the pursuit of those interests, exploiting the peoples of the world. As President Khamenei commented, "Nations cannot be convinced to accept a situation whereby foreign pirates came here to usurp the rights of nations, leaving a portion for their own accomplices, without anything being left for the nations themselves."[21]

Moreover, given that the United States is perceived to be a great power, the clerics believe that it pursues its interests by hatching conspiracies, by surreptitiously controlling the world in order to realize its exploitative aims. This tendency to interpret the policies of the United States as being pursued in a conspiratorial fashion is not limited to the clerics in Iran, nor is it restricted to alleged conspiracies to overthrow the rule of the clerics. An Arab journalist commented on the discovery of oil in the Yemen Arab Republic by the U.S. Hunt Oil Corporation with less than the enthusiasm that such a discovery could be expected to elicit:

20. Hojatolislam Seyyid Ali Mussawi Khamenei, "The Big Powers Have Established a Global Tyrrany," *Kayhan International*, 10 Mar. 1985, p. 6. The implications of his referring to the United States as a female are yet to be analyzed.

21. Ibid.

The question of discovering oil and gas in an Arab land is in large part a political decision on the part of the United States. If the Americans decide they want to discover oil, they do. If they decide that the Arab country—any country—should remain without oil, even if rivers of oil run under its soil, then oil will not be found.[22]

Not only does the United States pursue its policies through conspiracies, but it is, as a result, responsible for whatever happens in the Islamic world. In this way responsibility is evaded by Muslims as blame is assigned to external forces over which the Islamic world has little or no control.

The United States is fully responsible for the present historical predicament that is gravely afflicting the entire Arab homeland, exerting unendurable pressure on Egypt, and generating the most serious elements of explosion inside Egypt. Neither the United States nor any of its officials can evade the responsibility for the economic and social crisis that is digging its teeth and claws into Egypt's flesh and into its people's bones. This is because the United States has participated in plunging the Israeli dagger into the Arab homeland; the poisonous blade of this black dagger was directed at its heart, Egypt.[23]

Thus a fifth theme, which is central to the ideas that characterize clerical rule, is the immense power of the United States and its ability to work its will through the use of that power.

The response of the clerics to this perception of great American power exercised through conspiracies designed to achieve American purposes at the expense of the exploited Muslim peoples constitutes the sixth central theme of the Islamic Republic. That theme centers on the need to respond through war: war against the United States and its allies, in particular Israel, but also against other states, ostensibly Islamic, that nonetheless carry out America's plots. Iraq, of course, is at the top of Iran's list of enemies. The states that assist Iraq are equally culpable, however. Saudi Arabia and Kuwait, in particular, are thereby defined as enemies of Iran. But Egypt, because it signed a treaty of peace with the hated Israelis, is an enemy as well.

It is, of course, true that it was Iraq that launched a massive ground invasion of Iran in September of 1980. That forced the clerics to mobilize their people for a major military effort to repel the invaders. In that way, Iran engaged in war without much choice. But it would be overstating the centrality of that invasion to attribute the war that Iran has effectively declared against its enemies to that act alone. Before the Iraqi armed forces crossed their border with Iran, the Iranian clerics had supported a number of political organizations in Iraq committed to the overthrow of President Saddam Hussein. They had also been linked to numerous bombings and terrorist attacks in Baghdad. Even earlier, of course, the clerics had stimulated and sustained the capture of the U.S. embassy with its entire contingent of diplomats who were held prisoner for those seemingly interminable 444 days. The point here is that war by conventional or terrorist means was adopted as a central strategy of the Islamic Republic long before its invasion by Iraq. That strategy was an extension of the means adopted by the

22. Fuad Matar, "Yemen and Oil," *Al-tamadun* (London), 11 Aug. 1984, in *Joint Publications Research Service*, JPRS-NEA-84-161, 29 Oct. 1984, p. 93.

23. Mustafa Shardi, "The One Going to the United States on Behalf of All Egyptians," *Al-Wafd* (Cairo), 21 Feb. 1985, in *Foreign Broadcast Information Service Daily Report: Middle East*, FBIS-MEA-85-040, 28 Feb. 1985, p. D5.

regime and its allies to win and stabilize their power. War has been an extension of the domestic policy design to eliminate internal opposition and mobilize the population for the regime's support.

Ayatollah Khomeini's slogan of the day is War, War until Victory. It is a slogan that has joined one of longer standing, Death to America; these together now constitute the fundamental policies of the Islamic Republic of Iran. While the mobilization for war is directed primarily toward mobilizing the resources of Iran against Iraq, there is every reason to believe that the war slogan represents a more lasting theme to position the Islamic Republic against all of its powerful, conspiratorial enemies.

A final theme, which is the complement to all the rest, is that God has promised victory to those who follow his will. In words that could have been spoken by Ayatollah Khomeini, Shaykh al-Ghazali declared,

> All of Europe—Germany, Austria, Spain, England, France, and Italy—had divisions which fought the Muslims. . . . But the Muslims at that time [during the Crusades] refused to accept a fait accompli and they rejected a disgraceful surrender. They decided to fight and this war lasted 90 years, until Jerusalem returned to the control of the Muslims. . . . Many other principalities and posts were controlled by the crusaders, but the Muslims were able to recover them one by one until they defeated their enemy. The basis was religious effort, persistance, refusing to despair, and rejecting worldly pleasures. . . . History repeats itself but only by the same unchangeable moral and religious realities. The Muslims were victorious on the day they were able to stick to their religion, but were defeated on the day they betrayed it.[24]

This is precisely the view of Ayatollah Khomeini. To the extent that the Islamic Republic adheres to Islam, to the constitution, and to his interpretations of the sacred texts, victory is assured. Victory over all its enemies—over the conspiracies and plots of its domestic and foreign opponents—is inevitable.

The cost will be enormous. Muslims must be prepared to pay for victory. Economic well-being may need to be sacrificed. More important, Muslims must be prepared to sacrifice their very lives to work God's will. Ayatollah Khomeini's call for martyrdom is justified, then, as a necessity for realizing His will. If individual Muslims do not survive to witness the day of Islamic victory, they will, in giving their lives, speed the day when the community of the faithful can witness that victory.

These themes characterize the rule of the clerics in Iran: grandiosity, the insistence on unity, an abundance of enemies whose great power make their ever-present conspiracies dangerous, the search for military solutions to political dilemmas, all to be crowned by ultimate victory.

CONCLUSION

The combination of a powerful ideology and a functioning Islamic regime has resulted in a large cadre of Islamic clerics who fulfill political roles. Assured of their own righteousness, they operate with a sense of great legitimacy. A variety of themes characterize their rule, all predicated on their great commitment to communal victory. In short, the Islamic Republic of Iran is a formidable adventure in government. Islamic

24. Muhammad al-Ghazali, "Avoiding Political and Social Resistance Is a Betrayal of the Nation," *Al-mujtama* (Kuwait), 9 Oct. 1984, trans. in *Joint Publications Research Service*, JPRS-NEA-85-024, 15 Feb. 1985, p. 62.

clerics can exercise political power with that ruthless determination born of acting in the name of God.

The replication of the Iranian experience in other Islamic states appears problematic. Shiite ideology is especially suited to clerical rule and to the production of clerics whose religious eminence leads to their becoming sources of emulation for their followers. But even more significant, the clerics in Iran came to power through the particular convergence of a variety of revolutionary forces around the figure of Ayatollah Khomeini. For many of those forces Khomeini was meant to be a front, to be used in the task of ousting the shah and then to be set aside as an obdurate, archaic old man. But Khomeini has demonstrated a capacity for leadership and mass mobilization that many had underrated. His roles in the Iranian revolution—both in deposing the shah and in keeping the clerics in power—were fulfilled in what appears to be a unique way. Leaders like Khomeini do not appear often. It is unlikely that other Islamic regimes can be realized without such leadership or without the assistance of the Islamic Republic of Iran.

* * *

QUESTIONS AND ANSWERS

Q (Naff): It is apparent that the Shiite leadership in Iran has employed those attributes of leadership that you described to take control of the infrastructure of government and of social services from the local to the national level and to get rid of any pockets or source of opposition. They are firmly in control currently and do not have to worry too much about any serious opposition. Having managed to take this kind of control, the Shiite leadership has begun a process of restructuring Iranian society. Do you think it will succeed in restructuring Iranian society in some basic way for generations to come? And if you do, in what significant ways?

A: It seems to me that the success of the revolution and in particular of Ayatollah Khomeini has in fact resulted in a fundamental restructuring of Iranian society that I believe will take at least 50 years to work itself through. Historically in Iran processes work themselves through Iranian society extraordinarily slowly. For example, following the Constitutional movement of 1905 there really was no meaningful central government until Reza Khan made his coup in 1921 and then it took a few years to establish the government.

Similarly, the Arabs believe that Khomeini's most fundamental change has been the injection of Islam into the center of public life in Iran, and I cannot imagine how any succeeding regime will be able to alter that change except over a very long period of time.

Another characteristic of Iranian society is that Iranians are capable of believing many different things simultaneously. It is therefore possible to have a switch that will bring about quite dramatic changes. Where did all the vocal anti-U.S. Muslims come from? The answer is that they were there before except that they were all wearing Western suits and neckties and thinking different things. It is possible, at least on theoretical grounds, to imagine a kind of psychological transformation. I personally do not see that such a transformation is likely and I see any regime that follows as having to integrate the forces of Islam in a very powerful way into Iranian public life.

It is nonetheless the case that the possibilities for violence must be considered to be high in the Iranian situation because of the differences in Iran between the neomodernists and neofundamentalist Shiites. In other words, the ones who are in power at this time, the neofundamentalists, are quite worried about what would happen if the neomodernists took power. A lot of those neofundamentalists think they would be put up against a wall and shot down. The neofundamentalists hold onto power not merely out of a cynical motive of protecting their jobs but also because they truly believe that they are carrying out God's will for his faithful on earth. That becomes a very explosive mixture. We know that the *pasdaran* ("revolutionary guards") in Iran are not particularly unified. In fact, they are characterized by a number of serious splits that make it appear that individual commanders run individual segments of that body; it is therefore easy to imagine that the situation would disintegrate into rather severe violence in Iran.

Q (Zia Hashmi, Georgia Southern College, Statesboro): From your presentation, I did not get the idea that in Iran the clergy is split or, especially, that the difference between Ayatollah Khomeini and Ayatollah Shariat-Madari is a very important difference or a very central issue. You made a comparison between a Shiite clergy and a Sunni clergy. You did not mention one Sunni neofundamentalist in Pakistan, Maulana Maudoodi, who died in 1979; would you give your opinion about Maudoodi and his concept of Islamic revival.

A: Let me first say something about Ayatollah Shariat-Madari, but in a larger sense let me say something about the doctrine of *velayat-e faqih*, which I suppose can be translated most easily as "the rule of the jurist." This doctrine has been enshrined in the Islamic constitution of Iran. It does not exist, to my knowledge, anywhere other than in the writings of Ayatollah Khomeini and in the writings of the conveners of the constitutional assembly of Iran, which guarantees supreme authority within the regime to the rightly guided jurist.

The constitution specifies the mechanisms by which the rightly guided jurist will be identified, and in the case of Ayatollah Khomeini it is, of course, by divine election. There are now mechanisms in place for choosing the successor to Ayatollah Khomeini. The leading candidate is Mr. Montazeri. Unfortunately he does not seem to have a tremendous amount of power outside of a very narrow circle.

What is striking to me about Mr. Maudoodi is that he is an exemplar of a fundamentalist approach. I find it noteworthy that although Islam is capable of supporting the burden of both a modernist and a neofundamentalist corpus of interpretation, it is everywhere the case that those individuals that succeed are the neofundamentalists. I would put in that camp both Mr. Maudoodi and Rashid Rida as well as other leading Islamic theologians and philosophers about whom we know so much nowadays.

The reason the neofundamentalists are succeeding is unclear, and I think that the answer that is presented by Islamic theologians is unclear. We can begin to form an answer by thinking about the role of Islam as a protest ideology and as the protector of the cultural authenticity of the people who practice it against the onslaught of both the West and the East, or, in other words, against the onslaught of American imperialism and Soviet imperialism. Insofar as Islam is a protest ideology, it seems to me that a literalist, fundamentalist interpretation of the Quran and its use will be an interesting vehicle for a political mobilization of populations against the onslaught of Eastern and Western threats.

Q (Marvin Weinbaum, University of Illinois, Urbana): The usual view is that the church-state conflict in the Sunni branch was resolved at least by the fourteenth century, if not before, whereas in the Shiite, essentially in the Iranian context, that conflict was never resolved. It was never decided whether the *ulama* had a legitimate claim on political power. With that in mind, it strikes me that—Maudoodi aside—there is no good example in the recent past of a charismatic political neofundamentalist type coming to power in a Sunni context. Indeed, what we see in the Egyptian situation is a fragmentation, and most everywhere we see fragmentation and a legitimacy for the secular side that are not present in the Iranian context. I wonder whether you can so easily bridge what has been the conventional view that the Sunni and Shiite do have some things in common but not the concept of a man who is speaking God's words and who is the shadow of God; there is no parallel to that in the Sunni faith.

A: I think that you add a very important emendation. You suggest why it is the case that if one would have guessed 20 years ago where in the world a charismatic Islamic divine would most likely be found as the head of state, one would have guessed Iran. As absurd as that would have seemed 20 years ago, it would have seemed less absurd than it would to have expected a charismatic Islamic head in a Sunni society. This occurrence, as you point out quite rightly, had to do with certain basic notions of charisma in leadership within Shiite thought that are quite distinct from tenets in Sunni thought. Given the differences between the two religious branches, it is noteworthy that disintegration characterizes the unity of the Sunni clerics as well as the Shiite clerics.

I find Ayatollah Khomeini to be an extraordinary character. I am not a great devotee of the ayatollah but I do believe that this human being is truly a charismatic figure, and he is the only one whom I have ever met who is. There is a light around Ayatollah Khomeini. I think it is only the power of that charisma that has made it possible to overcome the differences among the clerics. It is inconceivable to me that with the death of Ayatollah Khomeini another Shiite cleric with the same kind of charisma will arise. As a result, there will be the same kind of disintegration of the unity of the ruling stratum of Iran as that which characterizes the Sunni clergy.

COMMENT: There seems to have been another such character who was a charismatic leader.

A: Imam Musa al-Sadr, in my opinion, failed. He was only saved from manifest failure by his felicitous disappearance in the deserts of Libya, and had he not so disappeared I think he would have lost the support of his followers.

Q: It should be recognized that in Sunni Islam there is no clergy. In Sunni Islam what we have are learned people, whereas in Shiite Islam the clergy has been institutionalized and there are many ayatollahs. Any comparison between Shiite and Sunni is therefore misleading. In Sunni Islam, power is given to the entire community, so that there is no charismatic leader in Sunni Islam as there is in Shiite Islam.

A: Imam Musa al-Sadr, as he was known by his followers, despite his failure retained his charisma. He was an extraordinary leader who maintained a cadre of people around him even after the failure represented by the civil war. Furthermore, he apparently retained a rather important following in Iran. I understand that he was perhaps one of the most popular religious figures in Iran. There are some who even link the current Iranian leadership to his disappearance. It seems that the charismatic figure may fall but the charisma is nevertheless sustained.

There is a man on the Lebanese scene right now named Muhammad Hussein Fadlallah. He is very much associated in the minds of many people in the West with Hezbollah, at least as something of an ideologue.

Q (Renze L. Hoeksema, Hope College, Holland, Michigan): If the present regime in Iran is going to take 50 years to change, would it not be in the interest of the United States to warm up to Iran as fast as possible, since Iran shares a long border with the Soviet Union? We have dealt with people like Stalin, and it would seem to me that we could deal with a person like Khomeini.

A: I meant to say not that this regime would last for 50 years but that the forces that this regime has set in motion will still be present on the Iranian scene in 50 years, irrespective of the particular regime.

Why is the United States not warming up to Iran? The answer is very much on a par with why the Israelis did not succeed in working things out with the Shiites before they withdrew from Lebanon. The United States has made a variety of overtures to Iran—all, of course, private and implicit and none public—seeking to explore the possibilities for so-called more normal relations with the Islamic Republic. Our basic interests in Iran can be served by a regime that is committed to three goals: selling oil; maintaining the unity of the territory; and serving as an anti-Soviet power. The present regime in Iran meets all three of these goals, which seem to me to be America's basic interest in Iran. The response to each U.S. overture is that no one in Iran is yet ready to undertake even the beginnings of a discussion of what normalization would be like. It is clear that the revolutionary fervor, the outrage, the hatred—the narcissistic wounds—are still too deep for any Iranian officials to contemplate such discussion unless he wanted to be executed.

There are some people in the regime that Americans can talk to but they are clearly not going to talk to Americans, just as members of Amal would like to talk to the Israelis but are not going to take the risk. I am sure normal relations will be established if this regime stays in power, but I do not know when.

Q (Candace Briggs, Warren County Community College, Washington, New Jersey): As of at least a decade or so ago, 10 percent of the population in Iran was Jewish. What impact has the Iranian revolution and the tremendous power that is now wielded by the Shiites had on this population?

A: There have been lengthy debates within Israel about the advisability of supplying weapons to the regime of the Islamic Republic; until very recently the decision of Israeli military and political leaders favored weapons supply. There were a number of justifications for supplying such weapons to Iran, one of which was to protect the Jewish community that resides in Iran. There is still a very sizable Jewish community in Iran, although its numbers are tremendously depleted.

The Islamic Republic lifted its restrictions on travel. One pretty much has to leave one's wealth behind, but one can at least take one's person out of the country. No census has been conducted in Iran since 1976, which is to say, not since the founding of the Islamic Republic, so it is very difficult to know the number of Jews in Iran. The numbers that I have seen range from 20,000 to 40,000 Jews. In Tehran, 25,000 to 35,000 Jews remain. The conditions of their lives are trying, insofar as the basic commitment to the Islamic Republic carries with it a commitment to the destruction of Zionism. Ayatollah Khomeini, true to some of his Islamic heritage, has made a very clear distinction between Jews in Iran and Zionists in Iran. As the Jewish community bends over backward to demonstrate that it is a Jewish, not Zionist community and not a locus of Zionist activities, it has been allowed to continue its basic activities. The Ayatollah receives delegations of Jewish leaders on appropriate occasions and says the appropriate things. It is also true, however, that the state has begun to impose restrictions on the operations of all religious minorities; in this case, the Jews are not in any way particular. For example, all minority schools in Iran have been eliminated. There used to be Armenian schools, Assyrian schools, and Jewish schools; there were schools for a large number of Christian minorities as well as Jewish minorities. Those schools have essentially been eliminated because the regime insists that not only a standard set of textbooks be used in every grade in every school but, in addition, that all children, irrespective of their religions, must undergo training in Islam. They are also allowed to undergo training in their own faith. It is not as if they are forbidden to practice their own faith or forbidden to have lessons, but they must have classes in Islam during school hours. Finally, the languages of the minority groups may no longer be used as a language of instruction in the school system. Under the shah, there were Jewish schools that used Hebrew, Armenian schools that used Armenian, and English schools that used English, but that is now disallowed and Persian is the only language permitted. Both the religion and the language of the minority schools have suffered to the point where most of them have been closed and are being incorporated into the public school system.

Q (Dario Scuka, Library of Congress, Washington, D.C.): The present Iranian stance against the imperialist enemies appears to be directed more at the United States than at European countries.

Does the Iranian position center more on past economic exploitation or on the effect of Western industrialization on Iran's social structure? Does the focus on imperialist enemies act as a unifying factor within domestic politics?

A: Several theoretical frameworks can be used to address these issues. Let me answer from a psychoanalytic perspective. One way in which I understand the intense hostility that one sees on the part of Iranians toward the United States is as a reaction formation to a very powerful longing for and attraction to Western culture as exemplified by the United States. It is not surprising that many followers of the line of the *imam*—the same young men and women who captured the U.S. embassy and held American diplomats incarcerated for so long—have applied for visas to come to the United States. A lot of these students who took over the American embassy were, of course, left-wing students, members of the Mujahedin and other groups not now in favor in Khomeini's Iran. Those are the very people who, when they have to go someplace in order to flee Iran, go to the United States.

Within another framework, Iran's anti-imperialism responds to the incredible influence that the United States had over the transformation of Iranian culture, particularly beginning in 1963 and then with a special intensity in 1970. Part of that influence was the power of American culture; part of it was the wealth of the United States and its attraction for Iranian students. Some of it certainly was the major participation in the Iranian economy of American corporations as well as the subservience of the shah to the American political system. U.S. influence was reflected, for instance, in the military of Iran being increasingly trained by the United States.

Q (Duygu Sezer, Columbia University, New York City): I have a methodological question. Would you please comment on terrorism in Turkey and terrorism against Turkey in the form of Armenian terrorism or domestic terrorism, which was one of the causes of the military intervention several years ago.

A (David Long, U.S. Department of State, Washington, D.C.): There has not been a body of methodological work yet produced on terrorism. A few methodological works are beginning to appear, but most of them are not terribly good. They are mostly anecdotal and mostly from a decided point of view of somebody who is trying to show why the other people are really worse than human. A methodological study of terrorism ought to look instead at why terrorism occurs. Religion is a variable that is examined. There have been and there are Christian terrorists in the Middle East; Armenians are an example. There have been and there are Muslim terrorists, Shiites in Lebanon and Sunnis elsewhere. There have been and there are Jewish terrorists; Yitzhak Shamir was a very effective terrorist. There is now a very curious organization in Israel called Terrorism to End Terrorism, and it is a terrorist organization. The question is, What is there about religion that adds to whatever else there is out there that makes a person want to blow up somebody that is not a member of the same religion? There are a lot of people, generally nonbelievers, who can show why certain religionists have in their religion something that makes them want to kill people. Daniel Pipes or Bernard Lewis would say very plainly that there are certain elements in Islam that give rise to behavior that is conducive to violence. I do not believe it. Likewise, some Arab *mullah*s and *imam*s will say that there is something intrinsic to Christianity and Judaism that is conducive to violence. I think that violence begets violence, and that violence has behavioral roots rather than theological roots. In the case of the Armenians, as in the case of the confessional groups in Lebanon, it is more the sociological grouping than the theological profession that leads them to terrorism. Along with sociological factors, the political environment must be examined. To take it a step further, one of the new elements that has appeared in the last decade has been the rise of fundamentalism. Most people usually say "Islamic fundamentalism" as a single word, but the Islamic is not the only fundamentalism. There are 30 million Hindu fundamentalists in India. The Sikhs are currently raising cain in India. There are confessional acts of incredible barbarity going on right now in Sri Lanka. It is a nasty little war in Sri Lanka, both sides of which want us to label the other as terrorists.

Fundamentalism has spread all over the world. One of the reasons for its popularity appears to be that people are looking for roots, for something to hang on to. Unfortunately when there is a puritan movement, to the pure all things are impure. If one person is pure and another person holds opposite views, then the other person is impure and the first person must kill the second person to make the second person clean. This is one of the elements of the growth of radicalism, the growth of intolerance, the growth of fanaticism throughout a part of the world—the Middle East; their confessionalism is a way of life. Fundamentalism's spread does not augur well because what it tells us is that the trend will probably grow rather than decline because frustration with one's life in general is growing, just in the processes of modernity.

I think Meir Kahane is an aberration; he is on the lunatic fringe. That he is allowed to be in Israel is evidence that democracy works there. But there is a somber side to it: there is not a growth in Israel of sentiment favoring Meir Kahane, but there is a growing acceptance in Israel of the right of people to be increasingly less tolerant and less flexible. This condition is being paralleled on the Arab side by people who are becoming less tolerant and less flexible, and unless the people who are tolerant and flexible can find solutions to lower the frustration level, this kind of inflexibility and fanaticism is likely to increase rather than decrease. It will increase the tragedy of people in the Middle East and it will also increase the risk of all people—Americans, Europeans, Africans, and Asians—who have interests beyond their own borders.

Q (Wolfgang): Grievances and frustrations indeed are part of the patterns and profiles of terrorists on both the Right and the Left; however, the presence of those ingredients is not very helpful for prediction purposes because a lot of people have grievances, but I doubt they would resort to terrorism. Is there any collaboration, subterranean or more visible, between those particular states that sponsor terrorism and the more private, nonstate terrorists, such as the Red Brigade in Italy? Is there any sharing of weaponry, financing, or training between the state and the nonstate terrorists?

A (Long): There is cooperation among groups at certain times and in certain circumstances. Given the nature of the subject, evidence must be circumstantial. This evidence indicates that from time to time there has been cooperation on operations on an ad hoc basis among various groups: the Red Brigade, the Red Army in Japan, Baader-Meinhof, and some of the Arab groups. There has probably been no cooperation, organizational or ideological, among groups such as the Armenian groups. Each group works its own side of the street and has its own agenda. There might be cooperation for one specific operation if the agendas overlap. But from that cooperation it should not be assumed that there is a closer relationship in an organizational or ideological realm. It does show, though, that the idea of radical on the Left and radical on the Right does not hold up as much as we thought when it comes down to operations.

Q (Thomas Harlick, Orange County Community College, Middletown, New York): First, to what extent are terroristic acts in Lebanon committed against the will of the ones committing them? Second, we talked about states that support terrorist activities; could you comment on states that support terrorist activities that are provoked by the state? I am thinking of American support for the shah, who, in a sense, used terrorist activities against his own citizens, and thereby may have created the alienation and terrorism that resulted.

A (Long): There has not been any international agreement on a definition of terrorism. What is the difference between an insurgency and terrorism, for example? There will never be a hard-and-fast definition of terrorism.

Politics is the art of the possible. We get what we can get, not what we would like. It is a very imperfect world. We have heard from Dr. Rustow that one can safely assume that all countries will not have American-style democracies by the end of this decade. We will therefore have to face the fact that there will be a lot of countries that use violence and intimidation with their citizens. It is probably more legitimate to try to address those kinds of activities as human rights violations than as terrorism. There is a universal declaration of human rights and there is legislation. There are several issues that can be dealt with by talking about these kinds of acts in terms of the human rights of the victim that have been violated. The area of a regime's relations with its own citizens is not, by and large, in the realm of international relations but of the domestic affairs of another country, which is a Pandora's box better left unopened. It is cleaner to pursue terroristic activity by states in a human-rights context, and in the State Department there is a Bureau of Human Rights that does just that.

Regarding the responsibility of actors for the acts of terrorism that they commit, there are parallels in U.S. criminal justice for denial of responsibility: the perpetrator had a bad childhood or did not really mean to commit the act, for example. Some of those circumstances are valid; some are not. But excusing actors from responsibility opens up a wide variety of questions—more questions than answers—about motivation.

I would say that whereas extenuating circumstances do exist, the fact is that the relatively high incidence of people who are willing to commit terrorism is predicated on an environment that includes a tremendous and deep-seated sense of grievance. Having that grievance and living in an area of political instability may not automatically make a person a terrorist, but they may increase the chances of the commission of a terrorist act if a gun is put into the actor's hand or if the actor is listening to a charismatic and persuasive speaker advocate the act. Conditions that promote fanaticism are not limited to Lebanon, as evidenced by the Israeli Gush Emunim. To me, living in an environment of stress, frustration, and instability and having a deep-seated sense of grievance are more important to look at than why one person or another person in an anecdotal situation accepts or denies responsibility for an act.

ANNALS, *AAPSS*, **482**, November 1985

Changing Actors and Leadership among the Shiites of Lebanon

By AUGUSTUS RICHARD NORTON

ABSTRACT: Scarcely three years ago there was little scholarly or policy interest in the Shiite community of Lebanon. Long irrelevant politically within Lebanon, the Shiites languished under the firm control of traditional leaders who were not seriously challenged until the 1960s. By the mid-1960s, however, the Shiites were becoming politicized. The most important role in mobilizing them was played by a charismatic Iranian cleric of Lebanese descent, Sayyid Musa al-Sadr. His efforts were disrupted by the war of 1975-76, and it was not until 1978 that the movement he started enjoyed a revival, in part because of his mysterious disappearance. By the eve of the Israeli invasion of 1982, al-Sadr's organization, Amal, was the most important political grouping among the Shiites. However, since the events of 1982, the Amal movement—an essentially moderate formation—has been challenged by a number of more extreme organizations, including Hezbollah, which seeks an Islamic solution to the plight of the Shiites. As of mid-1985, Amal was arguably the leading Shiite organization, but the ravages of further frustration and radicalization may shift the balance of power.

Augustus Richard Norton is associate professor of comparative politics at the United States Military Academy, West Point, New York. He earned his Ph.D. at the University of Chicago, where he wrote his dissertation on the Amal movement. He conducted field research in Lebanon, including the south, from 1980 to 1982. His book-length study of the Lebanese Shiites will be published in late 1985, and his many articles on Lebanon have been published by leading newspapers as well as in a number of professional journals and edited volumes.

NOTE: The opinions expressed by the author should not be construed to represent the position or policy of any institution or branch of the U.S. government.

AFTER centuries of political irrelevance, the Shiite Muslim community of Lebanon has enjoyed a remarkable transformation. Long consigned to footnotes in scholarly tomes, the Shiites are suddenly front-page news. Scarcely three years ago, there was little interest in this Shiite community, among either scholars or policymakers, but the momentous events following Israel's 1982 invasion of Lebanon have helped to propel the Shiites to center stage.

By early 1984, Shiite militiamen had seized control of West Beirut and thwarted the apparent intention of a Maronite president to ignore their demands for serious political reform. Despite a heavy commitment of U.S. troops, matériel, and prestige, the Shiites played a central role in precipitating the withdrawal of the Multinational Force and bringing about the abrogation of the American-sponsored agreement of 17 May 1983 between Israel and Lebanon. In south Lebanon, where Shiite fighters had openly combatted the armed Palestinian presence from 1979 to 1982, the Shiites turned their guns on the Israeli occupation forces. In January 1985, in the face of increasing armed resistance, especially on the part of the Shiites, and mounting Israeli casualties, the Israeli cabinet announced its decision to withdraw from Lebanon, thus signaling a major defeat for the Israeli armed forces and a stunning failure of Israeli policy objectives in Lebanon.[1] No doubt, Israel's painful experience in Lebanon will have a lasting impact on its security policy, and the example of the loosely coordinated, locally based Shiite resistance may well have a dramatic spillover effect in the territories occupied by Israel since 1967, not to mention the Middle East as a whole. All of these major developments certainly justify the new-found interest in the Lebanese Shiites; however, they constitute only the most sensational part of the story. There is another aspect, and that is the chronicle of economic, social, and political change among the Shiites, change that will not only permanently affect the conduct of politics in Lebanon, but will also ensure that the Shiites of Lebanon will have to be taken into account by any state dealing with their country.

THE ROOTS OF IMPOVERISHMENT

When Lebanon achieved independence in 1943 the Shiites could be, and were, largely taken for granted by Lebanese political leaders. Although they were officially recognized—on the basis of a suspect census taken in 1932—as the republic's third largest community, trailing behind the Maronite Christians and the Sunni Muslims, the Shiites remained relatively powerless well into the late 1950s and 1960s.

In part, the paucity of Shiite political power was explained by the Sunni-Maronite domination of the political system, in which virtually all significant offices—from parliamentary seats to senior army and bureaucratic posts—were distributed according to confessional—which is to say, ascriptive

1. Israel's policies in south Lebanon are examined in several of my articles, including "Israel and South Lebanon," *American-Arab Affairs*, no. 4, pp. 23-32 (Spring 1983); "Making Enemies in South Lebanon: Harakat Amal, the IDF, and South Lebanon," *Middle East Insight*, 3(3):13-20 (Jan.-Feb. 1984); and "Occupational Risks and Planned Retirement: The Israeli Withdrawal from Lebanon," *Middle East Insight*, 4(1):14-18 (Mar.-Apr. 1985).

sectarian—criteria. At the apex of national politics, the Maronites were accorded the presidency and the Sunnis the prime ministership, while the Shiites were only allocated the post of parliamentry Speaker, a position richer traditionally in patronage possibilities than significant political power. Despite a half-century's demographic changes, which saw the Shiites replace the Maronites as the largest confessional group in Lebanon, the structure of politics proved to be inflexible. Although the Shiites accounted for 30 percent or more of the Lebanese population as early as 20 years ago, only some 20 percent of the seats in the National Assembly—Lebanon's parliament—are assigned to Shiites. In the present Assembly, elected in 1972, 19 of 99 seats are held by Shiites.

But the structure of Lebanese politics was not the fundamental cause of the Shiites' second-class status. The structure merely reflected underlying socioeconomic realities.[2] The roots of their political impoverishment were in their social and economic underdevelopment. By any of the standard measures of socioeconomic status, the Shiites were the most deprived community in Lebanon. They were the poorest, the least well educated, and the least likely to benefit from government-provided services such as health facilities or public utilities. While some Shiites lived in the southern Beirut suburbs, most were village dwellers engaged in subsistence farming or sharecropping. Living on the geographic margins of Lebanon, in the Jebel Amel region of the south, which borders Israel, or in the undeveloped Bekaa Valley, they enjoyed a disproportionately small share of government expenditures.

Even discussing the Shiites as a community two or three decades ago would have been something of a misnomer. Lacking a developed political consciousness and a sense of community, the Shiites were fragmented politically into geographic segments that were dominated by a handful of traditional political bosses known as *zaims*.[3] The *zaims* were often men who had parlayed land wealth and tax collection concessions—dating from the Ottoman period—into political clout. Political power in Lebanon is distributed by sect, and, especially in the case of the Shiites, the sect's share of political power was not much more than the shares clutched by the *zaims*, who often enjoyed the perquisites of office and the many rewards of political influence without much more than cursory accountability to their constituents. In such a system, which today survives only in a much weakened form, citizens do not seek political rewards as their legal right, but as a favor granted by the *zaim*, who, in return, expects his clients to reciprocate his largess in myriad ways ranging from electoral support to payment in labor.

Until the 1960s, the *zaims* had few serious clerical or secular competitors. While Islam has been a persistent and cohesive cultural force among the Shiites, the Shiite clergy (*ulama*) lacked an independent financial base, and in many instances they were heavily dependent upon a *zaim* for financial support. Thus,

2. A more detailed discussion of the socioeconomic status of the Shiites may be found in Augustus Richard Norton, "Harakat Amal (The Movement of Hope)," in *Religion and Politics*, ed. Myron J. Aronoff (New Brunswick, NJ: Transaction Books, 1984), pp. 105-31.

3. The seminal analysis of the *zaim* (plural: *zuama*) is found in Arnold Hottinger, "*Zu'ama'* in Historical Perspective," in *Politics in Lebanon*, ed. Leonard Binder (New York: John Wiley, 1966), pp. 85-106.

much in contrast to Iran, where the *ulama* controlled a well-developed system of income-producing religious trusts (*awgaf*), in Lebanon the Shiite *ulama* lacked autonomous financial resources.[4] Nor, it should be emphasized, had the Shiite religious leaders of Lebanon established a historical record of political protest or opposition to secular political authorities on anything even approaching the scale of their Iranian or Iraqi cohorts.[5]

THE STIRRINGS OF CHANGE

In retrospect, the emergence of the Shiites as a political force can be traced to the 1950s, when the traditional structure of politics began to crack under the pressure of modernization. The 1950s were a decade of enormous social and economic change in Lebanon, and although the Shiites continued to lag behind Lebanon's other sects in terms of socioeconomic status, they were nonetheless profoundly affected by the changes that marked the country. The Shiite villagers' isolation was being broken by a growing exposure to various aspects of modernity, including increased access to education, enhanced internal transportation networks, and growing exposure to the news media, especially radio.

It should be emphasized that Lebanon is a small country, smaller than the state of Connecticut, and its modest scale has the effect of intensifying the impact of change. By road, all but the most isolated villages were within an easy three-to-four-hour drive of Beirut. Thus, even the villagers who never ventured very far from their homes and fields found it difficult to avoid the march of change.

Most important were patterns of internal and external migration, which contributed to a steady growth in the Shiite population of the Beirut suburbs, as well as impressive numbers of Shiite men relocating to the Gulf and to West Africa where they attempted to make their fortunes as peddlers, tradesmen, and even petty bureaucrats.[6] Initially, the most important impetus for migration was the prospect of gainful employment. Subsequently, especially after the displacement of the Palestine Liberation Organization (PLO) from Jordan to south Lebanon in 1970, the deteriorating security in the south not only seriously disrupted the economy of the area, but led many to flee simply for the sake of self-preservation.

The migrations had several ramifications that impaired and decreased the power of the *zaims*. Shiites leaving their villages, whether they moved to the environs of the capital or abroad, had ever more complex needs that could not be readily met by the *zaims*. For that matter, the anachronistic political bosses could hardly be expected to define their interests in terms of helping erstwhile clients break the bonds that tied them to their *zaims*. Thus, many of the new slum dwellers—accounting for as much as 40 percent of the total Shiite population in Lebanon—found themselves cast adrift without employment and without a tra-

4. Useful insights are found in Tarif Khalidi, "Shaykh Ahmad 'Arif al-Zayn and al-'Irfan," in *Intellectual Life in the Arab East, 1890-1939*, ed. Marwan R. Buheiry (Beirut: Center for Arab and Middle East Studies, 1981), pp. 110-24.

5. For a thoughtful collection of case studies and comparative treatments, see Nikki Keddie and Juan Cole, eds. *Shi'ism and Social Protest* (New Haven, CT: Yale University Press, forthcoming).

6. See Augustus Richard Norton, "Harakat Amal and the Political Mobilization of the Shi'a of Lebanon" (Ph.D. diss., University of Chicago, 1984), esp. pp. 19-63.

ditional patron. Not surprisingly, the poor Shiite migrants to the city came to constitute a prime recruitment pool for a wide range of political parties that promised to assuage their despair.

While many of the new migrants to the city lived in miserable poverty, those who left Lebanon—typically with the expectation of return—often accumulated at least modest savings, and many Shiites gained considerable wealth. It is worth emphasizing that we should not allow stereotypes about Shiite poverty to mask the fact that there is considerable wealth in the community, a fact that many analysts ignore. Indeed, well-to-do Shiites provided significant financial support to political movements that challenged the power and the leadership of the traditional power brokers.

By the mid-1960s a number of political parties and movements were competing for the newly politicized Shiites. Most of the competing organizations were avowedly secular in orientation, such as the Lebanese Communist Party, but one of the organizations appealed to the Shiites qua Shiites. This latter group was led by an Iranian cleric, Sayyid Musa al-Sadr, who at the age of 31 had become the *mufti*, or religious judge, in the southern port city of Tyre, the only major city in Lebanon where the Shiites predominate. Although Iranian by birth, Musa al-Sadr was a Lebanese by descent. In fact, his grandfather's tomb is in Maraka, a south Lebanon village that was an important center of resistance, both to the PLO, prior to the 1982 invasion, and to the Israel Defense Force subsequently. Musa al-Sadr quickly proved to be a skillful and charismatic shepherd for the nascent political consciousness of the Shiites.[7] Al-Sadr's followers—and even some of his adversaries—note that he was not only tolerant of religious traditions outside of Shiism, but that he extolled Lebanon as an example of intercommunal toleration. As one of his close associates wrote in 1984:

> The Imam believed that Lebanon represented a unique example to the world to prove the Oneness of God despite its plurality of religions.
>
> For him religions were but different ways to reach God, just like the different ways to reach the peak of a mountain. The Imam does not deny that each way to God has its own and proper characteristics, but in their essence all ways are alike because they lead to the same end. Therefore he rejected estrangement among believers in the name of religion, and he insistently preached the harmonization among them.
>
> The Imam was greatly involved in the salvation of Lebanon, because for him Lebanon is the country of dialogue, of tolerance, and of harmony, in one word, the country of freedom. There is no doubt that the Imam wanted the social and political evolution of Lebanon, but on condition that this evolution would be brought about by peaceful, moral and non-violent means.[8]

In the decade and a half preceding the civil war of 1975-76, Imam Musa—as al-Sadr came to be called by his followers—established himself as a formidable political actor. Courted by the Maronite Christians, who saw him as a reasonable and intelligent reformer committed to Lebanon, and the PLO, which recognized his growing influence among the Shiites, Musa al-Sadr proved himself capable of shifting alliance partners at opportune moments. Within

7. See Augustus Richard Norton, "Shi'ism and Social Protest in Lebanon," in *Shi'ism and Social Protest*, ed. Keddie and Cole.

8. Private communication.

the Shiite community, he skillfully employed the central symbols of Shiism, especially the martyrdom of Muhammad's grandson, Imam Hussein, to mobilize support among the masses. Hussein's tragic end in A.D. 680 at Karbala, in present-day Iraq, was held up as a fitting example of the selfless bravery and commitment that the Shiites could strive to emulate in the face of oppression.[9] At the same time, he attracted a dedicated cadre of Shiite nouveaux riches who saw in Imam Musa a means of reducing the power of the traditional Shiite leadership and concomitantly increasing their own role in politics.

Musa al-Sadr's bête noire was Kamel al-Asad, *zaim* par excellence, who quickly became his prime rival and target. To be sure, Kamel al-Asad was not without resources or victories, but by the end of the 1960s Musa al-Sadr had clearly shown himself more than a match for the clever *zaim*. For instance, in a notable political success, Imam Musa took over the presidency of the Supreme Shiite Council upon its establishment in 1969. The newly created council put the Shiites—for the first time—on an equal institutional footing with the Sunni Muslims, and with the council under his control Imam Musa occupied a post that nearly rivaled al-Asad's position as speaker of the Chamber of Deputies, which was later renamed the National Assembly.

Notwithstanding Musa al-Sadr's victories, it should be emphasized that no single organization dominated Shiite politics during this crucial period. Indeed, in the years preceding the civil war there was intense competition among a number of parties that were hectically recruiting from the growing pool of newly politicized Shiites. By the eve of the civil war in 1975, the Shiites were represented in a number of political parties, ranging from Musa al-Sadr's Movement of the Deprived, established in 1974, to the Syrian Social Nationalist Party and various leftist parties.

Initially aligned with a coalition of Palestinian organizations and various Muslim reform-oriented and radical parties, Musa al-Sadr broke with his allies in June 1976, when the Syrian army intervened to prevent the defeat of the Maronite militia forces. Al-Sadr's calculus was plain. Given the choice of a *fedayeen* victory that could radicalize and destroy Lebanon, he sought to preserve the state, which was the locus of his ambitions for reform.[10]

RESCUE FROM OBSCURITY

In effect, the onset of fighting in 1975 interrupted Imam Musa's efforts, just as the Israeli invasion of 1982 would later short-circuit the political exertions of his successors. Although some of Musa al-Sadr's followers played a minor role in the fighting, the strength of his movement was not that of an effective militia force. His movement was one of social protest, and the din of battle almost smothered it. By 1978 it seemed that al-Sadr's populist campaign to mobilize Shiites was fading into near obscurity, but several developments intervened in 1978 and 1979 to rescue it. His movement came to be known as the

9. For an insightful discussion of the appropriation of Shiite ritual for political purposes in south Lebanon, see Elizabeth Picard, "From 'Community-Class' to 'Patriotic Struggle'" (Paper delivered at the Annual Meeting of the Middle East Studies Association, San Francisco, Dec. 1984).

10. See Karim Pakradouni, *La paix manquée* [The unfound peace] (in French) (Beirut: Editions FMA, 1983), pp. 105-7.

Amal movement, although this name originally applied to the militia adjunct to the Movement of the Deprived.[11]

The new Hidden Imam

Al-Sadr disappeared during an August 1978 visit to Libya, never to be heard from again. Although a panoply of conspiracies has been offered as explanations for the disappearance, their common denominator is that Muammar el-Quaddafi, the mercurial Libyan leader, played a central role in killing the Lebanese leader.

Ironically, Imam Musa's disappearance was the single most important factor in reviving the Amal movement. He now transcended the bickering and competition of the Lebanese political scene and became a larger-than-life hero for the Shiites. Notably, the first significant evidence of Amal's revival was a national strike called in 1979—and repeated annually—to mark the anniversary of Imam Musa's disappearance. Moreover, the very mystery surrounding his probable demise added to his cultural authenticity and power as a symbol. One of the central myths of Shiism is that of the Hidden Imam and it was a myth made to order for Imam Musa. As Fouad Ajami notes in a recent and important article:

> In the Shia [Shiite] myth, the Twelfth Imam—religious and political successor to the Prophet—vanished to the eyes of ordinary men in 873-74, to return at the "end of time" to fill the earth with justice. This is the doctrine of the *Ghaiba*, the absence, the occultation, of the Hidden Imam. Musa al Sadr embodied the myth in modern times. He left inheritors and followers sitting under posters, repeating his words, awaiting his "return."[12]

Self-defense

Meanwhile, the security situation was deteriorating seriously in the south—the religious locus of the Shiite sect in Lebanon—where battles between Israel and the *fedayeen* were trapping increasing numbers of Shiites in the cross fire, especially after the Israeli Litani Operation of 1978, which seemed to mark an upsurge in Israeli intervention in the south.[13] While the Shiites had once been aligned with the Palestinian fighters, by the late 1970s they had lost their patience with the *fedayeen* and they were taking up arms in self-defense, both in the south and in the heavily Shiite suburbs of Beirut. Obviously, both Israel and the Palestinians exacted casualties in the south, but it was the force whose presence was seen and felt daily—the PLO—which was the target for Shiite resentment. It is still not adequately appreciated outside of Lebanon that the Shiites were quite literally at war with the PLO in the period preceding the Israeli invasion. Indeed, it is fair to conjecture that had Israel not invaded to extricate the PLO, the Shiites may well have ended up in a quiet alliance with Israel. The organization that symbolized the anti-PLO campaign of the Shiites was the Amal movement, which unlike its organizational competitors was not besmirched by association with

11. I have analyzed the critical events of 1978-79 in much greater detail elsewhere, including Edward Azar et al., *The Emergence of a New Lebanon: Fantasy or Reality?* (New York: Praeger, 1984).

12. Fouad Ajami, "Lebanon and Its Inheritors," *Foreign Affairs,* 63(4):783 (Spring 1985).

13. See Augustus Richard Norton, "Lebanon's Shiites," *New York Times*, 16 Apr. 1982; and idem, "Militant Protest and Political Violence under the Banner of Islam," *Armed Forces and Society,* 9(1):14-16 (Fall 1982).

the PLO. With every indignation, every provocation, and every incident involving the PLO, Amal seemed to gain new members.

The Islamic revolution in Iran

Finally, the Islamic revolution in Iran provided an exemplar for concerted Shiite political action against oppression. The events in Iran demonstrated dramatically that a well-organized and mobilized Shiite community might accomplish incredible feats, and the traditionally close ties between the two Shiite communities helped to ensure that the overthrow of the shah would reverberate in Lebanon. There is no denying that the Shiites revered Ayatollah Khomeini, yet for most of the Shiites there was no desire to replicate Iran's new Islamic Republic. After the disappointments and the radicalization of the post-1982 period, the Iranian solution would attract more followers, although it remains a minority movement in the community.

In any event, the three developments just summarized combined to revitalize and validate the Amal movement, which could now claim a powerful affective symbol, an effective model for action, and a populist cause uncomplicated by a sophisticated political program. Between 1978 and 1982 the Amal movement enjoyed impressive growth, and on the eve of the Israeli invasion of 1982 it was undoubtedly the most important Shiite political movement in Lebanon.

For the most part, al-Sadr's successors in the movement were centrist, secularly oriented men who were committed to the survival of Lebanon, as long as gradual progress was made in meeting Shiite demands for political reform, such as reallocation of state resources, recognition of the Shiites as the plurality in Lebanon, and eventual elimination of sectarianism in politics. With the Israeli invasion, and the expulsion of the hated and feared PLO, there was widespread hope for an end to the internal conflict, as well as the expectation that a government committed to reform would be installed.

FRACTURED HOPE

It would be difficult to exaggerate the ebullient and optimistic mood that gripped Lebanon following the extrication of the PLO from Beirut in August 1982. For many years the Lebanese had been waiting for the last battle to be fought, and now, finally, the war seemed to be over. Within the Shiite community there was a deep sense of relief that the PLO yoke had been lifted from its shoulders. Even the ominous events of September 1982—the massacres in the Sabra and Shatila camps that claimed the lives of hundreds of poor Shiites as well as Palestinians, and the assassination of the president-elect, Bashir Gemayel—did not dampen the hopes shared by so many. The new president, Amin Gemayel, was seen as a moderate who would pursue reconciliation and reform.[14]

The leadership of the Amal movement—Nabih Berri, Aqif Haidar, and their associates—adopted a patient stance. Berri had served in the short-lived Committee of National Salvation, which had been formed in July 1982 by President Elias Sarkis in the midst of the Israeli invasion, and he clearly expected that his service on the committee was a

14. See Augustus Richard Norton, "The Political Mood in Lebanon," *Middle East Insight,* 2(5):9-13 (Jan.-Feb. 1983).

harbinger for a central role in the reconciliation process. He was wrong.

By late 1982 it became clear that the last battle had yet to be fought. In fact, many additional battles loomed. The new president, enjoying only a weak following among the Maronites, was unable to generate support within the Lebanese Forces, the heavily Maronite militia that had been Bashir's organizational base. It was the memory of Bashir that reigned, and Amin was unable to evoke his brother's martyrdom to his own advantage. Moreover, the militant Maronites wore Israel's seeming victory as their own, and they had no intention of making magnanimous gestures to any other community. Throughout the fall of 1982, the Shiites living in and around Beirut found themselves the target of arbitrary arrests and capricious harassment at the hands of Maronite militiamen and Lebanese soldiers acting in apparent concert with the Lebanese Forces. Instead of striving to meet the needs of those dwelling in the mean Shiite slums of Beirut, the government may have decided to partially depopulate the slums and to send the inhabitants back to their villages of origin.[15] Whatever the impetus for the government's response to the Shiites—whether it was thought through or thoughtless—it had serious effects in exacerbating the alienation of the Shiite Lebanese from their government. As one young Shiite told me in October 1982, "I am afraid to even approach an army checkpoint. Because I wear a beard I am automatically assumed to be a militant, and because my wife dresses modestly she is subjected to slander." In such circumstances patience frays quickly.

15. See Ajami, "Lebanon and Its Inheritors," p. 789.

Amin Gemayel, discomfited by the demands of the newly assertive Shiites, simply chose to ignore them. Rather than dealing with the ascendant Shiite leaders, President Gemayel fatefully chose to deal with official communal representatives, who also happened to be serious rivals of Nabih Berri. This was a crucial miscalculation. Thus, Kamel al-Asad, the Speaker of the parliament who was reviled by so many Shiites, found himself in the paradoxical position of speaking for those who saw him as the very symbol of their subjugation. In addition, Gemayel attempted to build firm political ties with the respected, if somewhat staid, Mufti Muhammad Mahdi Shamseddine, another Berri rival. In short, the essentially moderate Amal leadership came up empty-handed while some of its political competitors were being assiduously stroked by the president. Only in the fall of 1983 was Nabih Berri brought into the national reconciliation dialogue, and then half-heartedly and apparently as a result of pressure from the United States.

Until his disappearance in 1978, Musa al-Sadr had dominated two distinct political organizations. On the one hand, he led the Amal movement, and on the other, he was the president of the Supreme Shiite Council. The former was a populist movement with grassroots support, and the latter was an institution of the state that brought together Shiite notables, clerics, politicians, and members of the professional class.

Upon al-Sadr's disappearance, the two leadership posts were split, roughly along clerical-secular lines. The leadership of the council fell to Shamseddine, an establishment cleric who was hardly a man of the street. The leadership of

Amal initially went to Hussein Husseini, a member of parliament who eventually deposed Kamel al-Asad from the speakership in October 1984. However, by 1980 Husseini had left the movement to the leadership of Nabih Berri and had aligned with Shamseddine. Proper relations, if not always cordial ones, were maintained between the council and Amal until 1983, when Shamseddine publicly split with the movement, dismissing it as a militia and claiming the mantle of communal leadership in concert with Husseini. The split is an important one because it cleaved the moderate center of Shiite politics. With minor exceptions, there are few policy differences between the two sides; the clash is simply one of political ambitions. Although followers of both sides have urged reconciliation, the split persists.

While Berri and Shamseddine were jockeying for power, the political substrata were shifting beneath them. As it became clear that the post-invasion period did not signal any substantial amelioration of the Shiites' plight, despair and frustration took their toll and substantial numbers of Shiites turned away from the centrist leaders and lent their support to more radical organizations. Chief among these radical Shiite organizations has been Hezbollah ("the Party of God"), led by a loose grouping of firebrand clerics who offer their variant of activist Islam as a refuge and an answer. In its major programmatic statement, Hezbollah dedicates itself to establishing the rule of Islam in Lebanon and acknowledges organic links with the Islamic revolution of Iran. For the righteous Hezbollah there is to be no compromise in the confrontation with evil, of which the root is America and the regional manifestation is the Zionist state of Israel. Long dissatisfied with the impiety—not to mention the moderation—of the Amal leadership, Iran's Islamic Republic under Ayatollah Khomeini has apparently thrown its support to Hezbollah.

It is not at all clear to what extent Hezbollah has been actively involved in the anti-Western terrorist bombings and rampant kipnappings that have occurred in Lebanon since 1982, but there is no denying the anger and vitriol that marks the party's public statements.

> Imam Khomeini, the leader [*al-qaid*], has emphasized repeatedly that America is the reason for all of our catastrophes and the source of all evil. By fighting it we are merely exercising our legitimate right to defend our Islam and the dignity of our nation.
>
> We frankly and clearly declare that we are a nation that fears only God and that does not accept tyranny, aggression and humiliation. America and its allies from the North Atlantic Alliance, and the Zionist entity that has usurped the sacred land of Palestine, have engaged and continue to engage in constant aggression against us and are working constantly to humiliate us. Therefore, we are in a state of constant and accelerating preparedness for the sake of repelling the aggression and defending our religion, existence and dignity.[16]

Hezbollah is not the only radical Shiite group operating in Lebanon, but it is clearly the most significant. In fact, some informed observers believe that Hezbollah has absorbed many of the smaller radical factions, such as the Islamic Amal organization, which is thought to have been implicated in some of the attacks on American targets in

16. *Nass al-risala al-mattuha allati wajjuhaha hizb allah ila al-mustadafin fi lubnan wa al-alam* [Text of the open message that the Party of God sends to the oppressed in Lebanon and the world] (in Arabic) (distributed in Lebanon in Feb. 1985), p. 9.

Lebanon.[17] It is worth noting, however, that Western concepts of membership are often misleading when applied to such groups. We are not dealing with well-defined groups, replete with membership lists and membership cards. Instead, the phenomenon is very different. Many of the newly politicized Shiites do not belong to any organization, although they may identify with the message of this or that group. In effect, affiliation is loose and fluid; it is a political state of mind.

A charismatic figure who can exploit the political tenor of the moment thus often exerts an influence that transcends organizational boundaries. In the present circumstances, Muhammad Hussein Fadlallah is such a figure. Born near the Israeli border in Ainata, trained in the religious schools of Najaf, Iraq, long resident in the suburbs of Beirut, Fadlallah is one of the most influential Shiite clerics in Lebanon, and his influence extends to the Gulf as well.

Some journalists have reported that Fadlallah is the leader of Hezbollah, and others have alleged that he was centrally involved in the anti-U.S. terrorist bombings that took more than 250 American lives. As to the first charge, Fadlallah has consistently claimed that he is not the leader of any party or movement, although he acknowledges his own influence among the Shiites. It is unimportant whether he is the leader of Hezbollah or not, although I do not believe that he is. The important fact is that his message resonates throughout the Shiite community, especially in the environs of Beirut. Moreover, it should be added that his message is one that combines a call for intercommunal tolerance with the adherence of Muslims to Islamic law. While he does not deny that he would like to live in an Islamic state—in fact, he aspires to do so—he does not think that the conditions in socially heterogeneous Lebanon are appropriate currently for the establishment of such a state. During his last visit to Iran, in February 1985, his refusal to demand the immediate establishment of an Islamic state in Lebanon reputedly led to a cool reception. Much has been written about Fadlallah's views, but the fact is that in comparison to many of his *ulama* cohorts, he is no fanatic. Indeed, his interviews are lucid, substantive, and detailed expositions that leave at least some room for dialogue.[18] Some at the center of Shiite politics believe that Fadlallah has a crucial role to play in consolidating the leadership of the community.

As to the second charge, that Fadlallah has played a role in spawning or directing terrorist attacks, the simple fact is that probably no one in the West knows who is responsible for the attacks.[19] There is no denying that the shaykh's message has inspired opposition to the United States and Israel—he concedes as much—but whether he has taken a more direct role is at least uncertain. Quite independent of his role in any specific incident, Fadlallah has his

17. See Augustus Richard Norton, "Political Violence and Shi'a Factionalism in Lebanon," *Middle East Insight*, 3(2):9-16 (Aug.-Oct. 1983).

18. A fascinating and lengthy interview with Fadlallah is found in *Middle East Insight*, 4(2):10-19 (June-July 1985).

19. The best informed account of Shiite political violence in the Middle East, including its roots and rationale, is Robin Wright, *Sacred Rage: The Crusade of Modern Islam* (New York: Simon & Schuster, forthcoming). Wright's book is based in part on rare interviews with Shiite activists and principals. The reader desiring a shorter treatment is invited to consult Augustus Richard Norton, *Political and Religious Extremism in the Middle East*, Middle East Institute Executive Report, no. 7 (Washington, DC: Middle East Institute, 1985).

share of enemies, as was tragically demonstrated in March 1985, when 80 persons were killed by a car bomb detonated near his office in Bir al-Abid. Meanwhile, Fadlallah's following is growing, and although the memory of Musa al-Sadr is still vibrant and powerful, Muhammad Hussein Fadlallah may yet prove to be his heir.

AN UNCERTAIN FUTURE

Nabih Berri's Amal movement seized control of West Beirut in February 1984 as much to preserve its loosening political grip as to confront a regime that seemed to consider its Shiite constituents as enemies. In mid-1985 Amal seemed to be succeeding in taking a large measure of credit—some of it undeserved—for the expulsion of Israel from south Lebanon, and its success in maintaining a semblance of order both in Beirut and in the south surprised some skeptics.

The outcome of the organizational competition among the Shiites, however, is anything but certain. Amal seems to hold the edge, but in an environment in which particularistic identity has been sharply reinforced by Shiite demagoguery, Maronite arrogance, Israeli clumsiness, and steady encouragement from Tehran, there are no guarantees. Syria's penchant for malleable clients will be a factor in the equation. Despite sporadic support for the radicals, Damascus seems much more comfortable with the pragmatic Shiite political figures such as Berri, Shamseddine, and Husseini, but Syria will not be able to impose any leader who does not have a substantial following within the community. Extremism feeds on extremism, and until the incentives for it are removed, we can expect political centrists to remain on the endangered species list.

While the outcome of the political competition for the leadership of the Shiites cannot be predicted with great confidence, it is unmistakably clear that the Shiites have left behind their long period of political irrelevance.

* * *

QUESTIONS AND ANSWERS

Q (David Brook, Jersey City State College, New Jersey): Have you noticed any close relationships between the present regime in Iran and the Shiite movement in Lebanon?

A: If by "Shiite movement" you mean the Amal movement, the answer to your question is no. The Amal movement has very poor relations with the government in Tehran, in large part because the centrist leaders of the movement do not want to create an Islamic state after the image of any Iranian ayatollah or theologian. In short, Amal's commitment to a secular solution is quite clear. We should also remember that Amal has not had to depend on Tehran—or any outside power—for financial support. There are significant pockets of wealth within the Lebanese Shiite community and wealthy Shiites have not been stingy in their support for Amal.

Obviously, however, Amal does not account for all Lebanese Shiites. There are groups of Shiite terrorists with apparent links to Iran, and as many as 1000 Iranian *pasadaran* ("revolutionary guards") have been operating in the Baalbek area since mid-1982. The evidence is sometimes skimpy, but it is widely believed that the shadowy Islamic Jihad organization, which has taken credit for the terrorist bombings of 1983 and 1984, enjoys something more than moral support from Iran. I should add that it is not fair to say that the Islamic Jihad terrorists represent the Shiite community.

The subterranean links of the terrorists to Iran are difficult to pinpoint, but it is not difficult to identify the close relations between Hezbollah and Iran. Hezbollah, in clear contrast to Amal, espouses the establishment of an Islamic state in Lebanon, and its political program calls forthrightly for close relations with the Islamic Republic of Iran. The clerics who lead Hezbollah are not a monolithic body, but many of them are influenced keenly by Iran. Shaykh Ibrahim al-Amin, for example, speaks as if he were deputized to speak on behalf of Ayatollah Khomeini. On the other hand, Shaykh Muhammad Hussein Fadlallah, who has been in the news quite frequently of late, seems to be very much his own man; in fact, when he was in Iran recently, he was received coolly because he has not been fully supportive of the Iranian view.

It is fair to say that to the extent that Hezbollah has gained supporters at the expense of the Amal movement, Tehran gains as well. The stakes for Iran are transparent, and we should not be surprised to find Tehran doing what it might to thicken its relations with Shiite coreligionists in Lebanon.

Q (Renze L. Hoeksema, Hope College, Michigan): I would say that the Amal is thinking more and more in terms of taking over the state. It seems that it is waiting to take over the state, but I got the opposite impression from Professor Norton's comment. I would think that nationalism was growing at a fantastic rate in Amal and among the Shiites in Lebanon.

A: There is no question that there is a sense of exuberance in the Shiite community with respect to some recent events. There is a sense that victory is in the hands of the community. I misspoke, however, when I said that the Shiites are the plurality in Lebanon. The plurality comprises all those groups who oppose the Shiites. There has not been any development in recent days in Lebanon that has generated more fear and distress than the activism of the Shiites. The Sunni community sees the Shiites as contending for their share of power. The Druzes are operating with a different agenda, and so are the Maronites.

I think that there is within the centrist leadership in the Shiite community at large an understanding that the Shiites are not going to be able to dominate Lebanon. They will only be able to participate in the governing of Lebanon. There is also an understanding even among those whom I would describe as quite optimistic—and there are not many left—that Lebanon is not a society that will be put back together anytime soon. In a sense we are dealing with a process of reconciliation that will last perhaps well into the end of this century. Discussions of anybody taking over the state are therefore premature. Many of the journalistic comments that have been made recently about Lebanon's changing political formula and the emergence of the Shiites as the great arbiter of politics in Lebanon are sensational and based on an incomplete understanding of the dynamics of the political milieu in Lebanon.

ANNALS, *AAPSS*, **482**, November 1985

Elections and Legitimacy in the Middle East

By DANKWART A. RUSTOW

ABSTRACT: Israel is an immigrant democracy, not unlike the United States; and its traditions and adverse circumstances have hastened assimilation and have softened the ideological differences so vocally expressed by its party system. In Turkey, democracy had to wait until a generation after it became a nation-state. Whereas the vast majority of voters supported moderate, centrist parties, the election system first encouraged majority tyranny and next gave exaggerated leverage to the extremist parties repudiated at the polls. These weaknesses of the political system—and periodic economic crises—gave rise to periodic military interventions but appear at last to have been overcome by the liberal and popular program of Turgut Özal. Elsewhere in the Middle East, the interlude of Western colonialism and the futile search for pan-Arab unity have delayed the advent of democracy; and in Lebanon, armed denominational rivalries have destroyed the political system. More recently, boundaries and regimes have stabilized throughout most of the region. Elections and parliamentary meetings have reflected the consolidation of Iran's charismatic revolutionary regime and the continuing quest of military or monarchic regimes in Egypt, Jordan, and Kuwait for greater legitimacy at home and abroad.

Dankwart A. Rustow (Ph.D., Yale) is Distinguished Professor of Political Science at the Graduate School of the City University of New York. Earlier he taught at Princeton and Columbia, served on the senior staff of the Brookings Institution, and was vice-president of the Middle East Studies Association and the American Political Science Association. Among his publications are The Politics of Compromise *(1955),* A World of Nations *(1967),* Philosophers and Kings *(editor, 1970),* Middle Eastern Political Systems *(1971),* OPEC: Success and Prospects *(with J.F. Mugno, 1976), and* Oil and Turmoil: America Faces OPEC and the Middle East *(1982).*

THE Middle East, centrally located at the junction of the three continents of the Old World, may be variously defined. In this article, it will be taken to include the Arabic-language countries—except those of the Maghreb, or Northwest Africa—as well as Israel, Turkey, and Iran. Among those 18 countries, from Turkey to the Sudan and from Iran to Libya, there are only two democracies: Israel, a full-fledged democracy, and Turkey, a country in which democracy for the past 35 years has alternated with interludes of military rule.

The forms of government prevalent throughout the Middle East are instead monarchic or military. There are seven hereditary monarchies: Bahrain, Jordan, Kuwait, Oman, Qatar, Saudi Arabia, and the United Arab Emirates, this last a federation of such monarchies. There are six military dictatorships: Egypt, Iraq, Libya, Sudan, Syria, and North Yemen. With the exception of Jordan, monarchies are found in those parts of the Arabian peninsula that remained untouched by European colonialism, or where British imperial rule established protectorate relationships with indigenous dynasties. By contrast, military coups became the major avenue to power in those parts of the Middle East that passed from Ottoman to European imperial rule and became independent with the collapse of the French and British empires after World War II.

This leaves three Middle Eastern countries that are neither democracies, nor monarchies, nor military regimes: Iran, South Yemen, and Lebanon. Of these, Iran has a government with distinct theocratic elements but that, following Max Weber's terminology, may perhaps be best described as a charismatic revolutionary regime in the process of "routinization."[1] South Yemen, upon attaining independence in 1967, proclaimed itself the People's Republic of Southern Yemen, and in 1970 the People's Democratic Republic of Yemen, the new, pleonastic terminology reflecting the victory of a Moscow-backed faction in a prolonged internal power struggle as well as an irredentist claim to North Yemen.

Finally, there is Lebanon, which, upon attaining independence in 1946, continued a parliamentary regime delicately balanced among religious factions. That balance was restored after the civil war of 1958, but shattered for good by the arrival of military contingents of the Palestine Liberation Organization (PLO) in the early 1970s, the fiercer civil war of 1975-76, and the intervention of Syria since 1976 and Israel in 1978 and from 1981 to 1985. As a result, Lebanon has dissolved into a congeries of military and hereditary fiefdoms based on those same denominational factions. Among all the countries of the world, Lebanon's form of nongovernment today comes closest to the "state of nature," where "masterless men," as Hobbes put it, find their lives to be "poor, nasty, brutish, and short."[2]

THE REQUISITES OF DEMOCRACY AND THEIR HISTORY IN THE MIDDLE EAST

Democracy remains rare in the Middle East; yet elections have played a considerable role as devices of legitima-

1. See Max Weber, *Wirtschaft und Gesellschaft* (1922) [The theory of social and economic organization], ed. T. Parsons (New York: Free Press, 1957), pp. 363-73.

2. Thomas Hobbes, *Leviathan* (1651), pt. 1, chap. 13.

tion, real, attempted, or pretended. They are one of the means by which—in Samuel Butler's phrase—"vice pays homage to virtue." Throughout much of the Middle East, that is to say, elections have served as little more than a political tactic. Hence the following analysis will concentrate mainly on Israel and Turkey, where elections have been at the very core of the political process. A comparison of the origins of democracy in those two countries, and of its difficulties in the Arab countries and Iran, can serve to test a number of crucial hypotheses about the nature of democracy as a historic institution of human politics. Similarly, the electoral experience of Israel, Turkey, and even Lebanon illustrates the effect of various voting systems on political parties and parliamentary governments.[3] And even the tactical uses of recent elections, or meetings of elected bodies, in nondemocratic countries such as Egypt, Iran, Kuwait, Jordan, and Lebanon can tell us much about the basis of power and the search for legitimacy in the Third World.

Democracy means government by the people, or, more specifically, by representatives elected by popular majorities in free and competitive elections, and this implies two essential requisites. First, there must be a settled sense of national identity: "the people cannot decide until somebody decides who are the people," as a British constitutional lawyer remarked—cuttingly but accurately enough—in commenting on the recent quest of colonies for self-government;[4] second, there must be a self-reinforcing pattern of political and social competition providing constant pressure for political equality. Two major patterns of democratic evolution may thus be distinguished, depending on the sequence in which these two requisites of identity and equality were attained.

In much of western and northern Europe, the achievement of national identity preceded the struggle for equality. From the thirteenth to sixteenth centuries dynastic wars and marriages fixed the boundaries of such European nations as France, Britain, and the Scandinavian countries; and, within such stabilized boundaries, the use of a single standardized language by the expanding royal bureaucracies helped to solidify the linguistic identity of the populations. Then, a number of sharp internal contests—in Britain from the civil war to the class conflicts of the nineteenth century, in France the violent changes in regimes from 1789 to 1870, and in Sweden the lesser upheavals from 1718 to 1905—completed the transition to democracy.[5]

In sharp contrast to this pattern of democratization of bureaucratic monarchies stands the evolution of democracy in immigrant countries such as the United States, Australia, New Zealand, or Israel. Here equality was guaranteed, by and large, by the equal experience of persecution or suffering in the old country and political and social competition in the new. If the elders of a first immigrant community such as Massachusetts

3. For a comparative study of voting systems in Turkey, Lebanon, and Israel, see Jacob M. Landau et al., *Electoral Politics in the Middle East* (London: Croom Helm, 1980).

4. Ivor Jennings, *The Approach to Self-Government* (Cambridge: Cambridge University Press, 1956), p. 56.

5. See Dankwart A. Rustow, "Transitions to Democracy: Toward a Dynamic Model," *Comparative Politics*, 2:337-63 (Apr. 1970); for a more recent discussion, see Samuel P. Huntington, "Will More Countries Become Democratic?" *Political Science Quarterly*, 99(2):193-218 (Summer 1984).

Bay proved too autocratic, the dissidents could always move on to new locations such as Providence. Meanwhile, the task of building and defending communities in the new country strengthened the immigrants' common sense of identity.

Germany and Italy offer an important variant of the first pattern. Here modern linguistic identity developed in the train of Dante's and Luther's achievements in the fourteenth and sixteenth centuries; yet there was no monarchic-bureaucratic centralization. The stirrings of egalitarian sentiment in the wake of the French Revolution were soon overshadowed by the military threat from outside and the quest for national unification within, these being the tragedy of the abortive German and Italian revolutions of 1848. And when the merger of the petty principalities into a linguistic nation-state was brought about between 1860 and 1871 through aggressive wars launched by the largest of them, it would serve to emphasize the conservative and antidemocratic elements in the political tradition—from Cavour and Bismarck to Mussolini and Hitler. In sum, whereas countries such as Britain, France, and Sweden achieved national identity first and equality next, the struggle for both at once delayed the advent of German and Italian democracy until after their military defeats in World War II. In the Middle East, the Arab experience after 1945 offers some significant analogies to this German-Italian theme.

Turkey, as we shall see, offers yet another variant of the basic western European pattern, one in which democracy was delayed not by the problems of a multistate nation but of a multinational state caught up in the throes of defensive modernization.

IMMIGRANT DEMOCRACY IN ISRAEL

Israel began holding elections early in 1949, only a few moths after attaining statehood. It has continued to do so at regular intervals every four years, except when the Israeli Assembly, or Knesset, by majority vote dissolves itself sooner, as in 1951, 1965, and 1984. But the electoral tradition goes back much further: to Jewish self-government under the Palestinian mandate of 1922-48,[6] to the Zionist congresses at the turn of the century, to the socialist convictions of a majority of early Zionists, and to the absence of a priestly hierarchy in Judaism. How seriously the early Zionists took their parliamentary deliberations, and how little deference they paid to their leaders and founders, is illustrated by the resounding defeat suffered in 1904 by Theodor Herzl's own proposal of establishing the Jewish national home in Uganda.

If Zionist organizations furnished Israel's early political leadership, its electorate was soon supplied by the wave of mass immigration from the late 1940s to the early 1960s. Israel's democracy, that is to say, rests on a pioneering and egalitarian ethos of immigrants, much like that of the United States, Canada, Australia, or New Zealand.[7] To be sure, Israel's immigrants from Europe and the Middle East came from far more varied backgrounds than did the early settlers of New England; yet their assimilation proved far more rapid. They had

6. See J.C. Hurewitz, *The Struggle for Palestine* (New York: Norton, 1950).

7. Indeed, as Peter Grose's recent study has shown in vivid detail, the early North American settlers arrived in quest of their own Christian vision of the promised Zion. See Peter B. Grose, *Israel in the Mind of America* (New York: Knopf, 1983), pp. 3-22.

escaped from direr hardships and arrived within a far shorter period.[8] Their migration was motivated by their belief in Zionism and Judaism; and soon they were engaged in the monumental tasks of reviving an ancient language for daily use, building a modern agricultural and industrial economy from scarce resources, and organizing a viable defense in a hostile region. The foundation of the Israeli nation upon the principle of rapid assimilation of immigrants is reflected in the Israeli Laws of Return (1950) and of Nationality (1952), which extend to all Jews the right of immigration and confer upon them the status of citizen and potential voter from the time of arrival.

Ideological disputes have been prominent in the electoral and parliamentary battles among Israeli parties. The liberal founders of Zionism, such as Herzl and Chaim Weizmann, soon faced a mass movement of socialist Zionists from Eastern Europe. The socialists themselves were engaged in intense debates among moderates—Mapai—and radicals—Mapam—in the trade union movement and the *kibbutzim*. The struggle for Zionist self-assertion under the British mandate provoked bitter divisions between the diplomatic strategy of the mainstream Zionists such as Weizmann and David Ben-Gurion and the terrorist tactics of the revisionists led by Vladimir Jabotinsky and Menachem Begin. And since the creation of the state of Israel, the secular Zionists—socialist, liberal, radical, or moderate—have had to accommodate to the well-orgranized pressures of religious groups, including the religious Zionists of Mizrahi—the National Religious Party—the non-Zionist orthodox Agudah, their respective labor affiliates, and other more recent offshoots.

Proportional representation

The ideological divisions were accentuated by Israel's election system of proportional representation, whereby parties present their lists of candidates, voters choose among those lists, and Knesset seats are allocated in proportion to the votes obtained. The system closely resembles those of the Weimar Republic in Germany or the Fourth Republic in France, with the same result of government by unstable and shifting party coalitions.

Two features of the Israeli system are noteworthy. All systems of proportional representation remove the powerful incentive for party consolidation provided by the Anglo-American single-member plurality, winner-take-all system. But Israel's version of proportional representation treats the entire country as a single district, making the party-splintering effects even more pronounced than in Germany or France: any political group that commands a following of as little as 1 percent—such as the extremist followers of Rabbi Meir Kahane in 1984—is assured of getting its candidate elected to the Knesset. Conversely, even the recurrent strenuous efforts to form a majority grouping in preparation for

8. Of the 2.1 million immigrants arriving in Palestine or Israel between 1919 and 1977, 78.1 percent arrived after the formation of the state of Israel in May 1948—35.9 percent by 1954, 58.6 percent by 1964, and 75.1 percent by 1974. My calculations are from the table in Bernard Reich, "The State of Israel," in *The Government and Politics of the Middle East and North Africa*, ed. David E. Long and Bernard Reich (Boulder, CO: Westview Press, 1980), p. 280. Of the total number of immigrants, 60 percent came from Europe and America, and 40 percent from Asia and Africa, most of the latter from Morocco, Iraq, and Yemen.

election have proved abortive: the maximum obtained by the socialist Alignment in 1969 was 46 percent of the vote and 56 Knesset seats, and by Begin's right-wing Likud in 1981, 37 percent and 48 seats. The result is that any election is followed by a tedious process of negotiation among potential partners for a government coalition. This repeated haggling has strengthened the hand of the religious parties, which typically have been willing to enter governments of Left or Right in return for concessions on religious schooling and budgets.

The second notable feature of Israel's proportional representation is the list system, which leaves to each party the ranking of its individual candidates on the ballot and gives the voters a choice only among those party lists. The quadrennial contest for top places on the list gives much power to the party organization—and provides another strong motive for dissident factions to split off. The result has been an ebb and flow whereby recurrent attempts to form broad electoral coalitions—such as the socialist Alignment in 1965, the right-wing Gahal and Likud groupings in 1965 and 1973, or the centrist Democratic Movement for Change in 1977—have been followed by renewed divisions, leaving the number of parties in the Knesset fluctuating between 9, as in 1973, and as many as 16, as in 1984. Because of all these divisive effects of proportional representation, David Ben-Gurion in his latter days became a strong champion of electoral reform. It remains to be seen whether the national coalition formed in the fall of 1984 under Ben-Gurion's disciple Shimon Peres will be able to implement the corresponding plank in its program.

Unifying forces

All the Israeli political divisions are far less deep than the intermittent drumfire of ideological rhetoric or the jockeying for places on the party list and for seats in the cabinet might suggest. Socialists may justify their Zionism on nonreligious grounds—the need for a national home for a persecuted people, the hope of building the ideal society of the future—yet their choice of Palestine—rather than, say, Uganda—as the site for their efforts testifies to their deep attachment to the biblical promise of return. Conversely, the ultra-orthodox religious groups may condemn secular Zionism as a sacrilegious anticipation of the Messiah's task—yet their acceptance of Israeli citizenship and government office undercuts their own argument. Meanwhile the more practical issues between the secularist majority of Israelis and the orthodox and ultra-orthodox minorities have been resolved by a series of compromises: Israeli parents are given a choice of secular or religious schools—both are state supported—for their children, rabbinical law prevails in matters of marriage, and ultra-orthodox women remain exempt from military duty.

The recurrent pressure of international events, moreover, has been a powerful factor in helping to resolve policy differences among the parties. Thus the 1967 war resulted in a three-year wall-to-wall coalition, including all parties from the leftist-socialist Mapam to the right-wing Gahal; and a similar comprehensive coalition between Shimon Peres's Labor Alignment and Yitzhak Shamir's Likud was formed in 1984 under the pressure of the debacle in Lebanon and of a deepening economic crisis—although this time the Mapam faction separated from

TABLE 1
PARTIES ELECTED TO THE ISRAELI KNESSET, 1949-84 (Number of seats)

	1949	1951	1955	1959	1961	1965	1969	1973	1977	1981	1984
Communist											
Israel Communists (Maki)	4	5	6	3	5	1	1*	–			
Democratic Movement for Peace and Equality (Hadash)									5	4	4
New Communists (Rakah)						3	3	4			
Left											
Haolam Hazeh						1	2	–			
Shelli (Peace for Israel)									2		
Moked								1			
Citizens' Rights Movement (Ratz)								3	1	1	3
Shinui										2	3
Progressive List for Peace											2
Socialist											
Labor-affiliated Arab lists	2	5	5	5	4	4	4	3	1		
Mapam (Left Socialists)	19	15	9	9	9	8					
Ahdut Haavoda			10	7	8						
Alignment						45	56	51	32	47	44†
Mapai (Israel Labor Party)	46	45	40	47	42						
Rafi						10	–				
State List (D. Ben-Gurion)							4*				

Center											
Telem (M. Dayan)										2	
Ometz (Y. Hurwitz)											1
Democratic Movement for Change									15*		
Yahad (E. Weizman)											3
Independent Liberals					—	5	4	4	1		
Progressives	5	4	5	6							
Liberals					17*						
General Zionists	7	20	13	8							
Religious Parties											
Mizrahi Labor		8									
National Religious Party (Mafdal)			11	12	12	11	12	10	12	6	4
Mizrahi		2									
Morasha											2
Tami (A. Abuhatzeira)										3	1
United Religious Front	16										
Agudat Israel Labor		2			2	2	2		1		
Agudat Israel		3	6	6	4	4	4	5	4	4	2
Shas (Sephardi Torah Guardians)											4
Kach (M. Kahane)											1
Right											
Free Center							2*				
Gahal (Herut Liberal)						26	26				
Likud								39	43	48	41
Herut	14	8	15	17	17						
Shlomzion (A. Sharon)									2		
Tehiya										3	5
Others‡	7	3							1		

TABLE 1 (Continued)

	1949	1951	1955	1959	1961	1965	1969	1973	1977	1981	1984
Summary: Distribution of Popular Vote (percentage)											
Communist	3.5	4.0	4.5	2.8	4.2	3.4	4.0	3.4	4.6	3.4	3.4
Left	–	–	–	–	–	1.2	1.2	3.6	2.8	2.9	6.8
Socialist	52.1	54.5	54.2	55.0	52.3	54.6	52.8	42.1	26.0	36.6	34.9
Center	9.3	19.6	14.6	10.8	13.6	3.8	4.4	3.6	12.8	1.6	3.4
Religious parties	12.2	11.9	13.8	14.6	15.4	14.1	14.7	12.1	13.9	11.8	12.6
Right	11.5	6.6	12.6	13.6	13.7	21.3	22.9	30.2	35.3	39.4	35.9
Others	11.4	3.5	0.3	3.2	0.8	1.5	–	5.0	4.5	4.3	3.0
Summary: Distribution of Knesset Seats (Total: 120)											
Communist	4	5	6	3	5	4	4	4	5	4	4
Left	–	–	–	–	–	1	2	4	3	3	8
Socialist	67	65	64	68	63	67	64	54	33	47	44
Center	12	24	18	14	17	5	4	4	16	2	4
Religious parties	16	15	17	18	18	17	18	15	17	13	14
Right	14	8	15	17	17	26	28	39	45	51	46
Others	7	3	–	–	–	–	–	–	1	–	–

SOURCES: For 1949-77, adapted from Daniel Shimshoni, *Israeli Democracy: The Middle of the Journey* (New York: Free Press, 1892), pp. 494-95; and David E. Long and Bernard Reich, eds., *The Government and Politics of the Middle East and North Africa* (Boulder, CO: Westview Press, 1980), pp. 292-93. For 1981, Colin Legum, ed., *Middle East Contemporary Survey*, vol. 5, *1980-81* (New York: Holmes & Meier, 1982), p. 609; and Shimshoni, *Israeli Democracy*, pp. 491 ff. For 1984, *Jerusalem Post Weekly*, 5-11 Aug. 1984.

*Most party splits and mergers occurred within the groupings distinguished in this table and are indicated by braces, but note the following exceptions: Israel Communists merged with Moked on the left, 1973; State List merged with Likud on the right, 1973; Democratic Movement for Change split in 1981 and merged with Likud on the right and Shinui on the left; Liberals, except for Independent Liberals, merged with Gahal on the right, 1965; and Free Center split in 1973 and merged with Likud on the right and Democratic Movement for Change in the center.

†Split in Sept. 1984: Alignment, 38; Mapam, 6.

‡In 1949: Sephardim, 4; Women's International Zionist Organization, 1; Fighters' List, 1; Yemenites, 1. In 1951: Sephardim, 2; Yemenites, 1. In 1977, Flatto Sharon, 1.

the Labor Alignment and went into opposition.

In recent Israeli elections, the entrenched ideological distinctions have been overshadowed by the social contrast between the older European settlers and the more recent Sephardic immigrants from Morocco, Yemen, and other Middle Eastern countries. The Europeans, or Ashkenazim, for decades had dominated the political-economic establishment: government, army, the socialist party organizations, and the powerful Histadrut federation of labor with its many business subsidiaries. For that very reason, the Sephardim, who constitute a majority of the younger voters, tended to flock to the right-wing opposition led by Begin's Herut Party—and later by the combined right-wing lists of Gahal and Likud—ensuring the remarkable electoral upset of 1977. In the long run, however, these social divisions appear to be fading even more rapidly than those based on ideology as political parties compete for the Sephardic vote and as social mobility and intermarriage blur the Sephardic-Ashkenazic distinction.

In sum, Israelis, whatever their immigrant background or ideological persuasion, share a strong sense of identity that derives from millennia of Jewish tradition, from the experience of survival of holocaust and persecution, from the decision to make a new start in the land of Zion, and from prolonged conflict with the surrounding Arab nations. Against those powerful factors of community, none of the divisions just mentioned can compare to the sectional or ethnic-social conflicts that have pervaded U.S. history, or to the linguistic question in Canada. On the other hand, the major anomaly for Israel as a democratic nation in its de facto boundaries remains the military occupation regime in the West Bank and Gaza, whose population of over 1 million constitutes a disfranchised lower stratum of Israeli society.

DEMOCRATIC EVOLUTION IN TURKEY

Turkey has held eight competitive elections since 1950. Here democratic evolution has followed not the pattern of immigrant countries such as Israel or the United States, but rather a further variant of the European pattern discussed earlier. Whereas the problem in Germany and Italy was that of a linguistic nation divided into petty states, the Ottoman Empire had been a dynastic and multinational state thrown on the defensive in a century and a half of defeat and secession from 1768 to 1918.[9] It was only the final defeat in World War I and the victory in the subsequent War of Independence, from 1919 to 1923, that fully converted the Ottoman ruling class to a Turkish national consciousness. When the Republic of Turkey was founded by Kemal Atatürk in 1923,[10] it thus represented the combination of (1) a populist movement fresh

9. On the pattern of defensive modernization in the Ottoman Empire and Turkey, see Robert E. Ward and Dankwart A. Rustow, eds., *Political Modernization in Japan and Turkey* (Princeton, NJ: Princeton University Press, 1964).

10. On Atatürk, cf. Lord Kinross [Patrick Boufour], *Atatürk: A Biography of Mustafa Kemal, Father of Modern Turkey* (New York: William Morrow, 1965); Vamik D. Volkan and Norman Itzkowitz, *The Immortal Atatürk: A Psychobiography* (Chicago: University of Chicago Press, 1984); D.A. Rustow, "Atatürk as an Institution-Builder," in *Atatürk: Founder of a Modern State,* ed. Ali Kazancigil and Ergun Özbudun (London: C. Hurst, 1981); and D.A. Rustow, "Kemalism," in *Südost-Europa-Handbuch: Turkei*, ed. K.-D. Grothusen (Gottingen: Vandehoeck & Rupprecht, forthcoming).

from victory in a war for national independence and (2) a modernizing civil-military bureaucracy inherited from the preceding Ottoman regime.

This unique and somewhat precarious combination accounts for both the successes and the difficulties of Turkey's later democratic evolution. Whereas the transition in 1945 from a benevolent one-party regime to competitive democratic elections was seen by President İsmet İnönü and his compatriots as an implementation of Atatürk's populist principles, the subsequent interventions of the military—in 1960-61, 1971-73, and 1980-83—can be seen as a continuation of the military's tutelary role in the late Ottoman period.[11]

In the early Turkish elections, İnönü's Republican People's Party, the embodiment of the ruling bureaucratic elite, was successfully challenged—by the Democrat Party in the 1950s and by the Justice Party in the 1960s—in the name of commercial, agrarian, and provincial interests. By the 1970s, the Republican People's Party made a remarkable comeback by adopting a social democratic program and mustering new support among industrial workers, the poorer peasants, and urban intellectuals. Recent Turkish party alignments thus resemble those in Britain or the United States[12]—and with similar regional variations. In Turkey these have reflected the social differences between old residents and recent migrants, between Sunni and Alevi Muslims in central Anatolia, or between ethnic Turks and the Kurdish or Arab minorities in the southeast.

The remarkable result has been that these moderate parties and their various offshoots at the center have consistently polled between 80 and 90 percent of the vote, with the remainder divided among such groups as the quasi-Communist Turkish Labor Party, the Islamic conservative National Salvation Party, and the fascist Nationalist Movement Party. (For detailed figures, see Table 2.)

The limited appeal of the National Salvation Party is particularly noteworthy. Its high point of 9 percent to 12 percent of the vote was reached in the 1970s under the leadership of a graduate engineer, whose rhetoric identified Islam as the most modern and up-to-date religion.Turgut Özal, who once ran as an unsuccessful candidate for the same party, won his major electoral landslide of 1983 at the head of the Motherland Party on a program of explicit advocacy of free enterprise and implicit opposition to continued military rule.

In Turkey, as in many other democracies, the competitive appeal of parties for the lower-class vote has done much to bridge the earlier social gaps. The party politics of the 1950s inaugurated an intense effort of economic development, much of it financed with American aid: farm mechanization, roads to connect villages to towns and citites and to connect the interior of the country to the coasts, new schools in the larger villages and towns, and new universities in the major cities. The share of agriculture and industry had remained virtually unchanged under two decades of etatist policy; from 1955 to 1981, however, industry's share of the gross national prod-

11. On that historic tutelary role, see Nicholas Ludington and James W. Spain, "Dateline Turkey: The Case for Patience," *Foreign Policy,* no. 50, pp. 150-68 (Spring 1983); the statement is eloquent if somewhat partisan. Cf. "Letters," ibid., no. 52, pp. 187-90. (Fall 1983).

12. But note that in Turkey the Republican People's Party—dissolved in 1980—represented the left of center, and the Democrat, or Democratic, Party of Menderes, which existed from 1946 to 1960, represented the center right.

uct increased from 14 percent to 35 percent. Similarly, whereas the literacy rate between 1935 and 1950 had increased slowly from 20 percent to 30 percent, by 1980 it had jumped to 68 percent, including 80 percent of the men and 54 percent of the women.

Economic trends since the 1970s have powerfully reinforced these tendencies of social change. Thus the educational reforms of the Atatürk period mainly affected a small educated elite, leaving a continuing cultural gap between it and the mass of traditional, Islamic villagers. Yet since the late 1960s, well over a million of those very villagers have migrated to factory and service jobs in West Germany and other European countries, giving them a tangible stake in the policy of Westernization. Conversely, Turkey in the past decade has established close trade relations with Iran, Iraq, Saudi Arabia, and other Middle Eastern countries, thus bringing its educated elite of engineers, architects, and businessmen into renewed contact with their Islamic heritage.

These converging trends among social classes are the solid foundation for a broad policy consensus that has allowed 80 percent to 90 percent of the Turkish electorate to vote for center-left parties such as İsmet İnönü's and Bülent Ecevit's Republican People's Party and center-right parties such as Adnan Menderes's Democrat Party, Süleyman Demirel's Justice Party, or, most recently, Turgut Ozal's Motherland Party. In sharp contrast to the electorate's maturity and moderation, however, stands the weakness of the institutional framework for Turkey's democracy. Military interventions have come at about 10-year intervals—in 1960-61, 1971-73, and 1980-83—typically preceded by temporary sharp downturns in Turkey's rapid economic growth and marked increases in domestic violence.[13] In 1959 and 1960 the government of Adnan Menderes itself encourged violent confrontations between its followers and the opposition. When the police proved unable to maintain order, the armed forces—rather than act as Menderes's partisans—deposed him in a nonviolent coup. In 1971, there was a wave of street warfare between left-wing and right-wing gangs punctuated by occasional assassinations, while the parties in the Ankara legislature were mired in a deepening stalemate. This time the military, in what became known as a "coup by memorandum," persuaded parliament to yield to a bureaucratic ministry backed by the military, while martial law in the major cities enabled the armed forces to stop the arms smuggling and gang warfare.

During another economic downturn in the late 1970s, however, the deadlock in parliament and the violence in the streets grew worse than ever. Following the 1977 election, Ecevit's Republican People's Party was able to obtain a parliamentary vote of confidence only after attracting a sizable group of defectors from the opposition, most of them rewarded with newly created cabinet offices. And when some of the defectors redefected, Demirel's right-of-center Justice Party maintained itself in office by preventing parliamentary quorums and hence a vote of no confidence. By 1980, the parliament, over a six-month

13. For analyses of the Turkish political scene at various points in that sequence, see Dankwart A. Rustow, "Politics and Islam in Turkey," in *Islam and the West,* ed. Richard N. Frye (The Hague: Mouton, 1957), pp. 69-107; idem, "Turkey's Second Try at Democracy," *Yale Review,* 52(4): 518-58 (Summer 1963); idem, "Turkey's Travails," *Foreign Affairs,* 58(1):82-102 (Fall 1979); and idem, "Turkey's Liberal Revolution," *Middle East Review,* 17(3):33-43 (Spring 1985).

TABLE 2
PARTIES ELECTED TO THE TURKISH NATIONAL ASSEMBLY, 1950-83

Party and Years of Existence	First Constitution				Second Constitution				Third Constitution	
	1950	1954	1957	1961	1965	1969	1973	1977	1983	1984*
	Percentage of Popular Vote									
Left										
Turkish Labor, 1961-71, 1975-80					3.0	2.8		0.1		
Center-left										
Republican People's, 1923-80	39.3	34.8	40.6	38.4	28.7	27.4	33.3	41.3		
Democratic Left, 1985-										
Social Democratic, 1983-										23.4
Center										
Populist, 1983-									30.5	8.8
Reliance, 1967-80						6.6	5.3	1.9		
Freedom, 1955-60			3.8							
New Turkey, 1961-73				12.0	3.7	2.2				
Democratic, 1970-80							11.9	1.9		
Nationalist Democracy, 1983-									23.8	7.1
Center-right										
Democrat, 1945-60	53.3	56.6	47.3							
Justice, 1961-80				34.6	52.9	46.5	29.8	36.9		
Motherland, 1983-									45.2	41.4
True Path, 1983-										13.4
Right										
Unity, 1966-80						2.8	1.1	0.4		
Nation, 1948-53, 1954-58, 1962-80	3.1	4.8	7.0		6.3	3.2	0.6			
National Salvation, 1972-80							11.8	8.5		
Welfare, 1984-										4.8
Republican Peasants' Nation, 1958-69				14.2	2.2					
Nationalist Movement, 1969-80						3.0	3.4	6.4		
Other parties and independents	4.8	3.8	1.3	0.8	3.2	5.6	2.8	2.5		1.2
Voting participation (percentage of voters)				81.4	71.3	64.3	66.8	72.4	92.3	

Assembly Seats

Left									
Turkish Labor					15	2			
Center-left									
Republican People's	63	31	178	173	134	143	185	213	
Center									
Populist									117
Reliance						15	13	3	
Freedom			4						
New Turkey				65	19	6			
Democratic							45	1	
Nationalist Democracy									67
Center-right									
Democrat	420	505	424						
Justice				158	240	256	149	189	
Motherland									211
Right									
Unity						8	1		
Nation	1	5	4		31	6			
National Salvation							48	24	
Republican Peasants' Nation				54	11				
Nationalist Movement						1	3	16	
Independents	3	1				13	6	4	4
Total seats	487	542	610	450	450	450	449	450	400†

NOTE: The final word "Party" in each party name is omitted.

SOURCES: For 1950-77, İlnur Cevik, ed., *Turkey Almanac 1983* (Ankara: Turkish Daily News, 1983), pp. 182, 195ff; for 1983, *News from Turkey* (Dec. 1983); for local elections, 25 Mar. 1984, *Keesing's Contemporary Archives*, p. 32925 (June 1984).

*Local elections.

†Includes one vacancy.

period, proved unable to fill a vacancy in the presidency of the republic; at the same time violence throughout the country mounted, claiming on occasion as many as 20 victims in one day, until it was stopped once again by the military, this time in the coup of September 1980.

Changing political rules and personnel

Turkey's military coups, backed by the armed forces as a whole, have been nonviolent. Each time, moreover, the generals kept their promise of returning to democracy—but not without improving, according to their lights, the personnel and operations of the political process. The trial in 1961 of ex-Premier Menderes for systematic violations of the constitution was amply justified by the evidence presented; yet the vindictive sentences of death by hanging against Menderes and two of his associates, carried out in 1961, embittered the subsequent political contest without changing the long-run outcome. Within a few years, a party—pointedly calling itself the Justice Party—recaptured most of the former Democrat vote with a more efficient party organization.

Avoiding the harsh 1961 precedent, the military junta of 1980-83 contented itself with banning the future political participation of the parties and leaders of the preceding regime. Yet by 1984 Demirel's associates had founded a continuation of the Justice Party—now called the True Path Party—and the former Republican People's Party organization had reemerged as the Social Democrat Party (Sodep) under the leadership of Erdal İnönü, a prominent physicist and son of the original leader of the Republican People's Party, İsmet Inonu. And by 1985, former Prime Minister Bulent Ecevit himself prepared his political comeback. He employed the simple device of having his wife coordinate the founding of the new Democratic Left Party.

In sum, the recurrent efforts to allow free elections while artificially narrowing the voters' choice have proven self-contradictory and futile.[14] Even less effective, in the event, was the attempt by members of the 1980-83 junta to reshape positively the political contest by encouraging the formation of new parties under handpicked leaders—Necdet Calp's Populist Party and the Nationalist Democracy of the amiable and inept ex-general Turgut Sunalp. The net beneficiary, this time, turned out to be Turgut Özal's Motherland Party, which to the surprise of the generals entered the election campaign just before the legal deadline, and, as the only party truly independent of the military, won by a landslide.

It is to Prime Minister Özal's credit that, once in office, he insisted on scheduling early local elections in which the bona fide successors of the older parties were once again allowed to participate. The result broadly confirmed Özal's earlier victory and established Sodep and the True Path Party as the more popular opposition groups. The Populists and National Democrats, reduced to fourth and fifth place in the local election and to less than one-third of their previous following, continued as parliamentary opposition groups—under the implicit threat that Özal might call an early general election.

14. As early as 1954, Premier Menderes had banned the Nation Party from running in the election, because of its alleged violation of the constitutional ban on separation of religion and politics, only to find himself confronting the Republican Nation Party, with a sanitized program, minimally altered leadership, and increased voter appeal.

Of greater import than the military's attempts to control the personnel of politics were the changes in political rules. Thus the constitutional assembly of 1960-61 devised a careful system of checks and balances—a bicameral legislature and a weak executive, guaranteed rights and a strengthened judiciary—that contributed to the political deadlock of the next decades. By contrast, the 1982 constitution provides for a strong presidency, somewhat on the model of the French Fifth Republic; and the short-term result has been that Turkey's government since 1983 has resembled a system of dual controls, with President Kenan Evren in charge of military and security policies, Prime Minister Özal and his legislative majority in undisputed authority over economic matters, and other concerns such as freedom of expression and educational policy in something of a shadow zone.[15]

The most important changes of 1961 and 1982 concerned the electoral rules. The elections of 1950 were held by a system of plurality in multiple-member constituencies, which—much as in the U.S. electoral college—resulted in a heavy overrepresentation of the largest party. Specifically, Menderes's Democrat Party obtained 53 percent, 57 percent, and 47 percent of the popular vote in 1950, 1954, and 1957, respectively, thereby securing as much as 86 percent, 93 percent, and 70 percent of the parliamentary seats, a disproportion that did much to encourage his party's tendency toward majority dictatorship. The Second Republic went to the opposite extreme of holding its national elections under a system of proportional representation, similar to that of Israel, Weimar, or the French Fourth Republic. This meant that of the five national polls of the 1960s and 1970s, only two produced a legislative majority; the other three resulted in incongruous coalitions of the larger parties with the smaller antidemocratic—Islamic and fascist—groups, or else periods of complete parliamentary deadlock and rising violence. By contrast, Turkey's third republican constitution of 1982 has been based on single-member plurality elections that, much as in Britain, have provided majority support for a strong government. This constitution gives Turkey at long last an election system capable of translating the moderation and common sense of its voters into effective government.

15. See Kenneth Mackenzie's perceptive analysis, *Turkey in Transition: The West's Neglected Ally* (London: Institute for European Defence and Strategic Studies, 1984).

ELECTIONS AND QUASI ELECTIONS IN IRAN AND THE ARAB COUNTRIES

Nowhere else in the Middle East has there been any equivalent of Israel's democratic elections as the very core of the political system, nor have Turkey's successive periods of elections in a continuing struggle for political freedom and stability been duplicated in the region. In some of the Arab countries there have been intervals of political pluralism and tolerance; yet the twilight of colonial rule and the competition between pan-Arab loyalties and allegiance to the separate states did not allow any consistent development toward democracy. In Iran, on the contrary, there has been a solid sense of national identity, but no tradition of tolerance of political divisions.

Iran's national tradition goes back more than a thousand years. Alone among the countries of the Middle East and North Africa conquered by the Islamic Arab armies of the seventh century A.D., Iran retained its own Persian language, which experienced its most impressive flowering in the classical literature from Firdausi to Omar Khayyám and Hafiz. Iranian national consciousness in those centuries became closely identified with the Shiite version of Islam, with its intense belief in martyrdom and the return of the Hidden Imam, and its explicit clerical hierarchy. In 1905 Iran also became one of the first Middle Eastern countries to adopt a representative constitution—not, as in the Ottoman Empire in 1876, as a gift from the ruler, but rather as the outcome of a prolonged political contest.

Soon, however, this constitutional life was squelched by a combination of monarchic reaction and foreign pressure—partition into British and Russian spheres of interest in 1907, suspension of the constitution in 1908, invasions by various belligerents during and after World War I, a military dictatorship under Reza Khan—later proclaimed shah—from 1921 to 1941, and occupation by British and Soviet troops from 1941 to 1947. Another movement toward parliamentary government in the years from 1944 to 1953 was abruptly ended by the reimposition, with the help of the American Central Intelligence Agency, of an even more repressive rule by Mohammad Reza Shah, who in the next quarter century managed to stamp out all secular opposition and left as the major political alternative the Shiite clerical establishment that was to emerge victorious in the revolution of 1978-79.

In some of the Arab countries, as in Iran between 1908 and 1953, there was an intense interplay between domestic aspirations for representative government and foreign imperial pressures. Thus the British invasion of Egypt in 1882 was prompted by the populist coup of Urabi Pasha, who emphasized the ruler's responsibility to parliament, and who, it was feared, might have repudiated Egypt's foreign debt. In 1919 a spontaneous mass movement insisted on holding Britain to its promise of postwar independence for Egypt and on sending a Wafdist delegation from Egypt to the peace conference at Paris. After vain attempts at repression, the British continued their rule for another quarter century, now in alliance with the nationalists of the Wafd Party and now with the autocratic king—a shifting arrangement that tended to discredit colonial rule, royal government, and parliamentary institutions alike. As the historian Bernard Lewis has strikingly put it in assessing the prospects of democracy in the Middle East following the imperial withdrawal:

> There is a case to be made for or against the imperial rule as a stage in political evolution. . . . But there is little that can be said in defense of the half-hearted, pussy-footing imperialism encountered by most of the peoples of the Middle East—an imperialism of interference without responsibility, which would neither create nor permit stable and orderly government.[16]

Following the British departure, a colonels' conspiracy seized power in 1952—with Gamal Abdel Nasser proclaiming his ambition to unify the Arab nation from the Atlantic to the Indian Ocean, from Morocco to Oman. Nonetheless, these Arab states were far larger and more independent than the German or Italian principalities of the early nineteenth century; and, at any rate, Egypt's military and political resources were far

16. Bernard Lewis, "Democracy in the Middle East: Its State and Prospects," *Middle Eastern Affairs,* 6(4):105 (Apr. 1955).

from adequate to make Nasser into an Arab Bismarck or Cavour. Egyptian armies suffered humiliating defeats against Israel in 1956 and 1967 and against mountain guerrillas in Yemen in the 1960s; and Nasser's one tangible political success, the proclamation of the United Arab Republic with Syria, dissolved in 1961 after only three years.

A similar disillusionment befell the Arab countries of the Fertile Crescent. The monarchy in Transjordan and the parliamentary monarchy in Iraq—both sponsored by the British—remained as suspect as did the division of the region into three League of Nations mandates, in Palestine—including Transjordan—and Iraq, which were ruled by the British, and in Syria, which was ruled by the French. The divide-and-rule principle was carried further by the French, who organized Syria into separate states for the regions populated by the Sunni Muslim majority and the Alawi Muslim and Druze minorities. The French also carefully gerrymandered the Christian district of Mount Lebanon into a Greater Lebanon, with a bare Christian majority, comprising Maronite, Greek Orthodox, and Catholic and other Christian groups, and minorities composed of Sunni and Shiite Muslims and Druzes.

Military coups did away with the parliamentary regimes established during the mandate periods in Syria and Iraq. In the struggle for Arab unification, the Syrian and Iraqi military dictators soon were caught in an intricate pattern of intrigue with Nasser of Egypt and the newly rich oil monarchies of the Arab penisula—a process that Malcolm Kerr has aptly characterized as the "Arab cold war."[17]

The only one of these Arab successor states in which an electoral regime took temporary root was Lebanon. The Lebanese election system adopted in 1943 divided all parliamentary and cabinet seats between Christians and Muslims on a ratio of six to five, reflecting the results of the country's only census in 1932. One of the more imaginative provisions of this electoral law required candidates to run for denominationally assigned seats but for the voting to take place in multiple-member constituencies of mixed population. This placed a major premium on moderation, since it forced Maronite, Orthodox, Sunni, Shiite, and Druze candidates to make deals, and develop an appeal, both inside and outside their own religious group. One weakness of the arrangement was that the six-to-five ratio was known to be outdated, due to higher Muslim birthrates and heavier emigration of Christians. Yet, no cabinet or parliament would agree to a new census, which would have implied abdication by the Christians of their majority position. In Lebanon, as elsewhere, that is to say, an election system tends to engender the vested interests that will prevent its own reform. An even more decisive flaw of the Lebanese system was that, after the departure of the French imperial forces, no comparable formula could be found to guarantee effectiveness and moderation in the armed forces, which instead dissolved into denominational militias, as already noted.

Aside from Lebanon, the perennial deadlock in the inter-Arab national struggle and the massive inflow of foreign weapons into the region have had two striking effects: the consolidation of boundaries, however artificially drawn, and of political regimes, however illegitimate their origins.

17. Malcolm H. Kerr, *The Arab Cold War,* 2nd ed. (London: Oxford University Press, 1967).

After an intense period of instability, from about 1947 to 1967, the appeal of pan-Arabism receded and the external boundaries were stabilized. The temporary union of Egypt and Syria lasted only three years, and other Arab unity schemes, however pretentiously proclaimed, proved stillborn.[18] Remarkably, today's political boundaries throughout the Middle East, with insignificant exceptions,[19] are precisely the same as in the 1920s, including the partitions imposed by the British and French mandates. With many players competing in the game for Arab unity and for aggrandizement of individual states, the net result was a precisely balanced status quo and a consolidation of the political map. The further result was a gradual transfer of allegiances from pan-Arabism to the existing states, a change most strikingly apparent in the purely Egyptian policy pursued by Nasser's successor, Anwar el-Sadat.

The continuity of regimes, whether hereditary monarchies or imposed by military coup, has been just as remarkable: Egypt has had two peaceful successions—in 1970 and 1982—within its dictatorial systems; Muammar el-Qaddafi of Libya has been in power since 1969 and Hafez al-Assad of Syria since 1970; Iraq has had no violent coup since 1968; and Gaafar al-Nimeiry was overthrown in 1985, after ruling the Sudan for 16 years. Similarly, the Saudi monarchy in the last quarter century has survived the abdication of one king, the assassination of another, and the temporary occupation of its holiest shrine; and Jordan has enjoyed a remarkable era of stability under the tight but flexible rule of Kings Abdullah, from 1923 to 1951, and Hussein, since 1953.

The revolutionary upheaval in Iran, the precarious development of national allegiances in the Arab countries, and the consolidation of monarchies and dictatorships have left no more than a tentative and limited basis for elections. The Iranian elections of 1980 marked the first vigorous electoral struggle in three decades, but they served only as a phase in the consolidation of Ayatollah Khomeini's dictatorship. In the following years, that regime eliminated its major rivals, such as the secular nationalists under Abolhasan Bani-Sadr, the moderate revolutionaries under Mehdi Bazargan, the strong-arm Mujahedin, and the Communist Tudeh Party; the ongoing war with Iraq since 1980 aided in that consolidation. The elections that followed, in the spring of 1984, thus were restricted to candidates of the official Islamic Republican Party.

It happens that 1984 was a year of elections, or meetings of elected bodies, in about one-third of the countries of the Middle East. In some of the Arab countries, this may reflect in part the hopes widely placed on Western, and specifically American, support in the ongoing Iraq-Iran war and the diplomatic maneuvers toward Arab-Israeli peace; but the desire to demonstrate to fellow Arabs the popularity of a given regime and its policies was an even more obvious con-

18. For a more detailed review, see D. A. Rustow, *Oil and Turmoil: America Faces OPEC and the Middle East* (New York: Norton, 1982), pp. 42-49.

19. The exceptions are the cession of the *sanjak* of Alexandrette (Iskenderun) from the French-ruled Syria to Turkey in 1938, and Israel's annexation of the Golan Heights in 1981. Israel's other de facto boundaries are those of the Palestine mandate after its separation in 1920 from Transjordan. On the Arabian peninsula, the last major change was the union in 1926 of Nejd and Hijaz under the Saudi monarchy.

sideration.[20] A rapid chronology of these events thus will illustrate the variety of uses of elections in the continued Middle Eastern struggle for legitimacy.

9 January. King Hussein reconvenes the parliament of Jordan after a lapse of 10 years; included are representatives of the Israeli-occupied West Bank. Hussein's major purpose would appear to be to prepare a reversal of the Arab League's 1974 decision proclaiming the PLO to be the "sole legitimate representative" of the Palestinian people, and thus to position himself as a plausible negotiator under the Reagan plan of 1982 for peace on the West Bank and in Gaza.

18 January. Municipal elections are held in Kuwait. These are part of a continuing effort of the princely family to formalize a process of consultation among Kuwaiti citizens, in view of the massive presence of foreign workers and professionals, and in view of the recurrent military threats from Iran and, before 1980, Iraq. Previously national legislatures were elected in 1971 and 1975, suspended in 1976, and elected once again in 1981.

25 March. Local elections in Turkey, with participation of parties banned in the preceding national elections, reconfirm the landslide victory of Turgut Özal's Motherland Party.

15 April-1 May. Two rounds of parliamentary elections take place in Iran. Only members of the Iranian Revolutionary Party are allowed, and in the run-offs most of the more conservative candidates lose.

20. For a more detailed assessment of the year's diplomatic and political developments, see Dankwart A. Rustow, "Realignments in the Middle East," *Foreign Affairs,* 63(3), *America and the World 1984,* pp. 581-601 (Feb. 1985).

27 May. Legislative elections are held in Egypt, the first since the 1981 assassination of Sadat by religious fundamentalists. They reflect President Mubarak's desire to open a safety valve to opposition, and to demonstrate popular support for his diplomatic strategy of maintaining the peace treaty with Israel and preserving close relations with the United States while preparing for a reconciliation with other Arab countries. Amidst widespread charges of coercion and tampering, 73 percent of the seats are won by the official National Democratic Party, and the remainder by the New Wafd opposition.

12 June. The Lebanese parliament, last elected in 1972 under the six-to-five rule reflecting results of the 1932 census, meets under armed escort to confirm a precariously negotiated coalition government. This government proves incapable of putting an end to the warfare of factional militias. The more significant political negotiations—still no more than exploratory—are held intermittently in neutral Switzerland or under Syrian aegis in Damascus.

23 July. Israeli national elections, called early as Shamir's right-wing coalition disintegrates, place the Labor Alignment slightly ahead of Likud and, by September, result in a national coalition.

22-29 November. The Palestin National Council meets in Amman, Jordan, and reelects PLO chairman Yasir Arafat to its presidency. The meeting in Jordan, from which the PLO was expelled in the Black September of 1970, reflects the failure of Arafat's previous military strategy and his active exploration of diplomatic alternatives.

It may well be that recent elections in such countries as Kuwait, Egypt, and even Iran will become the prelude of gradual developments in the direction of more representative government. If so, the relevant precedents in the history of Europe and the Middle East suggest that such an evolution will be protracted, far from smooth, and full of reversals. In the meantime, Turkey remains the only Middle Eastern country to have come close to achieving full democracy, and Israel the only country of the region to have practiced electoral legitimacy from its very inception.

* * *

QUESTIONS AND ANSWERS

Q (Naff): Within the last couple years or so, there has been an increasing number of elections or some processes with that label occurring in the Middle East. What do you think its significance is? Do you see a trend toward electoral processes as a means of obtaining political ends?

A: I am increasingly impressed with the fact that, for all the arms that pour into the Middle East, so little has been accomplished by force of arms. To be sure, people have been killed, and life for American diplomats and private citizens is unsafe in many parts of the Middle East. My friend Malcom Kerr, who became president of the American University of Beirut and refused to keep a bodyguard, paid with his life almost immediately. Indeed, Lebanon as a country has been thoroughly destroyed.

Let us reflect for a moment on what people normally want to achieve by force of arms. Almost every Middle Eastern country has some claims, real or fancied, to some of its neighbors' territories. And arms, of course, are a means not only of defending oneself against the aggressive designs of others, but also of pursuing such designs of one's own. Interestingly enough, no department of war ever calls itself a department of aggression; the common name is "department of defense." Still, one wonders why defense is needed when no one is doing the aggressing.

In the Middle East, one basic fact is that most countries do have designs on their neighbors, and this has led to the importation of enormous quantities of arms. Because there are so many countries in the region, the result is an interesting checkerboard pattern of alignment, whereby most Middle Eastern countries are at odds with their neighbors and, for that very reason, are ready to make some sort of deal with their neighbors once-removed. For example, the Syrians and the Iranians are drawn to each other, above all, by their common enmity toward Iraq.

A second basic fact is that the Middle Eastern map does not line up in neat checkerboard squares. This complicates the resulting alignments and produces an occasional dramatic reversal, such as Sadat's switch from Moscow toward Washington. Still, this intricate pattern of realignments in a highly militarized region adds up to an ever shifting balance of power and hence to a stabilization of the status quo.

The Iraq-Iran war provides a good illustration. There is no question that Iraq started the military action. Iraq's neighbors, joined in the Gulf Cooperation Council, as well as other Arab countries, came to Iraq's help—but not until the second round of the war, when Iran was ahead at the front and Iraq's weakness became obvious. A little later, assistance came from the Soviet Union and the United States: the Soviets resumed their military supplies to Iraq and the Americans resumed diplomatic relations. In sum, both the regional and extraregional powers tend to side with the weaker party in a given conflict and thus help preserve the status quo.

Perhaps I am dramatizing the picture a bit, but the basic features can readily be seen. Since every Middle Eastern country has three or four neighbors, and arms and alliances are readily available, the status quo forces are ahead by three or four to one. The result is a dawning recognition that force provides no solution. A remarkable instance is Yasir Arafat's Palestine Liberation Organization, which for over two decades has been single-mindedly dedicated to a violent solution to the problem of recouping Palestine for the Palestinians, what Arafat calls the Algerian, or war-or-liberation, strategy. In recent years, however, Arafat was besieged in Beirut by the Israelis and rescued by the Americans, and besieged again in Tripoli by the Syrians with yet another close escape—whereupon he practically had to go begging to find a place to hold his parliamentary meeting, until at last King Hussein invited him.

Arafat is a realist and a survivor. He is intelligent enough to realize that this is not the season for a violent solution, and that the diplomatic and parliamentary game must be given a chance. In other words, the many parliamentary meetings in recent years—and the elections that supply the parliamentarians—are in part an effect of the growing recognition that violence does not achieve its purposes.

Now, in places like Egypt and Kuwait and even Jordan, there is more to it. There is a desire on the part of Mubarak and King Hussein to mobilize some visible popular support, because there are many critics at home and opponents abroad. It is too soon to tell whether all this will eventually lead to any genuine democracy; considering that this development took two and a half centuries in a country such as Britain, I would not rule out the possibility. In that long-range perspective I am rather more optimistic in view of the fact that in Egypt the question of national identity seems to have been decided now in favor of an Egyptian, rather than a vaguely pan-Arab, identity.

Q: Could you elaborate on the phenomenon called Meir Kahane and the extent to which it fits into the Israeli system of democracy?

A: The percentage of Knesset seats held by the religious parties has been remarkably steady, the steadiest among all the major party groupings, in fact. It has ranged from a minimum of 11.9 percent to a maximum of 14 or 15 percent throughout the entire period of 11 Israeli elections since 1949. Elsewhere in the spectrum there have been shifts back and forth, the 1977 electoral upset being the most spectacular one. But in most Israeli political camps there has also been a kind of ebb and flow: first a desire to rally together and do better in the next election by forming a broader grouping such as the Labor Alignment or the Gahal or Likud groupings on the right, and next a renewed splintering.

Among the religious groups there has been some of that same rallying and splintering tendency. At one time there was the so-called United Religious Front, in which four religious groups went into the 1949 elections. Then they split four ways—Zionist and non-Zionist, Mizrahi and Mizrahi Labor, and so forth. Recently this splintering has been again most prominent among the religious groups, so that there are as many as six of them currently sharing the 14 or 15 percent of the total vote that goes to the religious parties. One seat among those is held by Meir Kahane.

It is well to remember that a single vote in the Knesset indicates a popular following of about 1 percent. There are 120 seats in the Knesset, and the whole country is one district where seats are allocated by proportional representation, and 1 percent of the popular vote is the minimum requirement for a party to be represented. Under no other election system except Israel's extreme form of proportional representation would a candidate like Kahane have been elected. It is true that his election has attracted a lot of attention because of the notoriety that his kind of violent direct action tends to bring with it. One major aim of terrorism is simply publicity, and it seems to me that we would be striking a blow against terrorism by not giving it quite as much publicity.

Q (Duygu Sezer, Columbia University, New York City): Would you comment on the relationship between religion and the democratic revolution in the evolution of the democratic process in Turkey? Turkey is not only a Middle Eastern country with a democratic tradition—despite interruptions—but it is also a Muslim country with a unique democratic performance. At the time of the revolution in Iran, there were some serious questions, both in Turkey and outside, about the possible impact of the social and religious revolution that was going on. What are the prospects for any impact on Turkey?

A: Certainly Turkey is a Muslim country: 98 percent or so of the population is Muslim. It is also true that the major emphasis of Atatürk's revolution was on secularism, which in many ways was perceived by the population of Turkey and other Muslim countries as anti-Islamic. In fairness we must say that Atatürk made it clear that he was not antireligious when he insisted on a secular state; and indeed the separation of government and Islam in Turkey is not as wide as that between church and state in the United States. Specifically, the religious establishment in Turkey continues to be paid from public funds, but it occupies a very subordinate position in the administrative hierarchy.

At the time of Turkey's first free and competitive elections in 1950, many observers in Turkey and abroad expected that the Islamic sentiment that had been pushed back for a quarter century would return in full force, that religion versus secularism would emerge as a central issue, and that secularism thus might become a victim of democracy. In fact, no such reversal occurred—for two reasons. İsmet İnönü, in preparing his one-party regime for the impending elections, made two major innovations. For the first time in Turkish republican history, foreign exchange was allowed for the pilgrimage to Mecca; Turks in earlier decades had abstained from the pilgrimage not because it was forbidden, but because it was not considered a valid claim for allocation of scarce foreign exchange. Also for the first time, a theological faculty was set up at the University of Ankara, so that Islam was studied—in strict scientific objectivity, to be sure—for the first time in an institution of higher education in the Turkish republic. The incoming government of Adnan Menderes in 1950 went one better by revoking the imposed translation of the Islamic prayer call, or *ezan,* into pure Turkish. Interestingly enough, an elaborate program had been instituted in 1932 to train the muezzins in this Turkicized version of the prayer call, but no training program was needed in 1950 to revert to the traditional, Arabic version of the prayer call; and everyone breathed a sigh of relief.

In some ways, these concessions made by the political establishment to popular Islamic sentiment managed to defuse the issue of secularism versus religion in Turkey. In addition, the processes of social mobility, secularization, and modern education have had the cumulative effect of weakening Islamic sentiment in Turkey. There is in Turkey less mosque attendance, less fasting, less prayer, and so on than in most other Islamic countries, with the same kind of social shadings and differences. For example, piety is more widespread among the lower classes and among the disadvantaged, but it is less on every specific count in Turkey than elsewhere in the Middle East. And piety is diminishing rather than increasing as a result of those same broad social and historic forces.

On the Turkish political scene, the striking fact is that there has always been at least one minor party that appeals to this religious antisecularist sentiment—but that that party in its various forms and guises has gone from a minimum of 3 percent of the popular vote in 1950 to a maximum of no more than 12 percent in 1973, and never higher. It is also worth remembering that the more militant Muslims in Turkey are Sunnis, and that as Sunnis they tend to take a somewhat jaundiced view of a Shiite militant movement such as the one in neighboring Iran.

Q (Mostapha Baligh, Bergen Community College, Paramus, New Jersey): Why does Israel, which is a democracy, not allow an Arab party?

A: The major defect and limitation of Israeli democracy is the military regime maintained over the Arabs in the West Bank and Gaza, who constitute roughly 30 percent of the total population of Israel in its post-1967 de facto boundaries and who are in effect a disfranchised lower class. In contrast, the Arabs who live within the pre-1967 boundaries and in greater Jerusalem do have Israeli citizenship and the right to vote. If every name change and every regrouping are counted, there have been seven or eight different Arab parties to represent these, most of them brought together under the designation of Labor- or Alignment-affiliated Arab lists. Since the Israeli election system encourages party splintering, these are the special Arab parties that appeal to the Arab residents around Nazareth and so on. Between the two major party groupings, it is clear that the Arab population prefers the Mapai and the Alignment to the Herut-Likud grouping. At the time of the last Israeli election, the authorities ruled one Arab party with a mixed Arab-Jewish list of candidates to be ineligible to participate in the ballot, but the election authorities were overruled by the courts. In the end the party did run, and it is represented, I believe, by two members in the Knesset.

In Jerusalem, Teddy Kollek has been very careful, as mayor of that city, to keep out of Israel's national politics in order to run the city in a peaceful way. I happened to be present some years ago when an agreement was negotiated in Jerusalem between Kollek and a leading Arab lawyer of the West Bank in preparation for the municipal election. The agreement was that the word would be passed among Arab residents of Jerusalem to vote for Kollek rather than the Herut candidate or the religious parties. But the agreement was kept under strict secrecy, and the Arab party to the negotiations made it clear that the deal would be off if anything got into the newspapers. In the most recent municipal election in Jerusalem, this Arab vote for Kollek was so out in the open that the common joke among Jerusalem residents was that just as in New York a candidate needs the Jewish vote to become mayor, so in Jerusalem a candidate needs the Arab vote.

ANNALS, *AAPSS*, **482**, November 1985

Businessmen's Associations in Egypt and Turkey

By ROBERT BIANCHI

ABSTRACT: Associations representing the special interests of the Egyptian business community have grown in number and variety during the last 15 years. The largest and most powerful of these interest groups are examined here. The persistent diversity of business organizations is explained by the discontinuous historical evolution of the private sector and by the changing political and economic strategies of Egypt's authoritarian regime. Finally, Egyptian business groups are compared briefly with Turkish business associations, which played a key role in the privatization of an economy once dominated by the state sector.

Robert Bianchi is assistant professor of political science at the University of Pennsylvania. He lived in Turkey for three years as a Peace Corps volunteer and a Fulbright-Hays fellow and then taught in Egypt for four years at the American University in Cairo. He speaks Turkish and Arabic. He is the author of Interest Groups and Political Development in Turkey *(1984) and is currently writing a book about associational life in modern Egypt.*

DESPITE its modest size and circumscribed range of activities, the Egyptian business community is organized in a remarkably diverse set of associations that have acquired great importance in the country's economic and political life. This article will provide a descriptive overview of the major interest groups in Egypt's private business sector, offer an explanation of the proliferation and increasing heterogeneity of these associations, and conclude with a brief comparison of Egyptian business groups with their counterparts in Turkey.

HETEROGENEITY AND CONFLICT AMONG BUSINESSMEN'S ASSOCIATIONS

The representation of Egyptian business interests comprises six principal associations with unusually diverse structural characteristics, ranging from older, corporatist groups, which are semiofficial and compulsory, to newer, pluralist groups, which are private and voluntary.[1]

Old corporatist groups

The two oldest and largest groups—the Federation of Chambers of Commerce and the Federation of Chambers of Industry—are corporatist structures that were inherited from the prerevolutionary period, refashioned into more explicitly state-controlled agents of economic regulation during the regime of Gamal Abdel Nasser, and granted a wider opportunity to express private-sector demands under the governments of Anwar el-Sadat and Hosni Mubarak. The chambers of commerce were transformed from private, voluntary organizations to semiofficial, corporatist groups during World War II. Since then they have operated primarily as bureaucratic instruments for policing the marketplace and only secondarily as representative associations for private businessmen. Under the Sadat regime the reemergence of partisan competition created new opportunities for chamber leaders to influence traditionally unresponsive government agencies through the intercession of the official party organization.

The eagerness of the ruling National Democratic Party to organize supporters in the chambers was heightened by the brief success of Mustafa Kamal Murad—now the leader of the right-of-center Liberal Party—in mobilizing discontent within the Cairo Chamber of Commerce against price controls on imported consumer goods. The ruling party has sought to prevent similar opposition inroads into the chambers by encouraging overlapping leaderships between the party and chamber organizations in most provincial capitals. These groups, in turn, have established a network of Popular Development Banks through which local entrepreneurs have received millions of dollars' worth of cheap credit and foreign aid for investments in food production, tourism, and land reclamation.[2]

Such practices have encouraged the many middle-sized provincial merchants to view the politically connected chambers as a useful device in meeting what they see as unfair competition from the

1. For definitions of "corporatism" and "pluralism," see Philippe C. Schmitter, "Still the Century of Corporatism?" *Review of Politics*, 36(1):85-131 (Jan. 1974).

2. See the 10-part series by Abdal-Qadir Shahib, "Haqiqat al-tanmiya al-shabiya" [The reality of popular development], *Al-shab*, 4 Jan.-15 Mar. 1983.

larger metropolitan firms that are less dependent on collective action and intermediaries to cut through red tape in acquiring financing, distributorships, and licenses. Thus, the enhanced position of the chambers of commerce is largely the result of a coincidence of interest between an authoritarian regime seeking a broader base of support in the provincial middle class and a rising group of merchants in provincial capitals and towns seeking political safeguards for their continued predominance in local markets.

The Federation of Chambers of Industry was undoubtedly Egypt's most powerful interest group before the Free Officers' Revolution of 1952. A few years before Nasser's nationalization of private industrial cartels, chambers of industry were reorganized into state-controlled corporatist structures along the lines of the previously corporatized chambers of commerce. When Sadat encouraged debate over the reorganization and possible divestiture of public-sector industries, the Federation of Chambers of Industry was surprisingly successful in formulating common demands for the managers of large public establishments and the far more numerous owners of small private firms. Their demands went well beyond proposals for administrative decentralization and greater reliance on market forces. The federation called for efforts to limit or eliminate such socialist reforms as worker participation in management, profit sharing, and job security. It advanced several proposals to permit private and foreign investors to acquire equity in and create joint ventures with profitable public firms. The federation also has prepared detailed demands for state subsidies and incentives to private industry that aim at a decisive shift in the balance of investment and power in Egypt's mixed economy in favor of private manufacturers.[3]

The remarkably swift reemergence of private business influence in a corporatist association designed to represent and control the technocratic and managerial elite of the public sector is attributable in part to the political vulnerability and economic opportunism of the managers themselves and in part to the peculiar blend of public and private interests encompassed by the federation. Sadat purged hundreds of managers who were sympathetic to rationalization and decentralization for the sake of greater efficiency, but who would have opposed attacks on the principle of public ownership of large industry. Their successors continued to portray themselves as stewards of the public sector, but they showed an alarming penchant for steering their enterprises into controversial joint ventures with foreign firms and then popping up on the local boards of those same corporations.

Moreover, private industrialists always have dominated the elected positions, which comprise two-thirds of the industry federation's executive committee, even though effective control has remained in the hands of the government-appointed minority. Thus when public policy began to encourage private manufacturing, the federation provided the business community with a ready-made mixed commission for reshaping industrial policy in close consultation with the state's key bankers, planners,

3. See, for example, the extensive coverage of the private sector in Egyptian Federation of Industries, *Al-kitab al-dhahabi lil-Ittihad al-sanaat al-misriya* [The golden book of the Egyptian Federation of Industries], (Cairo: Schindler, 1973), pp. 59-93.

and economic ministers. The dualistic structure of representation in the federation of industries has aided private manufacturers not only in recapturing their original associations, but also in penetrating government agencies that had become indifferent or hostile to their interests.

New corporatist groups

Two newer and more specialized groups—the Engineers' Syndicate and the Commercial Employees' Syndicate—are somewhat more autonomous corporatist associations in which intense factional rivalries frequently reflect struggles between supporters and opponents of government economic policies. In the case of the Engineers' Syndicate, the state intervened decisively to quash growing opposition by placing the association under the control of Uthman Ahmad Uthman, who personifies the symbiosis of the state bureaucracy, the ruling party, and the most opportunistic elements of the rising commercial bourgeoisie. Uthman soon began to transform the Engineers' Syndicate from a representative association into a business enterprise that would serve as the prototype of a new economic sector based on what might be called syndical capitalism. Many other corporatist occupational groups, including labor unions, have been induced and pressured to follow the example of the Engineers' Syndicate by renouncing demands for the more autonomous expression of special interests in exchange for opportunities to use pension funds and state grants to create new development banks, establish their own industrial enterprises, and enter into joint ventures with foreign capital.[4]

In the case of the Commercial Employees' Syndicate, however, banking and importing interests have found a more independent forum for criticizing what they regard as the half-hearted economic liberalization of the Sadat and Mubarak governments. In the last decade this syndicate has been led by two of the most important architects of Egypt's economic open-door policy, Abdal-Aziz Hijazi, a former prime minister, and Abdal-Razaq Abdal-Majid, a former minister of economy and foreign trade. Both men were forced from office by opponents who demanded greater state guidance for the expanding roles of private and foreign capital. Both men also eventually achieved political comebacks via the Commercial Employees' Syndicate, which Sadat originally had created in order to mobilize a pro-open-door constituency based on the rapidly growing number of accountants, clerks, and paraprofessionals working in private and joint-venture firms. By the end of the 1970s this state-initiated corporatist syndicate had become a forum for some of the most outspoken resistance to new policies seeking to reassert government controls over private banks, importers, and foreign investors.[5]

New pluralist groups

The two newest business organizations are purely private, voluntary groups, representing an important new tendency toward spontaneous and au-

4. Adal al-Mashad, "Al-ghazw al-istithmari lil-niqabat al-mihniya wa al-ummaliya" [The entrepreneurial invasion of professional and labor syndicates], *Al-shab*, 25 Jan. 1983.

5. Sharif Hassan Qasim, "Al-qissa al-kamila li intikhabat al-Tijariyin" [The complete story of the Commercial Employees' elections], *Al-ahali*, 7 Mar. 1984.

tonomous collective action in the private sector. The Egyptian Businessmen's Association and a clandestine network of black-market money changers are both important organizational responses of powerful segments of the business community to the Mubarak government's efforts to reorient Egypt's open-door policy from what the government sees as an anarchic and consumptive phase to what it calls a guided and productive phase. Whereas the Egyptian Businessmen's Association has sought to cooperate with and benefit from this shift in policy, the black marketeers have sought to challenge and subvert it.

The Egyptian Businessmen's Association is a new coalition of over 200 of the largest private firms in foreign trade, manufacturing, construction, banking, and consulting. It is quickly establishing itself as the major coordinator of big-business demands and as the private sector's principal bargaining agent vis-à-vis the state and foreign capital. Despite the diversity of its constituency, the association has welcomed Mubarak's interventionist policies to transfer private investment from commerce to industry, to shift importing from consumer goods to intermediate and capital goods, and to direct more foreign investment toward joint ventures with local firms.

The coalition's leaders have tried to persuade the government that there are elements of the private sector—more enlightened and competent, according to these leaders—that can be valuable allies in moving beyond the commercial profiteering, real estate speculation, and influence peddling that flourished under Sadat. The association is eager to demonstrate that big business is adapting as swiftly as possible to the emerging system that the government describes as guided capitalism and that implementation of the state's chosen priorities will be more successful if businessmen are more directly involved in the policy-making process. Accordingly, the group's leaders claim that one-half of the member firms in importing already have transferred the bulk of their activities to industrial raw materials and machinery and that one-half of the member firms in manufacturing are producing in branches other than food and textiles.[6]

The rapid emergence and growing influence of the Egyptian Businessmen's Association indicates the success of the bigger firms in creating an effective and attractive voluntary organization that is beginning to replace the traditional corporatist associations as the most authentic representative of the private sector. The association's leaders are determined to demonstrate that the local private business community has matured sufficiently to organize itself politically and that it is prepared to become a full partner with the state and foreign capital in a closer triple alliance that might indeed initiate the new phase of industrialization that was promised by the original proponents of the open-door policy.

An equally impressive new example of spontaneous collective action has arisen among considerably less benign segments of Egyptian free enterprise. By the late 1970s illegal trade in foreign exchange had reached an unprecedented volume and had spawned a broad organizational network connecting Egypt's villages with banks in Europe and the

6. Egyptian Businessmen's Association, *Al-taqrir al-sanawi wa dalil al-ada lil-Jamiya rijal al-amal al-misriyin* [Annual report and membership directory of the Egyptian Businessmen's Association] (Cairo: Dar al-alam al-arabi, 1983).

Persian Gulf. The growth of loosely regulated joint-venture banks, the insatiable demand for the dollar, which was becoming the preferred medium of exchange even in purely domestic transactions, and the rising remittances of Egyptian workers abroad created a bonanza for currency smugglers and black marketeers. Some operators were able to conspire with bank officials to obtain multimillion-dollar loans with little or no collateral. These funds were then added to the black market, loaned to dollar-hungry importers, including some government agencies and public-sector firms, or smuggled out of the country.[7]

When Mubarak's minister of economy, Mustafa al-Said, began to press for a new banking law to reestablish the Central Bank's control over the money supply, one of Sadat's former ministers met with the black-market leaders and asked them to suspend their operations temporarily so that the measure might be defeated. Instead of accepting this demand, the currency dealers asked him to convey to the government their own demand for an end to police harassment and for official recognition of their right to do business. Shortly thereafter the conflict between the government and the black marketeers escalated sharply, blossoming into a yearlong struggle for power that has caused great disruption in the economy. In the spring of 1984 Parliament invested the Central Bank and the minister of economy with sweeping new powers to regulate private and joint-venture banks. Then, in the fall, 18 of the largest currency dealers were put on trial; the chief defendant was accused of smuggling $3 billion out of the country within just 18 months.[8]

The week before the trials began, the black marketeers raised the price of the dollar more than 10 percent in only two days and called openly for Mustafa al-Said's resignation. With the real price of foreign exchange a full 20 percent higher than the official rate, importing slowed, inflation rose, and the government's goal of regaining control over the financial system seemed more elusive than ever. The government has continued with the trials, apparently unconcerned with the currency dealers' pledge to lower the price of the dollar to its previous level the day the minister of economy submits his resignation. The black-market leaders may yet have their way, however, given increasingly frequent press reports that the same demand is being made from within the cabinet itself.[9]

THE SOURCES OF ASSOCIATIONAL DIVERSITY

Why does Egypt have so few big businessmen and so many businessmen's organizations? Why are these groups not only so numerous, but so diverse in terms of their structures, the types of interests they represent, and

7. Mahmud Abdal-Fadil, *Taammulat fi al-masala al-iqtisadiya al-misriya* [Reflections on the Egyptian economic problem] (Cairo: Dar al-mustaqbal al-arabi, 1983), pp. 115-20.

8. Abdal-Rahman Aql, "Difa wazir al-iqtisad an tadil qanun al-bunuk" [The minister of economy's defense of the amendment of the banking law], *Al-ahram al-iqtisadi*, 2 Apr. 1984, pp. 6-9; and Yusuf al-Qaid, "Misr: Al-nizam al-masrafi fi khatar" [Egypt: The financial system in danger], *Al-mustaqbal*, 8(402):57-58 (3 Nov. 1984).

9. The minister of economy did indeed resign in April 1985 after all of the business groups mentioned here mounted intense resistance to new trade and banking regulations. "Tadil wizari wasi wa taraju shamil an al-islah al-iqtisadi" [A broad cabinet change and a sweeping retreat from economic reform], *Al-ahali*, 3 Apr. 1985.

their relationships with the political authorities? Part of the answer can be found in certain key characteristics of the Egyptian business community itself: its changing composition, its dissatisfaction with existing channels of representation, and its considerable resources for cultivating the art of association. Another part of the answer can be found in some important features of Egypt's current authoritarian regime, especially in its changing strategies of political domination and economic development.

Characteristics of the business community

The historical evolution of the private sector has been a highly discontinuous process, shaped by depression and world war, colonial occupation and national revolution, socialist transformation and neocapitalist revival. Entrepreneurs arose and prospered in each period, but often they were unable to consolidate their gains or pass them on to subsequent generations. It is not uncommon to meet older Egyptian businessmen making their second or third fortunes or younger ones trying to restore once-grand family estates. Nor is it unusual to see corporate executives who describe themselves as self-made men and yet have little or no business experience, having amassed wealth through land speculation, political connections, or extended employment in the Gulf.

The distinctly noncumulative formation of Egypt's private sector resembles Henri Pirenne's "staircase" conceptualization of successive stages in the social history of European capitalism. Economic development in the West, he argued, was not accomplished by a continuous capitalist class changing itself to suit changing circumstances, but by a multiplicity of "distinct and separate" capitalist classes that had arisen in succeeding "epochs."[10] Throughout the twentieth century the Egyptian business world has experienced abrupt shifts and frequent reversals in its sources of recruitment, concentration of ownership, sectoral distribution of investments, relative importance vis-à-vis state enterprise, and degree and direction of integration into foreign markets. The result has been a highly fragmented bourgeoisie, divided not only by such conventional cleavages as sector, region, size, and international competitiveness, but by equally important differences in age, education, ethics, family background, and, of course, political loyalty.

The postrevolutionary portions of Egypt's private-sector staircase have been only dimly lit by social historians. Nevertheless, it is clear that even the most rudimentary sketch of its current composition would have to include the following levels:

—families who were prominent in trade and industry before the nationalizations and who are making a comeback after temporary retreat into agribusiness and the free professions;

—engineers and former army officers who rose to form the managerial elite of the public sector and who by design or default have transferred to private business;

—the contractors, black marketeers, and suitcase merchants who thrived on the shortages and bottlenecks of the socialist and wartime economies;

10. Philippe C. Schmitter, "Modes of Interest Intermediation and Models of Societal Change in Western Europe," *Comparative Political Studies*, 10(1):24-26 (Apr. 1977).

—the open-door class of importers, builders, and bankers who fed the pent-up demand of middle-class consumers during Sadat's presidency;

—the thousands of small manufacturers who have hung on to their workshops despite repeated policy reversals that disrupted their supplies of inputs and their links with foreign outlets;

—newly prosperous provincial merchants, including many workers returned from abroad, competing for larger shares of their regional markets; and

—aspiring local industrialists, seeking an elusive combination of state protection and liberalization that would allow them to attract foreign partners without being swallowed by them.

All the foregoing types suggest far more structure and vitality than is implied in André Gunder Frank's dismal—although sometimes accurate—characterization of Third World capitalists as a "*lumpenbourgeoisie*."[11] But it also points to a hyperfragmentation that hinders any sustained and inclusive effort at collective action and leads us to anticipate just the sort of episodic, particularistic, and externally induced pattern of associational emergence that we described previously.

The continuous reformation of the private sector has been accompanied by a periodic restructuring of its representative associations as each generation of capitalists has reorganized itself from within or has been reorganized from above by successive political regimes. In general, previously dominant business elements were not violently displaced or eliminated by ascendant groups, but instead managed to become embedded in the expanding state bureaucracy. The result has been a gradual increase in both the number and variety of business associations that now comprise a curious mélange of corporatist, pluralist, and hybrid structures.

The most recent phase of associational reorganization since the early 1970s has been promoted by the growing dissatisfaction of nearly all major business elements with the contrived, inflexible, bureaucratic nature of preexisting corporatist groups. This dissatisfaction led to several parallel efforts to fashion new channels of representation that might serve as more accurate reflections of the still modest but increasingly differentiated business world. The externally imposed federations of commerce and industry were adapted to operate as mixed commissions and semiofficial networks for distributing public resources to private firms. The newer professional syndicates became more open arenas for political competition between rival factions of entrepreneurs even though the expression of such competition through the party system was still tightly restricted. And new pluralist associations, both legal and illegal, were created to be the special representatives of particularly influential groups seeking greater freedom of maneuver in both the marketplace and the political system.

Of course, private business is not the only sector that has become dissatisfied with the body of corporatist occupational groups that dominates associational life in Egypt. But businessmen have been far more successful than

11. André Gunder Frank, *Lumpenbourgeoisie: Lumpendevelopment* (New York: Monthly Review Press, 1971), passim.

professionals, workers, and farmers in refashioning their traditional organizations and initiating novel forms of collective action. They alone have had the combination of private resources and official tolerance necessary for cultivating the art of association in a seemingly inhospitable environment of weak capitalism and authoritarian rule. Internal fragmentation and external interference from the state have inhibited and delayed, but not prevented, their mobilization to translate their growing wealth into greater political influence.

The only other recent example of rapid associational proliferation and reorganization is in the area of religious groups. These also grew as a largely spontaneous expression of widespread dissatisfaction with the contrived nature of representative associations and limited outlets for the expression of political dissent. Whereas the sudden resurgence of autonomous organization among Muslims and Christians posed a brief yet fundamental challenge to the authoritarian regime, the emergence of more organized capitalists may present it with an important new partner whose support can be seen as particularly welcome as the traditional populist and socialist slogans of the revolution lose what little remains of their credibility.

Characteristics of the authoritarian regime

Several features of Egypt's political system also have been conducive to the proliferation and diversification of business groups. First of all, more numerous and diverse associations do not necessarily produce a more coherent and cohesive private sector. On the contrary, they simply may reflect and reinforce pervasive divisions and rivalries among specific subsectors. Thus by permitting and occasionally encouraging associational duplication and competition, the authoritarian elite is actually preserving a considerable degree of disorganization among capitalists and trying to maintain, at least temporarily, the state's relative autonomy from rapidly ascending socioeconomic groups. As long as businessmen lack inclusive and autonomous organizations they will not be able to represent themselves independently of a paternalistic ruling party.

The leaders of the National Democratic Party have been careful to preserve their role as the principal steering committee of the private sector, aggregating its demands, arbitrating its internal conflicts, and serving as its key to state largess. With the gradual reorganization of business associations in the last 15 years, the ruling party has become an increasingly important supplement to corporatism in maintaining authoritarian control over Egyptian capitalists. To be sure, the party is encountering more and more difficulty in performing its harmonizing role vis-à-vis business and the state. It has been forced to defend policies that clearly discriminate in favor of certain business interests and against others; it has been directly implicated in a string of spectacular business scandals; and it has been caught in the middle of the protracted trench warfare between the current minister of economy and his numerous opponents. Nevertheless, the party's ability to continue in such a key mediating role is largely attributable to the persistent disorganization that it has encouraged among increasingly pluralistic business groups.

The fragmenting strategy that the authoritarian elite has pursued toward the private sector, however, should not overshadow increasingly visible divisions within the state itself. Disagreements and rivalries among overlapping agencies of economic policymaking provide multiple points of access and influence for business associations that frequently are able to amend or reverse unfavorable government proposals despite their own weaknesses and mutual differences. Two lines of interagency cleavage are particularly persistent sources of bureaucratic infighting: (1) conflicts between coordinating ministries—Finance, Economy, Planning, and Interior—concerned with systemwide issues and virtually all other ministries, which are linked to particular constituencies; and (2) conflicts between regulatory ministries—Supply, Industry, Investment, Construction, Agriculture, Transportation, and Energy—heavily penetrated by special business interests and welfare ministries—Manpower, Social Affairs, Health, Education, Youth, Pious Foundations, and Cooperatives—which distribute benefits to much larger social categories.

There is, of course, an important third dimension of possible cleavages that, when activated, can sharply exacerbate the previous two dimensions: conflicts between the coordinating ministries and the numerous international aid and creditor agencies that can set the general limits, if not the specific lines, of many areas of economic policy. As these interagency disputes become entangled in a growing number of hotly contested issues, embattled ministers have greater incentives to seek support for their positions outside the government—and often outside the country. The widening interface of a more divided state bureaucracy and a more densely organized business community helps to explain much of the tentativeness, inconsistency, and drift of Egypt's recent economic policy.

Finally, the Mubarak government's changing strategy of economic development has sought to enhance the role of local private capital by providing its owners with most of the privileges and incentives previously reserved for foreign or joint-venture firms and by pressing foreign investors to enter into more partnerships with Egyptian entrepreneurs. Under Mubarak the state has intervened not only to encourage a shift of private investment into the manufacturing and exporting sectors, but also to strengthen the bargaining position of local businessmen vis-à-vis foreign competitors and partners. This new economic nationalism represents an attempt to moderate some of the tensions that had been accumulating in the nascent alliance among state, foreign, and local private capital, an alliance that Sadat created but could not consolidate and that Mubarak wishes to strengthen and refashion as an instrument for the reindustrialization of Egypt. The newly privatized chambers of industry, the entrepreneurial professional syndicates, and the exclusive Egyptian Businessmen's Association are the key mechanisms for integrating local capitalists into the regime's new developmental strategy.

In time it may appear to Egypt's military and technocratic elite that these same business associations can provide a strong enough base of social and economic support to allow a decisive shift in their strategy of authoritarian rule. As the Mubarak regime strengthens its ties with private business, local and foreign, it can expect further deterioration in its already tense relations with the workers and civil servants who were the main beneficiaries and supporters of the revolutionary order until the mid-1970s. In this case Egypt's expanding private sector together with its burgeoning associations could become instrumental in the transformation of a relatively tolerant, benign, and cooptive authoritarian regime into a far more ambitious and coercive system, a transformation that may resemble what several Latin American observers have described as the shift from "populist authoritarianism" to "bureaucratic authoritarianism."[12]

ORGANIZED CAPITALISTS IN EGYPT AND TURKEY

The differences between the private sectors of Egypt and Turkey are obvious and can be summarized easily. Turkey's private sector is larger, more evenly matched with public enterprises, more advanced in the process of import-substituting industrialization, and better prepared for a transition to capital-intensive, export-oriented manufacturing. The associations of Turkish capitalists are less numerous and more centralized; they enjoy more reciprocity in their relationships with government and party leaders and they possess a clearer advantage in their balance of power with organized labor.[13] Despite these differences in composition and relative strength, however, there are several striking similarities in the historical evolution and organizational development of the private sectors in the two countries.

First, in both countries private business has demonstrated a remarkable capacity to survive and flourish in the shadow of vastly superior public economic sectors. Egypt and Turkey are leading examples of state capitalist experiments that underwent extensive privatization as native entrepreneurs emerged from a nationalist revolution to replace expelled foreign minorities, carved out profitable niches as suppliers and contractors of public monopolies, and eventually joined with conservative politicians to lead a neocapitalist revival seeking to reestablish private enterprise as the leading force in rapid industrialization.

Second, in both cases the business community displayed a clear superiority over other social groups in its capacities for voluntary collective action. Businessmen were more successful in overcoming the rigidities of their traditional corporatist associations by reorganizing them from within and by quickly exploiting opportunities to create new and more flexible pluralist associations.

Third, in both Egypt and Turkey the emerging interest groups of private business succeeded in enlisting powerful political support in pursuit of ambitious goals that they could not have accomplished unilaterally. Business leaders became particularly dependent on high levels of American foreign aid to finance private investment, on the patronage of a right-of-center ruling party to moderate conflicts between rival factions of entrepreneurs, and on the more frequent and forceful use of state coercion to restrain or smash the power of organized labor.

Finally, there is considerable evidence that the experiences of Turkish

12. Guillermo O'Donnell, *Modernization and Bureaucratic-Authoritarianism* (Berkeley, CA: Institute of International Studies, 1979), pp. 51-76; and David Collier, ed., *The New Authoritarianism in Latin America* (Princeton, NJ: Princeton University Press, 1979), pp. 19-32.

13. Robert Bianchi, *Interest Groups and Political Development in Turkey* (Princeton, NJ: Princeton University Press, 1984), pp. 251-74.

business groups are diffusing to Egypt and that leaders of the Egyptian private sector wish to emulate certain organizations of their Turkish counterparts. This is especially noticeable in the case of the Egyptian Federation of Chambers of Commerce and the Egyptian Businessmen's Association, whose leaders express openly their admiration for the critical role of Turkish business groups in reshaping national economic policy in favor of free enterprise, rapid industrialization, and closer alliances with foreign capital.

* * *

QUESTIONS AND ANSWERS

Q: Given the growing role of the private sector in Turkey and Egypt and given the United States' strong commitment to both countries, is there a way to develop a better relationship between those two countries and U.S. interests?

A: U.S. relations with Turkey are much better than they are with Egypt, although people generally assume the opposite. There is some trouble in Egypt concerning what is perceived to be (1) American interference in economic decision making, and (2) American partisanship in favor of the private sector that may be an attempt to eradicate or seriously diminish what are regarded as the gains of socialism. In other words, there are now in Egypt a number of growing tensions between different social groups concerning economic policy. The United States is perceived as being a partisan in that polarization much as it has become perceived as partisan with respect to divisions in Lebanon. Only in one case the cleavages are based on communal and religious identities, and in this case they are based more on social and economic differences.

The role of the United States in participating in and exacerbating these conflicts in Egypt is like the role it played in Lebanon: the role involves a certain degree of intentionality. There is a desire to appear evenhanded or detached while in fact supporting one side a little more than the other. On the other hand, there is also some naiveté in thinking that one can be a little bit partisan and not get so deeply involved in internal conflicts that one's policies begin to backfire. There is a danger that this sort of involvement and backfiring could happen in Egypt, largely because the policies that Anwar el-Sadat was pursuing in terms of economic liberalization were perceived in the United States as being rational, but inefficient and long overdue. In Egypt, on the other hand, they are perceived as supporting a peculiarly corrupt and avaricious kind of capitalism that is not even tolerated in the United States or in supposedly clearly capitalist countries with mixed economies. Also, there is among Egyptian intellectuals—especially economists—a lot of resentment at what is perceived as the highly partisan role of the U.S. Agency for International Development and other agencies that refuse to fund any expansion or renewal of state economic enterprise. There is a feeling that American interests and the American funding of capitalism in Egypt and American private business interests are in many ways contrary to Egyptian interests and to a kind of economic nationalism. The United States might ease some of the tension by trying to understand Egyptian points of view a bit more and by not being quite so ideological in its approach to mixed economies.

Q (Dario Scuka, Library of Congress, Washington, D.C.): Economic aid is usually discussed as temporary aid, although it tends to last quite a long time. Given the amount of economic aid to Turkey and especially to Egypt and the aid's duration, could you comment on the addictive aspects of U.S. economic aid to fast-developing systems in the Middle East?

A: The aid is addictive in both directions. One reason that Mubarak has been able to accomplish some shift in his economic policy toward more protectionism and greater control over foreign capital and its role in the country is that he now believes that, as a result of this 10-year period of relatively unrestricted private-sector activity, it is not simply Egypt that is addicted to foreign imports but it is foreign producers who have become addicted to the Egyptian market. It is the point of view of Mubarak and his major economic advisors that Egypt can capitalize on the situation and that their use of protectionism and economic nationalist measures is not to deter foreign capital from coming to Egypt but rather to encourage it to come. But they want production to take place in Egypt, to create local employment and use local inputs to the greatest extent possible. The government has some leverage now in accomplishing these goals because it is clear that the Egyptian market is profitable. If confronted with the choice of losing access to the Egyptian market or accepting some limitations on their role in the Egyptian market, the foreign capitalists will choose the latter.

Mubarak has a great deal of support among private businessmen who feel that they have been discriminated against and that foreign capitalists have more rights and privileges for operating in Egypt than Egyptian businessmen do. Egyptian businessmen also realize that they cannot compete with foreign capitalists and that foreign capitalists can come to Egypt and not use local partners or intermediaries. They see the state's changing public policy as something that allows them to have a cut of the action, and the encouragement of joint ventures by the Egyptian government is something that has received a lot of support among the private sector. The building of triple alliances among foreign capital, the state, and local private enterprise is clearly visible in Egypt, just as it was in Turkey before and in Latin America before that. The process in Egypt is much more protracted, fitful, and conflictual. The role of foreign aid is critical. One of the most interesting things about the Egyptian experience as distinguished from Latin American cases and others that are a prototype of the triple-alliance formation is the role of the Agency for International Development (AID) in stepping in where private foreign capital, especially American capital, is not willingly put. AID leads reluctant capital into Egypt by giving all kinds of incentives and guarantees, including guaranteed profit margins. The hope is that the process will become self-sustaining and that official and international agencies can withdraw as multinational corporations replace them. Foreign aid is used not only in order to change the balance of power between domestic interest groups and between domestic social classes. It is also used to pave the way for the formation of joint ventures between foreign and local firms that would not arise spontaneously.

ANNALS, *AAPSS*, **482**, November 1985

Media Coverage of the Middle East: Perception and Foreign Policy

By JACK G. SHAHEEN

ABSTRACT: A distorted media image of the Arab people is becoming ingrained in American culture and continues to inhibit a resolution of the Middle East conflict. Seemingly innocuous vehicles of entertainment, such as television programs, motion pictures, novels, and comics, help promote the image to unsuspecting audiences, and these audiences relay the image to subsequent audiences. News correspondents' misperceptions of Arabs permeate their reports, policymakers' crucial decisions may be influenced by those unrealistic perceptions, and the public's stereotypical images may affect the formation and acceptance of policy. In order to show the extent of the harm caused by distorted images, examples from entertainment media and from news coverage will be offered. Pertinent to the image problem are illustrations of how misperceptions from the past have helped and continue to help influence policymakers' actions and decisions. Fair portrayals and accurate information are essential to foreign policy decisions; false images and incorrect information may corrupt the policymaking process.

Jack G. Shaheen is a journalist and professor of mass communications at Southern Illinois University, Edwardsville. He writes frequently on stereotypes, the television documentary, and media development in Third World countries for many publications, including the Wall Street Journal, *the* Washington Post, *and the* Journal of Broadcasting. *A recipient of two Fulbright-Hays Lectureship grants, Dr. Shaheen taught at the American University of Beirut and the University of Jordan. Under the auspices of the United States Information Service he offered numerous seminars for journalists and government officials throughout the Middle East.*

"THE subtlest and most pervasive of all influences," stated Walter Lippmann, "are those which create and maintain the repertory of stereotypes. We are told about the world before we see it. We imagine most things before we experience them. And those perceptions . . . govern deeply the whole process of perception."[1] Joseph Boskin, a professor of history and Afro-American studies at Boston University, elaborated on Lippmann's observations: "A stereotype is basically a standardized mental picture, or series of pictures, representing an oversimplified opinion . . . that is staggeringly tenacious in its hold over rational thinking." Boskin contends that a stereotype "gains its force by repetitive play, often presented in different guises so that the image it projects becomes firmly imbedded in reactive levels of thought and action."[2] "Once implanted in popular lore," notes Boskin, "an image attached to a group, an issue or event tends to pervade the deepest senses and profoundly affects behavioral action."[3] Thus, the stereotype endures in defiance of all evidence.

Today's most obvious stereotype is that of the Arab. It is magnified and given credence around the clock through television programs, motion pictures, novels, news reports, and even comic books. The image of the Arab is so pervasive that it threatens to engulf public opinion and ultimately influence American foreign policy in the Middle East.

The greater the distance we are from any group, including Arabs, the greater the reliance upon preconceived images about that group.[4] *Los Angeles Times* correspondent David Lamb has offered an explanation for the preconceived images of Arabs in the West: "In life-style, traditions and beliefs, the Arabs are 'different,' and any ethnic group that is 'different' tends to be stereotyped."[5] These conditions were identified by Henry Siegman, executive vice-president of the American Jewish Congress. "When Americans look at the surrounding Arab societies, they do not generally experience a similar sense of empathy and 'likeness.' To the contrary, these societies, their cultures and their values, evoke a sense of strangeness, of otherness, in most Americans."[6] The noted foreign service officer Laurence Pope has agreed with Siegman and has noted further that "one consequence is that Arabs and Muslims, their cultures and their values are fair game for racial stereotyping and bigotry of the crudest kind."[7]

"Most Americans," John R. Hayes, editor of the book *The Genius of Arab Civilization,* has observed, "don't know much about the Middle East." Americans lump together the diverse peoples and cultures of the area; they retain biases obtained "from European ancestors, from biased teachers, from bad books, from folklore. Many of their biases are superficial—simply the residue of poisonous entertainment."[8]

1. Walter Lippmann, *Public Opinion* (New York: Macmillan, 1922), pp. 59-70.

2. Joseph Boskin, "Denials: The Media View of Dark Skins and the City," in *Small Voices and Great Trumpets,* ed. Bernard Rubin (New York: Praeger, 1980), p. 141.

3. Ibid.

4. Susan Welch, "The American Press and Indochina, 1950-56," in *Communications in International Politics*, ed. Richard I. Merritt (Urbana: University of Illinois Press, 1972), pp. 227-28.

5. David Lamb, "A Bad Rap for the Arabs," *Courier-Journal* (Louisville, KY), 31 Mar. 1985.

6. Laurence Pope, "Flickers of Our Anti-Islam Bigotry," *Los Angeles Times*, 1 Mar. 1985.

7. Ibid.

8. John R. Hayes, "American Attitudes toward Arabs—Perceptions and Misperceptions"

The stereotyping of Arabs regularly appears in media designed to entertain. Communications scholar Erik Barnouw has pointed out that "the aura surrounding the word ["entertainment"] is important because it tends to lull critical faculties. . . . This enables 'entertainment' to play a leading role in shaping attitudes and ideas, including political ideas."[9] Poet and playwright Archibald MacLeish has suggested that images in entertainment programs are even more influential than information delivered in serious programs.[10]

THE PERCEPTION

Most Americans know little of the Arab people, their customs, or their accomplishments. The results of a national poll revealing American perceptions of Arabs were published by the Washington-based *Middle East Journal.* "Barbaric and cruel," "treacherous," "warlike," "rich," and "mistreaters of women" were descriptions frequently used.[11]

Many myths perpetrated by writers for television and film, novelists, cartoonists, and others promote false perceptions. Arabs are portrayed as extremely wealthy, as sex maniacs and white slavers. They are described as terrorists, their society as violent, and their religion, Islam, as radical.

In fact, however, Arabs on the average have annual per capita incomes of only $1000 or so.[12] The pillars of their religion, far from radical, are like those of Christianity: allegiance to God, compassion, and respect for the elderly. The radicalism emanates from those who pervert the religion.[13] Along with religion, the family is the basis for society. Most Arab husbands are monogamous, not sex maniacs. Slavery is outlawed.[14]

Only a minority of Arabs, Israelis, Europeans, Americans, and others resort to terror. As David Lamb pointed out, these few do not represent the whole "any more than the more than 19,000 murders committed in 1982 in the United States make America a nation of killers."[15] Furthermore, Arab society is surely not the most violent of societies. Arab cities have less violence and less crime than others. In Cairo, a city of 14 million, crimes against persons are all but unheard of. In Saudi Arabia, a visitor could leave a $100 bill on the street with his or her name attached and could reasonably expect to have it returned.[16]

It is claimed that Arabs are buying up America, but the U.S. Treasury reports that Arab investments in America are minimal compared with those of other groups. The leading investors are Dutch, British, Canadian, German, Swiss, French, and Japanese. Investments made

(Paper delivered at the conference "U.S.-Arab Relations: The Current Political Economic Commitment," Salt Lake City, UT, 27-29 Mar. 1985), p. 1.

9. Erik Barnouw, *The Sponsor* (New York: Oxford University Press, 1978), p. 101.

10. Archibald MacLeish, in *Broadcasting,* 28 September 1959, p. 90.

11. Lamb, "Bad Rap for the Arabs."

12. According to a 1981 World Bank Development Report, except for Saudi Arabia, Qatar, Kuwait, and the United Arab Emirates, the per capita income is less than $850 per year.

13. Lamb, "Bad Rap for the Arabs."

14. This information is based on my experiences in the Middle East as a Fulbright scholar. I taught mass communications at the American University of Beirut in 1974 and 1975 and at the University of Jordan in 1981 and 1982. Also, under the auspices of the United States Information Service, I traveled extensively throughout the region.

15. Lamb, "Bad Rap for the Arabs."

16. Ibid.

by Arabs are disparagingly tagged "Arab money" in a way that German marks and French francs are not.[17] The purchase of property in America by an Arab is sometimes turned into a minor scandal; the same purchase by a non-Arab is usually thought to be a sound investment. A European or Canadian who acquires an expensive painting is considered cultured and refined; an Arab who does the same is considered decadent.[18]

Iranians are classified often—and falsely—as Arabs. Rather, they are Persians. They speak not Arabic but Farsi, an Indo-European tongue that shares several characteristics with Western European languages. At the height of the Iranian hostage crisis, 70 percent of the Americans surveyed identified Iran as an Arab country, and 8 percent admitted that they did not know whether it was Arab or not.[19]

The Organization of Petroleum Exporting Countries (OPEC) is often taken as synonymous with Arab countries. In fact, only 7 of the 13 member nations are Arab.

The preceding myths are incorporated in the instant Arab kit, which includes belly dancers' outfits, headdresses, veils, dark sunglasses, flowing gowns and robes, oil wells, evil mysticism, limousines, and camels. We see Arabs as billionaires, bombers, or belly dancers—villains of choice.[20]

17. William K. Chung and Gregory G. Fouch, *Survey of Current Business,* pp. 31-41 (Aug. 1983).

18. Lamb, "Bad Rap for the Arabs."

19. Hayes, "American Attitudes toward Arabs," p. 12.

20. See Jack G. Shaheen, "Arabs—Villains of Choice," *Channels of Communication,* pp. 52, 53 (Mar.-Apr. 1984).

THE TELEVISION IMAGE

Images on television and motion picture screens convey powerful messages. Explained Walter Lippmann, "On the screen the whole process of observing, describing, reporting, and then imagining, has been accomplished for you. . . . The shadowy idea becomes vivid; your hazy notion . . . takes vivid shape. . . . Historically it may be the wrong shape, morally it may be a pernicious shape."[21]

Our most impressionable viewers, children, watch television more than 30 hours a week. Young adults spend at least a fifth of their waking hours in front of the television set, according to David Pearl, chief of the National Institute of Mental Health's Behavioral Sciences Research Bureau. By the time youngsters complete high school they will have spent twice as many hours watching television as they spent in classrooms—22,000 hours per child of accumulated television-viewing time and only 11,000 hours of classroom time.[22]

Children are not born with prejudice against races or religious groups. But, as pointed out by Carlos Cortes, a professor of history and chairman of Chicano studies at the University of California at Riverside, before many children reach school their attitudes about ethnic groups, "including prejudices and stereotypes," will be well formed. Cortes believes television has a particularly powerful impact, "often outweighing personal experience."[23]

21. Lippmann, *Public Opinion*, pp. 59-60.

22. "Today's Children Listen More to TV Than Teacher," *Christian Science Monitor,* 17 Oct. 1983.

23. Carlos Cortes, "The Societal Curriculum and the School Curriculum: Allies or Antagonists?" *Journal of Educational Leadership* (Apr. 1979).

Saturday morning cartoon shows feature scores of Arab heavies: Ali Boo-Boo; Abdul-O, the Un-Cool-O; the Desert Rat; and the Sheik in Wolf's Clothing. The animated rascals lurk in the shadows of the pyramids and harm the innocent. Television wrestling programs feature the Iron Sheik, Akbar the Great, and Abdullah the Butcher. The Iron Sheik shouts, "Russia No. 1. The U.S.A., blaaah. Uck!" He then spits on the floor.[24] Abdullah, a "despicable" wrestler, has been known to eat live chickens in front of a horrified audience. These so-called Arabs wrestle "for the sheer pleasure of inflicting pain on others," the ring announcers proclaim.

Situation comedies, such as *Alice,* perpetuate the illusion that Arabs have too much money and too many wives. One episode features Flo in an encounter with Ben, the oil baron. Alice states, "He's one of those Arabs who's coming over here to buy up the whole country." Ben wants to make Flo his fourth wife. Flo asks Ben if he indeed has a harem. He replies, "My goodness, no. It would be immodest of me to call three wives a harem."

In *CHiPs* we learn about what are portrayed as Arab customs. A reckless Arab playboy tries to bribe police officers with two envelopes full of $100 bills. When the officers resist, the Arab states, "You see, in my country this is custom."

In the dramatic series *Cagney and Lacey*, viewers see an oil-rich Arab run over an American Jew in his Rolls Royce, which bears a license plate that reads "OILBUX." The Arab has diplomatic immunity and refuses to pay the victim's hospital bills. What if the writer had switched the characters' identities and had telecast a rich Jew running down a poor Arab?

Some television documentaries do present balanced depictions. Documentaries such as *Oh, Tell the World What Happened; The Saudis; The Palestinians; Israel and the Palestinians: Will Reason Prevail?* and the Public Broadcasting Service (PBS) series *The Arabs and Israelis* show Arabs as individuals with rights and aspirations. These infrequent programs help foster an understanding of the Arab people.

THE MOTION PICTURE IMAGE

Cinema is an international language. Moviegoers in more than 130 international markets regularly view American films because the United States is a leading exporter of motion pictures. The Arab stereotype in American movies is subsequently viewed on video cassettes, cable systems, and government and private television networks. In time, a single film, distributed via several different media delivery systems in many nations, could reach between 500 million and 1 billion viewers.

The motion picture image of Arabs in the 1980s could be characterized in a film that would be entitled *The Arabs Are Coming, The Arabs Are Coming.* Arabs appear as serious threats to the world in the films *Network; The Formula; Rollover; Wrong Is Right;* and *Protocol.* In *Network*, actor Peter Finch warns that Arabs are "going to own what you read and what you see. There's not a single law in the land to stop them." *The Formula* reveals that ex-Nazis, the oil companies, and Arabs rule the world. Marlon Brando states, "Bribery is a way of life in the Middle East." Arabs destroy the American way of life in *Rollover* by causing a worldwide

24. *St. Louis Post-Dispatch*, 19 Apr. 1985.

depression. In *Wrong Is Right*, scores of Arabs willingly kill themselves in the name of a terrorist organization. In *Protocol,* Goldie Hawn warns that Arabs threaten America's security.

Another cinematic theme, that Arabs are sexually depraved, is perpetuated in the movies *Bolero; Protocol;* and *Sahara.* In *Bolero,* Bo Derek's would-be seducer—a shaykh—is counterfeit. Arabs ogle Goldie Hawn in *Protocol* and Brooke Shields in *Sahara*; Hawn, after all, has blond hair, and Shields has blue eyes, and, as the stale formula goes, Arabs are so depraved that they will do anything for a sexy blond or a blue-eyed nymph.

The Arab is regarded as less than human in *Time after Time; Things Are Tough All Over; Best Defense; Paradise;* and *Cannonball Run II.* In *Time after Time*, a woman wants to know if "London is really crawling with Arabs." The depraved Habib in *Things Are Tough All Over* has intercourse with a camel; he uses the same knife to clean his toenails and to eat his meal. In *Best Defense*, Kuwaiti children throw stones at Eddie Murphy's tank. Roars Murphy, "Okay, you desert rats, now you die." A shaykh massacres an entire village in *Paradise* simply because a young woman will not submit to "one of his slimy overtures." In *Cannonball Run II,* an ape kisses the Arab king, and the king smiles, "If only your mother could kiss like that!"

OTHER IMAGES

In the 1947 edition of *Webster's New International Dictionary,* "Arab" is defined as "one of the oldest and purest of peoples and with the Jews constitute the best modern representatives of the Semitic race." But today's dictionaries and thesauruses use the following synonyms for "Arab": "vagabond," "peddler," "bum," "derelict," and "tramp."[25]

The publishing industry perpetuates the stereotype in novels such as *The Haj; Key to Rebecca;* and *Evergreen.* Authors contend that Arabs are religious fanatics, warmongers, and inept assassins intent on destroying Israel and the West with nuclear weapons—even though Israel is the only nation in the Middle East with nuclear arms.

A novel that typically illustrates the image in fiction is *The World Rapers*, by Jonathan Black. The main character is an American Arab who kills innocent Israeli women and children and is an American draft dodger who ruthlessly deceives his friends. He seduces and causes the death of one friend's wife while achieving financial gain at the expense of the other. When he finally meets his fate, can we fault the reader for rejoicing?

Comic strips in newspapers are another means by which the public is misinformed about Arabs. They attract much attention. Millions of readers saw a popular cartoon character, Dennis the Menace, ridicule Arabs. Complained Dennis on Thanksgiving Day, "Dewey's family's havin' meatloaf. Some Arab is eating their turkey." In "Brenda Starr," we saw Sheik Oily-Oleum, an arrogant would-be seducer of Western women. "Spiderman" featured Dr. Mondo, a nuclear terrorist.

In a *Superman* comic book, Lois Lane is wooed by a romantic shaykh who turns out to be ruthless killer of several wives.[26] A brave American sergeant in *G.I. Combat* sets a TNT booby

25. *Merriam-Webster Thesaurus* (1978), s.v. "arab," "peddler," "vagabond."

26. "The Captive Princess," *Superman's Girl Friend, Lois Lane,* no. 58. pp. 1-8 (July 1965).

trap. Hordes of Arabs are killed and the sergeant boasts, "[The vultures will] feast on human [Arab] hyenas."[27]

We are less inclined to view the entertainment message as propaganda because entertainment is supposedly harmless. Yet entertainment may perform as propaganda precisely because audiences perceive the messages unknowingly and without suspicion.

Perceptions may also be rooted and perpetuated in news coverage of the Middle East. "I don't think one can point the finger to [entertainment] alone," said National Broadcasting Company (NBC) executive Jerome Stanley. "Television entertainment producers take their information from newspaper headlines, from editorial cartoons and from articles in magazines, rather than get the information for themselves. Some of the superficial stories in our newspapers and the exploitation of the Arab filter down to producers and writers," said Stanley. "Such information, though we would like to think otherwise, becomes a part of their philosophy; they accept it and use it in their programs."[28]

PICTURES AND WORDS

Perceptions acquired from pictures and words have far-reaching implications. In *The Press and Foreign Policy*, Bernard Cohen maintained that "the press is significantly more than a purveyor of information and opinion. It may not be successful much of the time in telling people what to think, but it is stunningly successful in telling people what to think about."[29] He observed, "If we do not see a story in the newspapers (or catch it on radio or television), it effectively has not happened so far as we are concerned."[30] He asserted that "the press is a significant part of the public audience for foreign policy."[31]

Some reporters contend that their job "is to perceive and point out the main directions of policy, or even the failings of policy."[32] Walter Lippmann noted that a reporter's "opinion is in some vital measure constructed out of his own stereotypes, according to his own code, and by the urgency of his own interest. He knows that he is seeing the world through subjective lenses."[33] This observation was confirmed by Cohen: "It is hard to find a reporter who carries the myth of objectivity to the point of erasing or denying his own policy preferences."[34] Thus, Lippmann and Cohen contend that the pictures and words put forth by print or broadcast journalists relate to perceptions and perhaps to subsequent foreign policy.

A reporter's perception has a direct effect on public opinion, which, in turn, can influence a policymaker's actions and decisions. George Christian recalled President Lyndon Johnson's distress upon hearing the following remark about the Vietnam war in 1968 from Walter Cronkite: "It is increasingly clear to this reporter that the only rational way out [of Vietnam] then will be to negotiate." Christian stated, "Because of Cronkite's credibility, [and] because of his perceived influence on the public, [Johnson's] reaction was that if he had lost

27. "God of Steel," *G. I. Combat,* 29(22):1-8 (Oct. 1980).

28. Interview with Jerome Stanley, NBC-TV, Burbank, CA, 14 July 1980.

29. Bernard C. Cohen, *The Press and Foreign Policy* (Princeton, NJ: Princeton University Press, 1963), p. 13.

30. Ibid.

31. Ibid., p. 253.

32. Ibid., p. 27.

33. Lippmann, *Public Opinion*, pp. 271-72.

34. Cohen, *Press and Foreign Policy,* p. 74.

Cronkite [he had] probably lost the public, and I think what he meant was that there was no turning back as far as bolstering public opinion, that [public support] could not be recaptured."[35]

Christian also said that television coverage "had a terrific impact on President Johnson, I know that. I think press coverage in general tended to close some options for him he might have had otherwise. . . . And, I think, [television] probably precipitated some of the actions he took." He added, "In terms of which influence in the media was the most pervasive on national policy during the period of Johnson's presidency, I'd say the *New York Times* probably was number one, and the . . . three networks probably ranked right behind that."[36]

Former Secretary of State Alexander Haig has cited one such perception. "During the Israeli invasion of Lebanon, . . . the [television] pictures seen in millions of American houses—including the white one at 1600 Pennsylvania Ave.—profoundly influenced U.S. policy. . . . pictures of Israeli forces pursuing what appeared to be a relentless war against Lebanese and Palestinian civilians, as well as the [Palestine Liberation Organization (PLO)] terrorists and their allies, engendered a groundswell of criticism here in the U.S. against Israel." To Haig, this coverage was "a concrete example of how America's foreign policy was directly affected by the pictures that TV news brought into our homes night after night."[37]

Correspondents necessarily deliver their own perspective of an event or situation. For example, Garrick Utley, a correspondent in the Sinai after the first major battle in October 1973, appeared on the *Today* program. Utley, who was wearing a battle jacket with "Utley" stitched over one pocket and "NBC NEWS" over the other, appeared with the Israelis. The camera revealed Israeli soldiers praying quietly in trenches on the Sabbath. Conversely, we saw Egyptians waving guns in the air and yelling, "Allah akhbar!"

Bias in television network pictures was clearly documented in a series of *TV Guide* articles on Palestinians and Israelis in October 1981. *TV Guide* reviewed nightly newscasts from the 10 months from July 1980 through April 1981 and found that

> there were 38 reports of raids on Palestinian targets in southern Lebanon. Only three of these reports—for a total of one minute, ten seconds—showed pictures of the effects of the Israeli attacks. None showed any Palestinian victims. On the other hand, 11 included pictures of Israeli victims, and the filmed reports totaled some 17 minutes.[38]

Patricia Karl, a specialist in Middle Eastern affairs, noted that although television pictures never showed Palestinian victims, neither did articles in the *TV Guide*. Readers saw only a picture of two Palestinian soldiers.[39] Karl also faulted the *TV Guide* reporter's use of language. When Palestinians were attacked, the reporter tagged them "targets," implying that military areas were being hit. When Israelis were attacked,

35. George Christian, in his appearance on *CBS Morning News*, 26 Apr. 1985.

36. Ibid.

37. Alexander Haig, "TV Can Derail Diplomacy," *TV Guide*, 9 Mar. 1985.

38. John Weisman, "Blind Spot in the Middle East: Why You Don't See More Palestinians on TV," *TV Guide*, 24 Oct. 1981.

39. Patricia Karl, "In the Middle of the Middle East: The Media and U.S. Foreign Policy," in *Split Vision*, ed. Edmund Ghareeb (Washington, DC: American Arab Affairs Council, 1983), p. 293.

the "state of Israel," a civilian area, was referred to by the reporter.[40]

Reporters often use the label "Islamic terrorists," forming a perception in the public's mind that all Muslims are terrorists. Yet, as Karl pointed out, the Baader-Meinhof gang are not tagged "Christian terrorists."[41] As Mark Twain said, "The difference between the right word and the almost-right word is the difference between lightning and the lightning bug."

Journalists—among them Philip Geyelin of the *Washington Post*, Bob Adams of the *St. Louis Post-Dispatch,* and William L. Chaze and John Barnes of *U.S. News and World Report*—equate Lebanese with terrorist in such sentences as Adams's "Israel has responded by declaring a curfew in south Lebanon's villages and destroying homes where terrorists are believed to live."[42] Programs on the three major television networks and articles in *U.S. News and World Report* paint as terrorists the Lebanese in occupied Lebanon who fight those who control their land. Palestinians living on the Israeli-occupied West Bank, when they are engaged in any conflict with Israelis, are also called terrorists.[43] Former President Jimmy Carter observed that "there is a stigma attached to Palestinians by many Israelis because [the Palestinians are] equated with terrorists. . . . This is obviously one of the obstacles before us."[44] The *Middle East International* reported:

> Scores of Shiite Moslems have been killed during raids on villages in South Lebanon. Several times the Israeli Army has invaded a village and then later withdrawn claiming to have killed 20 or 30 "terrorists." It is only when the bodies are inspected afterwards that so many "terrorists" turn out to be young girls or old shepherds or families trying to flee by car.[45]

Why label Palestinians and Lebanese terrorists? Are they not repelling the soldiers of an illegal occupying force? A Shiite Amal party leader, Abu Hassan, has asked, "Who are the terrorists, [we] or the Israelis? Who has gone into whose country and destroyed whose homes?"[46] Journalists do not label citizens of Afghanistan who fight to rid their land of Soviet invaders terrorists. Why the double standard?

Why is Israel tagged "our only friend" in the Middle East? Conversely, Arab nations are labeled "radical" or "moderate." A State Department or Foreign Service employee concentrating on Arab nations is called an "Arabist." What does "Arabist" connote? Is a government employee on the Israeli desk tagged "Israeli-ist"?

Buzzwords are taken so much for granted that we neglect to question what they actually mean. In print and on air, they seem harmless, but they often carry subliminal messages. Why do our media

40. Ibid.

41. Ibid., p. 287.

42. See Philip Geyelin, "Terrorism Labels Confound Diplomacy," *St. Louis Post-Dispatch*, 6 Apr. 1985; Bob Adams, "Balancing Act in Lebanon," *St. Louis Post-Dispatch,* 3 Mar. 1985; John Barnes, "As Israelis Start Pullback from Lebanon," *U.S. News and World Report*, 4 Mar. 1985, p. 37; William L. Chaze with John Barnes, "Hopes Fading, Violence Rising in Mideast," *U.S. News and World Report*, 25 Mar. 1985, pp. 33-34.

43. Barnes, "As Israelis Start Pullback from Lebanon"; Chaze with Barnes, "Hopes Fading, Violence Rising in Mideast."

44. Jimmy Carter, "Inquiry: The Middle East," Interview by John Hanchette, *USA Today,* 4 Apr. 1985.

45. Editorial, *Middle East International* (London) no. 247, p. 2 (5 Apr. 1985).

46. Rod Nordland, "Israel's Troubled Exit," *Newsweek*, 18 Mar. 1985, p. 35.

perpetuate buzzwords, such as "Lebanese terrorist," "Palestinian terrorist," "Muslim terrorist," "Shiite terrorist," "Judea and Samaria," and "Yom Kippur War"? Journalists refer to the Yom Kippur War, which took place on the Jewish holy day of Yom Kippur, but the war also occurred during the Muslim holy season of Ramadan. Why do journalists ignore the Arab equivalent—the "Ramadan War"?

The labeling of a people, which terms like "Palestinian terrorist" accomplish, may have devastating results. Israeli journalist Uri Avneri wrote, "Some PLO were called 'terrorists,' but then it started being applied to all PLO members, be they diplomats, officials, physicians, nurses." Avneri explained that "when a journalist lends a hand to the dehumanization of an entire people, then the blood of those people can be spilt freely. We, the Jews, know this better than anyone else. Once a Jew is described as a 'terrorist,' he can be bombed, shelled, expelled and denied human rights and dignity."[47]

OWNERSHIP AND OMISSIONS

Stereotypes could affect news judgments. We rely mostly on a handful of sources: network newscasts, the Associated Press and the United Press International wire services, and the *New York Times* and the *Washington Post* news agencies. If one major news organization exploits a stereotype, the chances are that others may do the same. Consider that "the judgments of importance [are] made by a comparatively few people, especially in the news agencies."[48] We should be concerned about "the potential influence and great responsibility [that] rest in just a few hands."[49]

Media ownership is becoming more concentrated. Only 50 corporations control most of our print and broadcast media. Over half the $7 billion in book sales for 1980 was received by 11 firms. A mere 10 corporations have over half the audience for commercial radio. Only 20 newspaper chains now control more than half of the daily newspaper sales. Of all newspapers, 98 percent are the only newspapers in their communities. Just over 50 percent of the annual magazine sales are credited to a mere 20 corporations.[50]

These data lead to Charles Rembar's thesis that "our press is obviously controlled by the people who own it."[51] There exists the possibility that a few owners will exert their personal political perspectives on the majority of the media. "The American press," noted Frances Fitzgerald, an author who contributes frequently to the *New Yorker,* "has no obligation to tell the truth about anything. . . . Nothing prevents a publisher [or broadcaster] from buying a newspaper [or magazine, or television or radio station] and turning it into a vehicle of political propaganda for one side or the other."[52] The *New Republic,* for instance, is totally predictable in its unquestioning defense of Israel. "Criticism of Israel is a 'no-no'," said a contributing editor, Ronald Steele. Former contributor Christopher Hitchens accused owner and editor in chief Martin

47. Uri Avneri, "What Is a Terrorist?" *Haolam hazeh*, 4 Aug. 1982.

48. Cohen, *Press and Foreign Policy*, p. 131.

49. Ibid., pp. 131-32.

50. See Ben Bagdikian, *The Media Monopoly* (Boston: Beacon Press, 1983), chap. 1.

51. Charles Rembar, quoted in "Can the Press Tell the Truth," *Harper's*, 270(1616):37-41 (Jan. 1985).

52. Frances Fitzgerald, quoted in "Can the Press Tell the Truth," *Harper's*, 270(1616):37-41 (Jan. 1985).

Peretz of having an "obsession with conservatism in one country (Israel) [that] has infected the whole magazine."[53]

The United States probably has the freest press of any society, but there are nonetheless some constraints. Constraints may come from policymakers when they try to promote an image in order to gain policy support from the public. An example is provided by the role of Robert Kintner, the former president of the NBC network, a member of the White House staff. As secretary to the Cabinet he advised President Johnson on press coverage of the Vietnam war. John Chancellor has noted that "Kintner . . . chastised his former network [NBC] for . . . its airing of sensational stories rather than political news on Vietnam." Kintner told Johnson that all it took to alter the coverage was "just a conversation between the head of NBC News and the person who gave him his job." Chancellor states, "There is no indication that such a talk ever took place, but there is no indication, either, that Johnson would have objected to pressure being put on a network.[54]

The omission of information may form false perceptions. Former President Carter has given the following example:

> We hear the Israeli position in our country quite consistently, and we rarely hear the countervailing arguments. Any time you present to the public, as accurately as possible, the policy of Syria, or the Palestinians in particular, it's almost inevitable you're going to be accused of being anti-Israel.[55]

Correspondent Georgie Ann Geyer found that if she wrote rationally on the Palestinian question and criticized Israel's treatment of the Palestinians, she was labeled an anti-Semite. An Israeli government news agency officer told her, "We've been watching you as you went around the Arab world. You certainly are an Arab lover."[56]

"In June 1982, Israel invaded to drive the PLO out. . . . More than 500 Israelis died; more than 240 U.S. Marines . . . were blown up," wrote journalist Bob Adams. As for Lebanese casualties, Adams simply stated, "Thousands of Lebanese were killed."[57] In fact, however, statistics reported by the Lebanese police to the *Christian Science Monitor* reveal a far more tragic, accurate account. Casualties occurring "between June 4 and August 31, 1982, a period ranging from the first Israeli bombing raids until completion of the Palestinian withdrawal, [were] 19,085 . . . killed and 30,302 . . . wounded. In Beirut alone 6,775 died—84% of them civilians—so the police reported."[58]

The *Oakland Tribune*, the *Chicago Sun-Times*, and the *Detroit Free Press* on 5 May 1984 all printed an Associated Press report out of Jerusalem that

> Israeli officials rejected what is believed to be the first public PLO offer for mutual recognition and direct negotiations on the future of the Israeli occupied West Bank. [But] the Israeli officials . . . reaffirmed Israel's longstanding refusal to recognize the Palestine Liberation Organization, calling it a terrorist organization.

The *New York Times* neither reported this initiative of Arafat's nor had any comment on it.

53. Jane Meyer, "The New Republic," *Wall Street Journal*, 6 Mar. 1985.
54. John Chancellor, "LBJ's Losing Battles," *Washington Journalism Review*, p. 64 (May 1985).
55. Carter, "Inquiry."
56. Georgie Ann Geyer, "The Middle East Conundrum," *Quill*, pp. 10, 12 (Feb. 1983).
57. Adams, "Balancing Act in Lebanon."
58. George W. Ball, *Error and Betrayal in Lebanon* (Washington, DC: Foundation for Middle East Peace, 1984), p. 47.

"There is no such thing as public opinion," wrote Winston Churchill, "there is only published opinion." Churchill's words are as true today as they were four decades ago: the press decides whose opinions will be heard and in what context.

PRECONCEIVED IMAGES AND POLICYMAKERS

The Federal Bureau of Investigation's ABSCAM ruse was a success, in part, because policymakers had a negative perception of Arabs.

Historically, perceptions have played a role in policymaking, as international affairs scholar Robert Jervis has pointed out. "People often preserve their images in the face of what seems in retrospect to have been clear evidence to the contrary. We ignore information that does not fit, twist it so that it confirms ... our beliefs, and deny its validity."[59] For example, John Foster Dulles accepted information—such as evidence of economic failure—about the USSR that conformed to his image of the country, but he required overwhelming evidence before he would seriously consider information that contradicted his views.[60]

When policymakers do not initially perceive evidence as conforming to their views, "they often explicitly interpret it as compatible with their beliefs. Dulles interpreted a Soviet troop cut not as evidence of softening Soviet intentions, but as the response of a hostile nation to economic difficulties."[61]

59. Robert Jervis, *Perception and Misperception in International Politics* (Princeton, NJ: Princeton University Press, 1976), p. 143.

60. Ole R. Holsti, David Finlay, and Richard R. Fagen, *Enemies in Politics* (Chicago: Rand McNally, 1967), p. 86.

61. Jervis, *Perception and Misperception in International Politics,* p. 145.

Harold Isaacs has noted that "events are shaped by social forces that are normally much larger and more powerful than any individual policy maker, but insofar as policy makers do play a role, then their images of the people concerned (like their images of themselves and their own nation) have some part in the process."[62] He says that "great events can result from . . . 'mistaken' arrangements and images and ideas in the minds of men in power." Examples of such ideas include

> conceptions of Russia and the United States on which Hitler based his course, . . . the belief of certain American leaders in 1945 that Japanese fanaticism would outweigh Japan's loss of capacity to wage war, [and] the belief of British and French leaders that they could impose their will by force on Egypt in 1956. . . . the consequences of such "miscalculations" can be quite formidable.[63]

The noted American historian Howard K. Beale criticized the perceptions and consequent behavior of Theodore Roosevelt. Roosevelt's "persistence in regarding [the Chinese], because of military weakness and industrial underdevelopment, as a 'backward people' destroyed the effectiveness of his policy in the Far East."[64]

Concerning the Middle East, former Secretary of State Henry Kissinger has observed that American policymakers "missed the meaning of the evacuation of Soviet civilians from Syria a few days before the Arab attack on Israel in October 1973. . . . The [U.S.] government was certain that the Arabs were

62. Harold R. Isaacs, *Scratches on Our Minds* (New York: John Day, 1958), p. 405.

63. Ibid., pp. 401-2.

64. Ibid., p. 402.

too weak to contemplate starting a war."[65]

Common also are cases of outright refusal to believe reports that contradict a firm belief. Consequently, "when the secretary of the navy [Frank Knox] was told of the Japanese attack on Pearl Harbor, he said, 'My God, this can't be true. This [message] must mean the Philippines.' " It is significant that Knox's reaction was not that the report was incorrect, but that it must have been incorrect.[66]

"One of the cruel paradoxes of international politics is that those decisions which require the most serious consideration of alternative interpretations of reality" are often the ones most influenced by stereotypes. "Wisdom in our world consists of maintaining an open mind under such pressures, for a realistic assessment of opportunities and risks in one's relation with . . . [others] appears to be a necessary, if not a sufficient, condition for survival."[67]

CONCLUSION

When one ethnic or minority group is degraded, for whatever reason, we all suffer. Such degradation is influenced by the means of mass communications. For example, the racism that led to the internment of Japanese Americans during World War II was created partly by the motion picture industry, which for years typecast Orientals as villains, and partly by the press, especially the newspapers of William Randolph Hearst.[68] The yellow-peril hysteria and the stereotyping that helped produce that myth have, fortunately, retreated into history.

As of this writing the all-pervasive Arab stereotype remains. American culture appears to have absorbed the Israeli stereotype of the Arab. Israelis believe "that Arabs are overly emotional, uneducated and still living in the Middle Ages, untrustworthy, [and that they] are all desert shieks who are avaricious, oversexed, bloodthirsty and dictatorial."[69]

"A dangerous state of mind . . . pervades American thinking when it comes to the Middle East," noted correspondent Jeffrey St. John of the Columbia Broadcasting System (CBS). "To Americans, Jew or Gentile, the Arab world is an illiterate, dirty and impoverished part of the globe. In sum, we look on the Arabs the same way the West looked upon the wandering Jew a century ago: as a stereotype."[70]

Today's Arab stereotype parallels that of the Jews in pre-Nazi Germany, when newspapers and films made them dark and threatening. The characterization of Jews as anarchists or devious financiers was intolerable. Yet this caricature has been transferred to another group of Semites, the Arabs. Now it wears a robe and a headdress, instead of a *yarmulke* and a star of David. Sadly, it is still fashionable to be anti-Semitic—provided, these days, that the Semites are Arabs.

65. Ole Holsti, "Cognitive Dynamics and Images of the Enemy," *Al-akhbar,* 14 Oct. 1974.

66. Jervis, *Perception and Misperception in International Politics,* p. 145.

67. Holsti, Finlay, and Fagen, *Enemies in Politics,* p. 96.

68. The Japanese internment is discussed in Jacobus ten Broek, Edward N. Barnhart, and Floyd M. Matson, *Prejudice, War, and the Constitution* (Berkeley: University of California Press, 1954).

69. Indar Jit Rikhye and John Volkmar, *The Middle East and the New Realism* (New York: New York International Peace Academy, 1975), pp. 11, 15, 65, 70, 75.

70. Jeffrey St. John, *CBS Morning News,* 16 Oct. 1973.

When considering the possible influence of perceptions on foreign policy, we should note the words of Amnon Rubinstein. Writing of the tragedy of the Jewish people, he reminds us, "Every racist generalization, every attempt to deprive others of their rights, is to be deplored and condemned. When [Rabbi] Kahane trumpets in Acre: 'Shalom to the dogs!' and 'Even a dead Arab is scum!' and his followers in Gush Emunim remain silent and by that silence show their support, they are helping to keep alive the universal phenomenon of hatred of the stranger, a phenomenon of which we [Jews] have been the chief victims."[71]

The stereotype in popular culture, the news media's selection of pictures and words, the omission of information, the possible consequences of monopoly, and the preconceptions of policymakers combine to render grave distortions for us. The gravity is magnified when the receiver of the distortions is not only John Q. Public, but an under secretary at the State Department, or a strategist at the Pentagon, or a national security adviser to the president. How often have we heard high-ranking officials explain their understanding of a diplomatic development by saying that they do not know much more than what they have seen in the news?

Despite the elaborate network of intelligence gathering at their disposal, policymakers acquire information from and form opinions based on media messages. These messages carry with them great pressure to accept stereotyped images.[72] Thus the media's portraits of the people, issues, and events of the Middle East help prevent a realistic approach to the foreign policy needed to resolve the Middle East conflict.

71. Amnon Rubinstein, "Anti-Semitism in Reverse," *Palestine Perspectives*, p. 5 (Feb. 1985).

72. Holsti, Finlay, and Fagen, *Enemies in Politics,* p. 96.

* * *

QUESTIONS AND ANSWERS

Q (Joseph Ostroy, Long Beach, New York): I would like Dr. Shaheen's comment on two situations. The first is the Protocols of the Elders of Zion, which are notorious, stereotyping, vicious attacks upon Jews. These are distributed by Arab countries throughout South America and the world. The second is the addresses by the Arab delegates to the United Nations, especially a recent address that the United States protested, in which the delegate said that the Jews suck the blood of Arab children.

A: I am not aware of the instances you mention, but if indeed what you say is true, I deplore that as much as I would an attack on any individual and on any group. There is just no room for such attacks among civilized men and women in our society.

COMMENT (Bernadette Wimberley, Goldey Beacon College, Wilmington, Delaware): I have two items to add to Dr. Shaheen's collection of stereotypes. If the Arab is perceived to be lecherous and rich, the Turk is generally perceived as being very vicious and cruel. In the recent reworking of *Midnight Express* on *Cover Story*, Theodore Bikel in a Russian-accented English played a wonderful Turkish commandant who was locking up American teenagers merely for drug running. The other item that I particularly savor concerns plastic figurines representing crusaders that are being sold in a national chain of shops. All the Turks are black.

COMMENT (Shaheen): From time to time a television network will call me for advice. Let me share with you a telephone call that I received in the winter of 1984-85 concerning a certain program. First of all, Turks were perceived to be Arabs. It took me 15 minutes to convince the person with the network that the two groups are different, with different languages and different cultures. Then we proceeded to the story. The story had about eight Turkish villains and one Turkish good guy who had attended the University of Southern California. I spent at least 55 minutes trying to soften the Turkish stereotype.

COMMENT (Dario Scuka, Library of Congress, Washington, D.C.): In 1973 when the oil crisis occurred, I was in the forefront of the gathering and distribution of information. The first information that came out indicated that it was the Organization of Petroleum Exporting Countries (OPEC) that implemented the so-called Arab oil embargo.

I have been battling the largest number of editors of the major newspapers in the United States trying to explain to them that historically OPEC did not implement the oil crisis, but the success is very scant. OPEC is seen as the perpetrator of the embargo simply because OPEC came into the news earlier, in 1971. By the time of the oil crisis, the OPEC image or name was already in the media and was grabbed and never let go. The depth to which OPEC has been incorrectly identified with embargo is revealed by the U.S. Congress's passing of a law in 1976 concerning foreign trade. OPEC was identified in the law as the perpetrator of the embargo. That's how far we go with misinformation in the media.

Q (Cavan Hogue, Permanent Mission of Australia to the United Nations, New York City): I think the stereotypes of Middle Eastern peoples that you identified are accurate in terms of the sexual and the violent images and so on. But we can go back to the operas of Mozart, such as *The Abduction from the Seraglio*; we can go back to Shakespeare, who indeed probably did not distinguish between Othello the Moor and Shylock the Jew in many ways. Of course, we can go back to the Crusades and the terrible Turk. Stereotyping is part of a great tradition that is not particularly American or particularly contemporary. My question is, Do you see what you were describing as something new and different, or is it really just part of tradition?

A: I think that unfortunately humankind has a propensity—a cancer—that at differet times makes us want to pick on someone; so to that extent I think nothing is new. There were over 1000 motion pictures made concerning cowboys and Indians; there is a marvelous book called *The Hollywood Indian*. In many history books today, a conflict between the cavalry and Indians that the U.S. Cavalry won is called a "battle"; a conflict won by the Indians is a "massacre." What is new? First, I think there is a tremendous amount of apathy about the stereotype of Middle Eastern peoples. Second, I do not think we realize the pervasiveness of the stereotype or that we are really sensitized to it. I think it has become so much a part of our psyches that we have grown to accept it.

Report of the Board of Directors to the Members of the American Academy of Political and Social Science for the Year 1984

MEMBERSHIP

MEMBERSHIP AS OF DECEMBER 31

Year	*Number*
1974	19,473
1975	16,923
1976	15,516
1977	14,202
1978	12,816
1979	10,884
1980	10,059
1981	9,874
1982	9,536
1983	8,904
1984	8,856

PUBLICATIONS

NUMBER OF VOLUMES OF *THE ANNALS* PRINTED (6 PER YEAR)

1974	120,397
1975	104,049
1976	101,789
1977	91,367
1978	85,605
1979	71,513
1980	65,153
1981	69,313
1982	74,211
1983	68,236
1984	52,154

FINANCES

SIZE OF SECURITIES PORTFOLIO

MARKET VALUE AS OF DECEMBER 31

1974	371,004
1975	440,450
1976	504,046
1977	451,545
1978	385,795
1979	377,915
1980	368,926
1981	351,886
1982	390,119
1983	485,809
1984	384,312

NUMBER OF VOLUMES OF *THE ANNALS* SOLD (IN ADDITION TO MEMBERSHIPS AND SUBSCRIPTIONS)

1974	13,153
1975	13,034
1976	12,235
1977	6,296
1978	8,124
1979	5,907
1980	8,751
1981	5,884
1982	7,562
1983	5,877
1984	5,230

STATEMENT OF INCOME AND RETAINED EARNINGS FOR THE YEAR ENDED DECEMBER 31, 1984

Income	
Royalty–Sage Publications	$118,333
Sales of review books	1,544
Royalties and reprint permissions	4,553
Annual meeting revenue	9,598
Miscellaneous	7,087
Total Income	141,115
Operating Expenses	
Salaries	84,630
Payroll taxes	10,412
Pension expense	15,528
Employee benefits	2,027
Annual meeting expense	19,602
Depreciation	5,933
Insurance	2,565
Miscellaneous	17,166
Postage	2,276
Repairs and maintenance	5,015
Supplies	2,036

Telephone	2,860
Utilities	5,807
Total Operating Expenses	175,857
Loss from Operations	(34,742)
Other Income (Expenses)	
Investment income (net)	13,953
Gains (loss) on sale of investments	(94,826)
Grant administration overhead	8,350
Total Other Income (Expense)	(72,523)
Net Income (Loss)	(107,265)
Retained Earnings–January 1	408,129
Retained Earnings–December 31	$300,864

Report of the Board of Directors

During 1984, the six volumes of THE ANNALS dealt with the following subjects:

January *Paying for Culture*, edited by Patricia A. McFate, President, The American-Scandinavian Foundation, New York City.

March *Polling and the Democratic Consensus*, edited by L. John Martin, Professor, College of Journalism, University of Maryland, College Park.

May *The Future of American Unionism*, edited by Louis A. Ferman, Professor of Social Work and Research Director, Institute of Labor and Industrial Relations, The University of Michigan, Ann Arbor.

July *Gambling: Views from the Social Sciences*, edited by James H. Frey, Associate Professor, Department of Sociology, University of Nevada, Las Vegas; and William R. Eadington, Professor, Department of Economics, University of Nevada, Reno.

September *Deindustrialization: Restructuring the Economy*, edited by Gene F. Summers, Professor and Chairman, Department of Rural Sociology, University of Wisconsin, Madison.

November *China in Transition*, edited by Marvin E. Wolfgang, President, American Academy of Political and Social Science, and Professor, Department of Social Systems Sciences, Department of Sociology, and Law School, University of Pennsylvania, Philadelphia.

The publication program for 1985 includes the following volumes:

January *The Insanity Defense*, edited by Richard Moran, Associate Professor, Department of Sociology and Anthropology, Mount Holyoke College, South Hadley, Massachusetts.

March *Our Crowded Prisons*, edited by the National Institute of Corrections, U.S. Department of Justice, Washington, D.C.

May *The Welfare State in America: Trends and Prospects*, edited by Mayer N. Zald, Professor and Chair, Department of Sociology, and Professor, School of Social Work; and Yeheskel Hasenfeld, Professor and Associate Dean, School of Social Work, and Professor, Department of Sociology, The University of Michigan, Ann Arbor.

July *Religion in America Today*, edited by Wade Clark Roof, Executive Secretary, Society for the Scientific Study of Religion, Department of Sociology, University of Massachusetts, Amherst.

September *Soviet Foreign Policy in an Uncertain World*, edited by John J. Stremlau, Acting Director, International Relations, The Rockefeller Foundation, New York City.

November *Changing Patterns of Power in the Middle East*, edited by Thomas Naff, Director, Middle East Research Institute, University of Pennsylvania; and Marvin E. Wolfgang, President, The American Academy of Political and Social Science, and Professor of Sociology and Law, University of Pennsylvania, Philadelphia.

During 1984, the Book Department published approximately 250 reviews. The majority of these were written by professors, but reviewers also included university presidents, members of private and university-sponsored organizations, government and public officials, and business professionals. Over 575 books were listed in the Other Books section.

Forty-two requests were granted to reprint material from THE ANNALS. These went to professors and other authors for use in books in preparation and to nonprofit organizations for educational purposes.

MEETINGS

The eighty-seventh annual meeting, which was held on April 27-28, 1984, had as its subject *China in Transition* and continued the tradition of our gatherings with respect to the diversity of organizations represented by delegates, the size of the audiences and the interest displayed. Thirteen embassies sent official delegations, as did nine United Nations missions and ten states, cities, and agencies of the federal government. Delegates were also sent by 103 American and foreign universities and colleges and 47 international, civic, scientific, and commercial organizations. More than 180 persons attended one or more sessions.

The theme of the eighty-eighth annual meeting, held April 26-27, 1985, at the Bellevue Stratford Hotel, Philadelphia, was *Changing Patterns of Power in the Middle East*. The November 1985 volume of THE ANNALS contains the papers presented at the meeting.

OFFICERS AND STAFF

The Board reelected the following officers: Marvin E. Wolfgang, President; Richard D. Lambert, Vice-President; Randall M. Whaley, Secretary; Elmer B. Staats, Treasurer; Henry W. Sawyer, III, Counsel. Reappointed were: Richard D. Lambert, Editor, and Alan W. Heston, Associate Editor. The following Board Members were reelected for a three-year term: Lloyd N. Cutler, Randall M. Whaley, Elmer B. Staats, and Thomas L. Hughes. Three new Board Members were elected for a three-year term: Henry W. Sawyer, III, William T. Coleman, Jr., and Anthony J. Scirica. Covey T. Oliver resigned due to attainment of retirement age.

Respectfully submitted,

THE BOARD OF DIRECTORS

Elmer B. Staats
Marvin E. Wolfgang
Lee Benson
Richard D. Lambert
Thomas L. Hughes
Randall M. Whaley
Lloyd N. Cutler
Henry W. Sawyer, III
William T. Coleman, Jr.
Anthony J. Scirica

Philadelphia, Pennsylvania
1 September 1985

Book Department

PAGE

INTERNATIONAL RELATIONS AND POLITICS

GILMORE, WILLIAM C. *The Grenada Intervention: Analysis and Documentation.* Pp. 116. New York: Facts on File, 1984. No price.

This slender volume is well worth knowing. Dispassionately prepared by a lecturer in public international law at the University of Edinburgh who once lived in the Caribbean area—having been a lecturer in law at the University of the West Indies in Barbados some years ago and actually there later at the time of the Grenada invasion—it also is well, even profusely, documented.

Although "warmly welcomed by the majority of the people of the Commonwealth Caribbean" and the people of Grenada itself "appear to have viewed the situation in much the same light," this multinational intervention was regretted, on the other hand, by Trinidad-Tobago, condemned by Guayana, referred to by Great Britain as an action uncalled for, and "deeply deplored" by the General Assembly of the United Nations 108 to 9, with 27 abstentions. The question considered here, however, is not these variations of opinion but "whether this action was justifiable in international law irrespective of the views of the people of the region."

After giving preliminary attention to the decolonization of Grenada; to certain developments following independence; and to the "anatomy" of this military intervention and the role of the United States in its genesis and execution, William C. Gilmore analyzes systematically the principal "justifications" offered by participants, namely, that the intervention (1) was in keeping with Article 8 of the treaty establishing the Organization of Eastern Caribbean States; (2) was needed to protect U.S. nationals residing on the island; and (3) was invited by Grenada's head of state, Governor General Sir Paul Scoon.

After a careful—and what Gilmore considers a sympathetic—analysis of each justification, he concludes that "although too short a time has elapsed . . . for the full factual background to have come to light," and "without calling into question the stated motivations of the interested states," there remain "serious reservations" regarding "the legality of the use of force in this instance," inasmuch as "little attention appears to have been paid to considerations of international law in advance."

Almost all the 326 footnotes refer to other studies or to textual documentation, approximately a third of the volume being given over to appended texts. These texts, some of which appear in full and some in part, include the treaty establishing the Organization of Eastern Caribbean States, declarations, memoranda of understanding, diplomatic notes, prime ministers' addresses, and press releases, all of Caribbean origin and reference, plus the pertinent resolutions of the United Nations General Assembly and Security Council.

Like some other writers, especially today, Gilmore tends to think and write "socialist," or "leftist," for "Communist." This confusion in terminology overlooks, consciously or unconsciously, significant variations in objectives, techniques of gaining power, and tenacity in holding on to it.

The Grenada incident is then treated principally as an isolated phenomenon, the larger geopolitical implications being realized but neglected. However, is the primary limitation of this quite scholarly and legally well-grounded study perhaps that of international law itself, in that the latter has not yet undertaken to deal with a geopolitical situation of the precise type involved here? That is, with a situation where a totalitarian government has come into power by way of a coup, followed by internecine strife among the new leaders, violence, civilian casualties, and the execution of the newest acting chief executive and several of his ministers, its leaders nevertheless all imbued with an imported political ideology and materially aided, on a day-to-day basis, by foreign collaborators from different countries but of the same political persuasion? And, in addition, all possessed of missionary zeal in propagating, in any way possible, inside and outside the country, this secular gospel? With correspondingly hostile intent, and either potentially—as in this case—or actually hostile action—as in other areas currently—toward neighboring countries with differing political structures? In other words, not yet undertaken to deal with a multinational civil war of extranational character?

DONALD PIERSON

Fruitland Park
Florida

GONG, GERRITT W. *The Standard of "Civilization" in International Society*. Pp. xvi, 267. New York: Oxford University Press, Clarendon Press, 1984. $37.50.

The transition from an international society based on European notions of civilized society to a global society of modern nation-states involved the collapse of the European imperialisms, the rise of non-European superpowers, and the revolt against white by colored peoples. In the creation of this world system, the concept of the standard of "civilization" in international law, according to Gerritt Gong, influenced the confrontation between European and non-European societies in the nineteenth and early twentieth centuries.

Distinguishing members from nonmembers, the standard of civilization shaped international society, itself measured by common values and practices. The standard of civilization regulated interaction between Europeans and non-European societies, justifying colonialism and fostering resentment among the subjugated. A liberal vision, the standard consisted of five elements, as delineated by Gong: (1) protection of life, liberty, property, and freedom to travel, trade, and practice religion; (2) organized and effective political bureaucracy; (3) adherence to European international law; (4) regular diplomatic interchange; and (5) compliance with so-called civilized social practices, like the prohibition of polygamy and slavery.

The need to protect life, liberty, and property in non-European areas as the Europeans expanded their dominion led to the standard's codification in treaties and law texts. Imposing European rights to trade, travel, and proselytize as well as non-European adherence to international law and diplomacy, the standard of civilization also revealed European *noblesse oblige* and self-confidence. At the same time, the inclusion, between 1895 and 1905, of the United States and Japan among the civilized and the increased secularization within European societies contributed to the standard being made explicit in universal principles.

Yet, why did non-European nations surrender to the European standard? As Gong argues in surveys based on secondary sources of Russia, the Ottoman Empire, Abyssinia, China, Japan, and Siam, non-European adoption of and accommodation to the European prescription for civilized society was pragmatic, a means to preserve their own survival and independence.

Today the concept of the standard of civilization has disappeared from international law. Most nations, Gong claims, now conform to the old standard. Moreover, the concept's biases against the Third World and its abuses by nonliberal European nations in this century undermined its credibility. Nonetheless, having provided secular principles for expanding international law's domain, the standard has given way to the imperative for more general criteria of nondiscrimination, such as human rights.

Finally, Gong's argument exaggerates the power of legal concepts. More likely, the notion of the standard of civilization reflected the changing power structure of international society itself. What shaped this structure involves important questions, neglected by Gong, about the meaning and sources of modernization and about the economic and political bases of relations between nations.

JOEL D. WOLFE

Georgetown University
Washington, D.C.

PAYNE, JAMES L. et al., *The Motivations of Politicians*. Pp. 214. Chicago: Nelson-Hall, 1984. $22.95. Paperbound, $9.95.

How incredibly helpful it would be to know what motivates politicians. Whenever one looked at or thought about President Reagan, Chairman Gorbachev, or their local councilperson, it would be of great comfort and even relief to have profound insights as to why they are behaving in a particular manner. In *The Motivations of Politicians* the five authors propose to unlock this mystery for us.

This is a very perplexing book. It is a good read, utilizing interesting snapshots of various political types—which the authors characterize in terms of the "incentives" that drive politicians—and it does take on a big issue. However, the efforts fall far short of clarifying matters. In fact, I found it for the most part to be disappointing.

The authors have identified five of the more common types of personal incentives that, based upon 15 years of research, they believe are found in politicians. These incentive types are: "status, program, conviviality, obligation, and game." To these essentially Western, developed types the authors add the "mission" and "adulation" varieties as "foreign" modes. Perhaps their most interesting and useful observation is that in most instances politicians tend to be solidly one type and not a mixture of numerous ingredients.

I am quite bothered by the primary assumption that undergirds the work. The authors have decided, without arguments to sustain this belief, that politics is psychology. That is, these incentives that motivate particular politicians determine what policy agendas will be created, which agenda choices will be made, and how they will be carried out. This grand reductionist schematic of politics must be demonstrated through more than what the authors provide, which is virtually nothing at all. To dismiss Plato, Madison, and Marx without benefit of discussion is simply bad form and poor argument. To have rendered the pursuit of interests and goals through the reduction of behavior to a sort of character analysis cannot be accepted on its face value. I found the entire work to be very vulnerable to the criticism that it is just too conceptually thin and distorting to be of much validity.

CARL F. PINKELE

Ohio Wesleyan University
Delaware
Ohio

SEDERBERG, PETER C. *The Politics of Meaning: Power and Explanation in the Construction of Social Reality*. Pp. xiii, 294. Tucson: University of Arizona Press, 1984. $22.50.

Peter C. Sederberg has written a solid, well-organized book around a straightforward thesis. The basic assumption is that meaning is embodied in response. Thus, political communities are groups of individuals who share mutually expected responses to political stimuli. Politics, then, is perceived as the deliberate attempt to control the shared meanings of political communities. From this perspective, Sederberg devotes a chapter to analyzing each of the following topics: the philosophy of social science, conflict, coercion and utopia, organization, leadership, freedom and order, and the entropy of meaning in today's politics and what this portends for the political future. The utilization of Sederberg's thoughtfully developed framework produces some thought-provoking results. But, as is always the case with a book of such wide scope, each reader will find weaknesses in this or that chapter according to his or her area of expertise. I will concentrate on some potential sources of disappointment.

First, the title of the book can mislead the reader by raising the false hope of a comprehensive discussion of "meaning." But this is not the case. We are simply told that individuals construct their own particular meanings of reality within the parameters of a field of possible responses. Exact responses cannot be predicted. Thus the meanings of various political events within and between political communities are never completely commensurate. Stated another way, all political communities exhibit varying degrees of instability and require different degrees of coercion to hold them together. This work could have benefited greatly by devoting a chapter to an analytical discussion of "meaning," to provide the theoretical warrant for the choice Sederberg made in his use of the concept.

Another source of disappointment is that a book with such great potential for theoretical excitement is really rather tortuous reading. There are two reasons for this. First, the book is unnecessarily jargon laden. Second, all too often Sederberg's theoretical discussions are devoid of concrete examples.

On balance, though, Sederberg's book is worth reading, and he is to be commended for assembling a book that does shed some new light on topics of perennial interest to political theorists. I recommend it for both professionals and students.

THOMAS J. MORTILLARO

Nicholls State University
Thibodaux
Louisiana

SNYDER, LOUIS L. *Macro-Nationalisms: A History of the Pan Movements.* Pp. xii, 308. Westport, CT: Greenwood Press, 1984. $35.00.

This rather obscure title should not confuse the intelligent layperson about an uncommonly interesting and well-written book. Admirably free of the usual social science double-talk jargon, *Macro-Nationalisms* presents an astonishing amount of information about transnational political and social movements around the world: Pan-Slavism, Pan-Germanism, Pan-Europeanism, the Pan-Turkish movements, Pan-Islamism, Zionism, Pan-Asianism, Pan-Americanism. All these movements have been attempts to go beyond nationalism as we think of it in our times, and to break out of the usual geographical boundaries toward the creation of a larger and more inclusive organization.

And yet, without exception, all such movements have so far either foundered, or at least failed to accomplish their stated goals. The culprit has been nationalism, which just about anyone who has thought seriously about the matter has to conclude is one of the greatest evils afflicting modern society.

Nationalism is usually considered to have started with the French Revolution and with Napoleon's marauding armies, which provoked savage resistance wherever they went. This is the kind of nationalism to which we object with seeming futility and that, with our European cultural blinders, we project in catastrophic error onto the rest of the world.

We are terribly mistaken to equate upheaval and dislocation in the non-Western world with the suicidal urges of the Western world. Nationalism in France and nationalism in China are not the same thing at all—and yet the appeal of nationalism, whether French or Chinese, is understandable. Ever since humans became social animals they have sought contact with those sharing common interests. They have sought security in a group; those outside were seen as hostile. Macro-nationalism failed to provide enough ties—whether geographical, political, economic, cultural, linguistic, psychological, or other kinds—to compete with nationalism. The astronomical acceleration of change arising out of science, technology, and communications in the last century only seems to have rooted nationalism more firmly. Can men find security in their new knowledge? Or are they condemned to continue falling into the patently false, even dangerous, oversimplifications of the fundamentalisms now sweeping the world?

The erudition that Snyder brings to this fairly short book is truly impressive. Spanning the globe as he does, I could not find even one generalization I cared to challenge.

JOHN F. MELBY

University of Guelph
Ontario
Canada

SPECTOR, LEONARD S. *Nuclear Proliferation Today*. Pp. xv, 478. Cambridge, MA: Ballinger, 1984. $25.00

CALDICOTT, HELEN. *Missile Envy*. Pp. 365. New York: William Morrow, 1984. $15.95.

Nuclear weapons proliferation spawns a seemingly endless number of books, commensurate with our justified concern. Spector's book deals with horizontal proliferation—that is, the increasing number of states possessing nuclear weapons—and Caldicott concerns herself with vertical proliferation—the superpowers' arms race.

Nuclear Proliferation Today is a very useful compendium, reviewing nuclear capabilities and motivations possessed by a number of states that have demonstrated unremitting resolve to achieve a nuclear weapons capability. Separate chapters are devoted to each of eight states—Argentina, Brazil, India, Iraq, Israel, Libya, Pakistan, and South Africa—in which the historical development of the state's nuclear capabilities are traced and current—as of the middle of 1984—assessments of skills and motivations are provided. Within this group of eight, some are clearly closer to having nuclear weapons than others. Spector feels that the most imminent proliferation threat resides in the Indian-Pakistan rivalry. India's explosion of a peaceful nuclear device in 1974 triggered a fervid determination in Pakistan to match the Indian achievement, and this effort may bear fruit soon. Spector claims that Israel and South Africa may already have a limited number of assembled or unassembled bombs "in the basement." The absence of any serious nuclear rival in either the Middle East—Iraqi and Libyan efforts have largely been thwarted to date—or Africa, however, is fortuitous. Finally, Brazil and Argentina each appear bent on obtaining full nuclear weapons capabilities, but they are at least a few years away from this achievement. Spector offers no new proof for all these assertions, but he has marshaled a strong case largely on the basis of a prodigious number of secondary sources.

The readers of *Nuclear Proliferation Today* may conclude, depending upon their own inclinations, that nonproliferation policies have produced a glass either half full or half empty. The popular press has emphasized the half-empty, highlighting the Israeli and South African cases and dwelling upon the potential for catastrophe elsewhere should these nations continue their quest for skilled manpower, sensitive nuclear facilities, and nuclear fuel. Nonproliferation policies to date have done nothing to eliminate the motivations these states have for acquiring a full nuclear weapons capability. On the other hand, Spector reminds us that there has been no new declared weapons state over the past 20 years—no mean feat—and that the nonproliferation treaty is still gaining adherents, albeit incrementally. More important, nuclear suppliers are increasingly becoming more restrictive, showing greater concern for proliferation risks in their export policies. And Spector asserts that the threat of sanctions by the United States and other countries in the event of a nuclear test explosion really is having a deterrent impact. Spector's good news-bad news assessment of the current situation may not satisfy those seeking simple, unambiguous policy conclusions, but it does nonetheless seem to reflect reality.

Spector offers no new policy intitiatives, as this book is intended to serve solely as a proliferation update. It does so admirably and provides a wealth of bibliographic material for the reader interested in going further.

Perhaps the less said about *Missile Envy,* the better. Caldicott is clearly a zealot arguing for the dismantlement of nuclear arsenals. Although many will argue, with some justification, that nothing short of zealotry is required to end the nuclear madness that confronts us, I seriously question whether the publication of this book helps rather than hinders the cause.

The book ostensibly deals with the basic forces that are driving the superpowers' arms race to increasingly higher and more dangerous levels. The forces—or culprits—Caldicott identifies are practically all on the American side, as the Soviets are seen as simply responding to American provocation. President Reagan and his administration are portrayed as warmongers busily planning a first strike against the Soviet Union; Caldicott even raises the bizarre notion that Reagan may have suffered debilitating strokes that now impair his thinking. She further identifies the insatiable U.S. imperialistic ethic manifest throughout the globe, the "rapacious greed exhibited by the military industries," and the "iron triangle" consisting of the Congress, the Pentagon, and the military-industrial complex. These we have heard of before; what is new is her linkage of sexuality with nuclear weapons policy. Caldicott asserts that typical male characteristics—for example, lack of emotion, a strong macho image—foster and sustain the arms race and that what is needed is the infusion of feminine—"nurturing"—influences and values.

There is no doubt that we need to be reminded of the untold horrors that would accompany nuclear war; that these deadly weapon systems are more than just chess pieces played across a global board; and that nuclear deterrence based upon bulging arsenals is an invitation to disaster. Caldicott's written attempt to convey this message is terribly flawed. Far more enlightening and compelling accounts can be found in the writings of Freeman Dyson and Jonathan Schell.

JACK BARKENBUS

Oak Ridge Associated Universities
Tennessee

AFRICA, ASIA, AND LATIN AMERICA

BALMORI, DIANA, STUART VOSS, and MILES WORTMAN. *Notable Family Networks in Latin America.* Pp. vii, 290. Chicago: University of Chicago Press, 1984. $27.00.

The family has been an important unit of analysis for historians of Latin America for at least a decade. What is novel about the present work is that a theoretical focus on the "notable family network" is provided to integrate the growing number of case studies on the marriage strategies, investment patterns, and political participation of Latin America's prominent families.

Family has been important in Iberian culture at least since medieval times, yet the notable family networks that arose in Latin America during the years 1750-1900, the period covered in this study, were a distinct historical phenomenon. They differed from prominent Latin American families of other times in their degree of cohesion "that allowed for concerted action and control at the highest levels of government." Furthermore, in defining the concept of the notable family network, Balmori, Voss, and Wortman challenge the truism in Latin American studies that extended family relationships operate on all layers of society. For Balmori and her coauthors, the extended family is the sine qua non of nineteenth-century notableness, whereas nonnotable families can only be described as households.

In this volume, the rise of the family networks in the 1750-1900 era is skillfully connected to changes in the nature of Spanish rule in Latin America and changes in the international economy. Due to Bourbon attempts to modernize their Latin American colonies in the mid-1700s, thousands of Spanish immigrants streamed into the region. Tensions arising from Latin America's economic awakening contributed in large part to successful independence bids by nations in the region. After independence, the family networks filled the power vacuum left by the collapse of Spanish colonial institutions and the weakening of the Catholic church, which had been the region's preeminent banker.

Balmori, Voss, and Wortman support their premises in case studies tracing the rise of family networks through three generations in diverse locations: Guatemala City, provincial Northwest Mexico, and the pampas region around Buenos Aires. A typical pattern is discerned in which the first-generation member, a Spanish immigrant merchant, marries into an established creole family in the same business. By the second generation, the family has developed a thriving import-export firm, tied to hacienda or mining holdings. They also marry into other family networks whose economic activities diversify their own. Third-generation members marry within the network to consolidate family holdings. In addition, second- and third-generation members turn to public officeholding as a necessary key to maintaining family influence.

The notable-family-network concept is significant in offering a convincing explanation of much collective action in nineteenth-century Latin America. Usually this period is analyzed in terms of ideological struggles between liberals and conservatives, traditionalists and modernizers, or in terms of class struggles among various socioeconomic groups. Close examination shows that ideological or class lines do not hold up well, "and where they nominally existed, individuals and groups continually moved back and forth across them." The notable family network as the analytical unit makes the intergroup or interclass movements more comprehensible, inasmuch as allegiance to family goals was consistently more important than allegiance to any political party or ideology.

The notable family networks lost their hegemony in the fourth generation largely due to the new social forces generated by industrialization and the depression of the 1930s. Although the networks have lost their undisputed dominance, they remain influential. Understanding the extent of their power in the nineteenth century and that their zenith was a mere two generations ago makes more evident the challenge facing other groups seeking a share of economic and political power.

SHERRIE L. BAVER

The City College of New York

GOLDMANN, ROBERT B. and JEYARATNAM WILSON, eds. *From Independence to Statehood: Managing Ethnic Conflict in Five African and Asian States.* Pp. x, 225. New York: St. Martin's Press, 1984. $27.50.

Many nations in Africa, Asia, and Europe became independent during and after World War II, and they inherited the old boundaries established by the major colonial powers. The new governments of these countries presently are trying to develop into nations people of different races, tribes, religions, languages, and cultural backgrounds. The leaders found that kinship and loyalty to an ethnic group were more important to their constituents than nationhood, and each group strived to develop its own social and economic welfare. The result was ethnic conflict, which caused governments to create policies that would aid the economic and social progress of one group to the detriment of another.

Ethnic conflict is the subject of this book, *From Independence to Statehood: Managing Ethnic Conflict in Five African and Asian States,* which emanated from a consensus developed by consultation with academic and public officials from Africa and Asia. The writers focus upon the ethnic conflict in their respective nations and discuss the policies and programs that were designed to ease group tensions. The five African and Asian states are Nigeria, India, Malaysia, Tanzania, and Sri Lanka.

There are two chapters on Nigeria. The first one examines structural changes and the problem of national cohesion in Nigeria. The writer states that until this century, Nigeria was composed of multiple subcultures or communities that were rivals among themselves, and the tension among these groups and the emergence of a national government created problems of national cohesion. "Regardless of how people came together in the first place or were brought together, National Cohesion is simply an acknowledgement of the minimum need to resolve the problems of social existence." The structural changes in the 1979 constitution stipulated how national cohesion would assist in the mediation of conflicts and promote cooperation between groups. The constitutional structure of Nigeria is discussed in greater depth in the second chapter. Nigeria's political history has been plagued by ethnic tension. The writer recalls the 30-month civil war and the 13 years of military rule. The war settle one issue, that Nigeria would remain a single entity. The writer feels that the constitutional structure brought about increased participation in the government and the affairs of the country, and the federal character has gained acceptance by the people.

The third chapter deals with positive discrimination in India with reference to education. The policy of positive discrimination basically refers to provisions and programs that aim at direct intervention through a system of quotas and reservations, for individuals from groups formerly discriminated against, in public and private office, education, administration, and employment.

The fourth and tenth chapters concentrate on economic issues—employment, business, and land—in Malaysia. Riots fueled by economic frustrations resulted in the New Economic Policy, which aims to eradicate poverty and to restructure society to correct interethnic inequalities.

The fifth chapter is about the pursuit of ethnic equality through preferential policies. The writer defines ethnic equality, equality of results, equality of treatment, and preferential policies. "Ethnic equality" refers to equality of opportunity, where individuals are not discriminated against due to their religion, race, sex, birth, caste, or any other ethnic category. The writer discusses the affirmative action programs of the United States that were used to equalize the races. The proponents saw them as a goal; the opponents saw them as a system of quotas and preferences. In turning to an examination of India's ethnic minorities, the writer indicates that the Indian position supports group rights rather than individual rights. The Indian constitution contains articles against discrimination on the grounds of race, caste, sex, descent, place of birth, residence, or any combination of these.

The next chapter concerns Tanzania. The author analyzes the problem of unequal geographical distribution of economic opportunities in Tanzania, and an affirmative policy of equalization as a solution.

Sri Lanka is the subject of six chapters, which focus on the friction between the Tamils and Sinhalese. The range of topics is varied and includes the background of the ethnic rivalry between the two groups since their settlement of Sri Lanka; university admissions; government employment opportunities; resource allocation in Sri Lankan society; and the District Development Councils Law.

The final chapter returns the reader to India. The writer takes a look at India's experiment of providing political participation for that country's most depressed groups through a system of political reservations. Arguments pro and con are examined, and the author concludes that "the device of legislative reservations designed to redistribute political power as an aspect of social justice, in fact, operates as an 'efficient and inexpensive' means of social control."

Ethnic tension and conflict seem to be constantly exploding upon the world scene. The Sikhs' assassination of Indira Gandhi in India; the political violence between the Tamils and Sinhalese in Sri Lanka; and the Afghan rebels in Afghanistan are just some of the ethnic minority conflicts occurring throughout the world.

Ethnic conflict is the only idea that remains constant throughout this collection. The numerous individual chapters do not provide this book with the kind of thematic unity or organization found in most books. This book, although repetitious, does offer a readable and analytical insight into the origin of the ethnic tensions, and possible solutions to them. It is recommended reading for scholars in the fields of African and Asian studies who want to gain an understanding of one of the awful scourges of our century, ethnic conflict in selected states.

EDWARD L. JONES

University of Washington
Seattle

HAYES, LOUIS D. *Politics in Pakistan: The Struggle for Legitimacy*. Pp. viii, 203. Boulder, CO: Westview Press, 1984. Paperbound, $19.00.

Pakistan's contemporary political dilemmas and its failure, in nearly four decades of independence, to develop a viable political system enhance the timeliness and relevance of the central theme of this book. Louis Hayes argues that "Pakistan's political system has failed because the foundations of the state and the requirements of modernization have not yet been bridgeable by any institutional arrangements yet employed." In pursuit of this thesis, he devotes his first chapter to a series of definitions of the concepts of authority, legitimacy, political culture, values, political recruitment, modernization, secularization, and democracy. Although he returns to some of these concepts in his brief conclusion, most of the intervening pages are predominantly descriptive and historical.

The descriptive chapters are generally readable and interesting. They are not strictly chronological, but they cover familiar topics: historical developments leading to the creation of Pakistan, in chapter 2; Islamic politics, in chapter 3; constitutional changes, in chapter 4; foreign relations, in chapter 8; and political events during the periods of Ayub Khan, in chapter 5, Yahya Khan, in chapter 6, the Bangladesh War, in chapter 7, and Z.A. Bhutto, in chapter 9. The discussion of constitutional developments is a succinct and useful summary. Perhaps the most interesting portions of the book are those dealing with the Bangladesh War, where Hayes presents an account considerably more sympathetic to Pakistan than those found in most other works on the subject.

Chapters 8 and 9 deliver somewhat less than they promise. At the beginning of his chapter on foreign policy, Hayes writes that he "will not review foreign relations as such but will attempt to show how these relations and the consequences of them influenced the course of Pakistan's politics." What follows, however, is largely a review of foreign relations without the promised attempt to show their impact on domestic politics. On a somewhat different plane, the title of chapter 9, "Bhutto and Bonapartism," would lead one to expect, following Marx's original use of the concept of Bonapartism in his *Eighteenth Brumaire,* some discussion of the manipulation of the various social classes by such authoritarian leaders as Ayub, Bhutto, and Zia.

A further criticism might be leveled at the several overgeneralizations or questionable statements found throughout this book. We are told, for instance, that in India after 1857, "there would be no more pretense of gentlemanly cooperation and understanding between ruler and ruled." The heterodox Ahmadiyas are referred to as "radically orthodox." The claim that jute and cotton, as major cash crops in pre-1971 Pakistan, "were limited to the East wing" is true of jute but not of cotton.

This book provides an interesting review of Pakistan's politics. Although the Pakistan specialist will probably find it less satisfying than earlier works on the same subject by Sayeed, Ziring, or Burki, the general reader will find it a useful and readable account.

WILLIAM L. RICHTER

Kansas State University
Manhattan

HAYES, MARGARET DALY. *Latin America and the U.S. National Interest: A Basis for U.S. Foreign Policy.* Pp. xvi, 295. Boulder, CO: Westview Press, 1984. $23.50. Paperbound, $11.95.

This book is the result of a study undertaken by Margaret Hayes for the Office of Assistant Secretary of Defense, International Security Affairs. Hayes was charged with the task of assessing the importance of Latin America to U.S. security, with a view toward establishing new policies appropriate to coping with dramatically changing Latin American conditions. Students of Latin American politics will find this work useful for understanding both how the Defense Department has defined security issues in the past and how this agency might react to present security problems. Although the Defense Department is but one of many govenmental agencies that shape U.S. policy toward Latin America, its importance rests in the historical fact that military intervention has been one of the cornerstones of U.S. policy toward Latin America since 1898. One of the central issues of this work is whether the United States' promotion of Latin American economic growth should replace the increasingly politically indefensible reliance on military intervention as the main thrust of U.S. foreign policy toward this region. Suffice it to say that Hayes is a firm advocate of growth as the panacea for the region's problems.

The theme of growth as the road to salvation is laid out in chapter 1, "Latin America and the United States' National Interest." Here Hayes notes that the special linkage between the United States and Latin America should be employed to promote economic prosperity, as this prosperity would lead Latin Americans to realize that it is in their best interests to remain as voluntary partners of the United States. Chapter 2, "Latin America's Expanding International Economic Role," treats the increasingly important position of Latin American economies both as purveyors of raw materials and, most critically to me, as world-class debtor nations, whose debt load threatens to sink the entire international financial structure. In chapter 3, "The Caribbean Basin: Focus of Immediate Concerns," Hayes observes the obvious: every country in that region in the U.S. orbit is virtually bankrupt, most are consequently politically unstable, and all have the Cuban alternative model to contemplate. If there is a case for growth, it should emerge in chapters 4 and 5, which deal with Mexico and Brazil, respectively. Both countries epitomize the best of the growth philosophy realized in all of Latin America, and Mexico has achieved growth with the same government in power for more than 60 years. Both have pretensions to the economic and political status of a world power. Clearly, these nations have arrived on the world scene. But their arrival through growth has plunged them into staggering indebtedness, unemployment, and increasing political instability. Mexico has reached the point where one of its most consistent exports is that of Mexicans to the United States, a trend likely to intensify with each passing year. Ironically, these two chapters expose the notion of growth for what it is: a justification for international financiers to make money in the name of prosperity for all, regardless of social and political consequences for any nations and peoples involved in the process.

In this context, the concluding chapter, "Dimensions of U.S. Security Interests in

Latin America," is anticlimactic, insofar as it is concerned with the Soviet threat to the prospects of growth in Latin America. If growth has proved to be a flop in the best of cases, what is left other than the habitual military intervention? If we were to follow the arguments of this work, arguments not necessarily belonging to Hayes, we could conclude that the intervention in Grenada is only a sneak preview of what the Department of Defense has in mind for Nicaragua and El Salvador in the very near future.

EDWARD C. HANSEN

Queens College
Flushing
New York

WHITE, RICHARD ALAN, *The Morass: United States Intervention in Central America.* Pp. xi, 319. New York: Harper & Row, 1984. $14.95. Paperbound, $6.95.

A recurrent fear and question of many Americans is whether U.S. intervention in Central America will lead to another Vietnam and a war that cannot be won. Richard Alan White—a project director of the Third World Center for Social and Economic Studies in Mexico City and a senior research fellow at the Council on Hemisphere Affairs in Washington, D.C.—feels that the question has already been answered. Beginning with the last years of the Carter administration, the United States has increasingly intervened in Central America and has sought to end and prevent the takeover of leftist regimes that look to Cuba and the Soviet Union for support. Through its continued machinations the United States has already become directly involved in the civil wars spreading throughout the region. Although Washington has tried to hide its role with behind-the-scenes manipulations and covert military activities, it has failed, and the story of the United States' nefarious intervention is readily available for anyone to read. White has compiled largely from newspaper accounts and interviews the regionwide scope of the Reagan administration's role and its close association with the right-wing forces. With these forces trained by the U.S. military and with the clandestine support of CIA agents, the administration seeks to defeat the rebels in El Salvador and Guatemala and to overthrow the Sandinista regime in Nicaragua. Not content to dominate these three countries, the administration has pressured and blackmailed Honduras and Costa Rica to fall in with its plans. In trying to defeat the rebels in El Salvador, White argues, the same mistakes the United States made in Vietnam are being repeated. Even those lessons in counterinsurgency that the U.S. military did learn from the Vietnam experience have been largely wasted on the Salvadoran military so that the rebel forces with their superior tactics are slowly winning both the military struggle and the support of the population.

This compilation of newspaper and other sources is presented in the manner of a white paper to prove the failure and underhanded nature of the United States' not very secret intervention into the countries of Central America to stop the spread of so-called Marxist regimes. White makes no attempt to evaluate the material; he just accepts the reports of journalists and others without question. He makes no attempt to present or give any credence to the Reagan administration's fears and policies, and he passes over the role played by Cuba, the Sandinistas, and the Soviet Union in the region. White's book is a completely one-sided condemnation of practically every policy and action taken by the United States in the area. Like so much of the writing on Latin America in general, it is a highly emotional appeal on behalf of one side of the struggles in the Americas south of the border.

This volume could have been much more persuasive if White had carefully sifted and evaluated the evidence and had more objectively argued his position. There have already been enough emotional appeals in the press and statements of the governments involved. What is needed is a study that carefully evaluates the evidence and the arguments on both sides. Unfortunately this book is not that study, even though in it there is assembled a large body of material that could begin to serve as a basis for an objective analysis.

DAVID T. CATTELL
University of California
Los Angeles

YANSANÉ, AGUIBOU Y. *Decolonization in West African States with French Colonial Legacy, Comparison and Contrast: Development in Guinea, the Ivory Coast, and Senegal 1945-80.* Pp. xix, 540. Cambridge, MA: Schenkman, 1984. $34.50. Paperbound, $15.95.

This is a most important addition to the literature of decolonization and development in West African states. Aguibou Yansané takes three states, Guinea, the Ivory Coast, and Senegal, and examines their contrasting strategies after the retreat of direct French colonialism. All three were members of the French West African Federation, and Yansané sees many of their problems arising as a result of the balkanization that occurred after the Loi Cadre of 1956, promoted partly by Félix Houphouët-Boigny of the Ivory Coast, but mainly by the French. Both Senegal and Guinea would have preferred to remain part of a wider grouping, but they in turn differed in that Sékou Touré's Guinea did not accept the French constitution and the Community established between 1958 and 1960, whereas Senghor's Senegal did. Although the three territories shared a tradition of an authoritarian president inherited from the French Fifth Republic, the developmental models promoted by each were very different. Guinea, attempting full economic decolonization and largely cut off from its neighbors, pursued internal development somewhat akin to Julius Nyerere's concept of self-reliance, complete with rural collectivization. The Ivory Coast created a full-blown state capitalism, paying particular attention to the coastal urban areas, welcoming foreign investment in what Yansané describes as a pragmatic and evolutionary approach to decolonization. Senegal, inhibited by its monocultural economy, pursued African socialism in association with the free-enterprise system.

The Ivory Coast produced dramatic growth rates in the sixties and seventies, qualifying the territory for the title of miracle economy of West Africa, but the social cost was great, particularly for the precarious fortunes of the immigrant workers sucked in from the poorer territories to the north, for the neglected rural areas, and for the disadvantaged in the resulting urban sprawl of Abidjan and other coastal towns. Such a system promoted and exacerbated wealth differentials in a society heavily influenced by expatriates and foreign decision makers. Guinea's system produced a more genuine escape from neocolonialism, but with considerable attendant hardships to its population. Generalized poverty was merely redistributed; corruption, black-marketing, and speculation were rife, as were plots and attempted coups. Serious supply breakdowns were experienced, too. Senegal attempted a more open society, including, more recently, a multiparty system, but found it difficult to escape the buyers' control of peanut and oil seed prices. This country found itself with a high food import bill, and efforts to grow more millet and rice have been vitiated by the serious worsening of weather conditions since the late seventies.

Yansané sees each of the original development strategies as being modified by hard experience. The idealism of the sixties in Guinea gave way to economic realism in the late seventies. Both Senegal and the Ivory Coast have adapted their systems to changed circumstances and all have become more aware of the need for regional cooperation. It is in this area that Yansané reaches his rather optimistic conclusion. He is enthusiastic about the Economic Community of West African States, which brings together both Anglophone and Francophone territories and which in his view offers hope for regional development strategies, for fruitful relationships with world bodies like the World Bank and the International Monetary Fund, and for a route to more open societies paying greater attention to human rights.

Yansané is himself a Guinean, but national bias never shows. His exploration of developmental strategies is balanced, clear, and full of valuable data, including figures down to 1980-81. It is a brave scholar who makes predictions in the face of a fast-moving situation. Since he wrote, the world recession has deepened, the Sahel problem has reached terrifying proportions, there have been considerable political developments in West Africa, particularly in Guinea and the Ivory Coast, and the West African economies generally have been plunged into greater crisis. Yet this transparently honest and concerned work should remain standard reading for all interested in West Africa and in world development in general.

JOHN M. MacKENZIE

University of Lancaster
Bailrigg
Great Britain

EUROPE

ALBA, RICHARD D. *Italian Americans: Into the Twilight of Ethnicity*. Pp. ix, 182. Englewood Cliff, NJ: Prentice-Hall, 1985. $15.95.

Richard Alba has written an important book. He argues that the recent revival of ethnicity for Italian Americans and others notwithstanding, ethnicity has entered a twilight phase, one that may be perdu indefinitely, but one that bespeaks a weakened sense of ethnic identity. With clarity and precision Alba traces the history and sociology of Italian Americans over the course of the past century and concludes that whereas Italian descent was once a major impediment to inclusion in American social life, it is no longer such an obstacle. Offering a detached, scholarly view of his subject, Alba maintains that ethnic-revival protagonists have misread what in fact was taking place: structural assimilation.

World War II served as the turning point for Italian Americans as the generation coming of age in the immediate postwar period made remarkable strides in various walks of life, such as education and professionalism. Even though they remained somewhat behind the WASP group moving into the 1970s, the gap had narrowed so much that differences were minor or virtually nonexistent. Analysis of statistical data such as the U.S. census of 1980 and the General Survey Poll leads Alba to the conclusion that the mentality of Italian Americans with respect to questions on abortion, premarital sex, and various other social issues is either very similar to the WASP response or even more liberal when compared to major differences in attitudes of an earlier generation. Moreover, the differences that do exist in a few categories can be explained by the inclusion of older cohorts. But when one measures the younger cohorts of Italian Americans their responses to questions regarding interests, attitudes, and so forth show the same pattern other mainline groups show in the same geographic area. Even the famed attachments to the family—so celebrated in literature and visual media as well as sociological studies—has not stood in the way of greater acceptance and assimilation.

Of all the observations Alba makes about present-day Italian Americans, his pronouncement about intermarriage rates is most provocative. Whereas marriage between Americans of Italian descent and those of non-Italian background were in a distinct minority a generation or two ago, they now constitute the vast majority. When dealing with a 70 percent rate of intermarriage, can the twilight of ethnicity be doubted? With indications of an accelerating rate of intermarriage, can what remains be more than symbolic ethnicity, a nostalgic notion about one's national roots without much significance as a life-sustaining influence?

Alba's prediction of the imminence of a decline in ethnicity seems reminiscent of earlier prognostications by sociologists who had been so certain of ethnicity's disappearance that by midcentury hardly any serious thought was given to the topic. Although Alba is careful to proclaim the differences between earlier projections and his own, he does not entirely avoid the temptation to register his own predictions. For example, he indulges in a presumption when he pronounces the debilitation of ethnicity as an inevitable consequence of intermarriage. At the same time he admits that intermarriage of Italian Americans is of such recent vintage that few studies on the topic have been conducted; therefore deduction—rather than empirical, evidential, and measurable work—is the basis for his conclusions. What is called for is more serious research that clearly demonstrates a sharp decline of ethnic interest among Italian Americans of mixed ancestry. Interestingly, the U.S. census of 1980 records a remarkable degree of residential concentration of mixed-ancestry Italian Americans with those of single ancestry, leading to the conclusion that mixed marriages have not led to a drastic change in residential patterns.

But I do not wish to dwell on what might be missing from Alba's work. What Alba has produced makes a strong case for the dimming of ethnicity, a case that cannot be easily dismissed because it may be disturbing. Although he may have failed in successfully refuting theories of ethnic revival, by his forcible reminder that the moving spirit of the Italian American ethos is little different from that of WASPs, were are compelled to give this book serious consideration.

SALVATORE J. LAGUMINA
Nassau Community College
Garden City
New York

HEWETT, ED A. *Energy, Economics, and Foreign Policy in the Soviet Union*. Pp. xi, 228. Washington, DC: Brookings Institution, 1984. $28.95. Paperbound, $10.95.

This up-to-date analysis of Soviet energy production and use clarifies a complex situation in a very helpful way. Hewett shows how to answer the question, Is the USSR likely to reach out for Middle Eastern oil in the next five or ten years? He explains in a detached, realistic, technically informed way that the answer depends not just on Soviet crude oil output prospects, but on the output of Soviet natural gas and other fuels, on Soviet domestic energy consumption, and on Soviet energy exports to Eastern Europe and other parts of the world. For each issue, Soviet decision makers face policy options that will shape the overall outcome.

Building on the pioneering work of Robert W. Campbell, Hewett makes judicious use of Soviet technical literature to review the Soviet energy record since 1960 and examine its prospects through 1990. In the process he appraises the ability of the Soviet economy to react efficiently to changes in energy supply and demand conditions, and he offers cautious judgments about the range of likely developments. Hewett makes projections for 1985 and 1990 based on low and high estimates of production and consumption, suggesting that in 1990 the former will rise less than 20 percent and the latter more than 20 percent over 1980 levels. Despite an printer's error on page 179, Hewett's bottom line is that, for 1990, his low estimate of net exports is 30 percent below and his high estimate 50 percent above the 4.4 million barrels per day achieved in 1980.

Everyone concerned about Soviet energy prospects will benefit from—even while enjoying—Hewett's thoughtful analysis of the interlocked aspects of this situation. His conclusions may be summarized, in overly terse form, as suggesting that:

—Soviet energy output will not turn down in the 1980s;

—the USSR will be a net energy exporter through the 1980s;

—Soviet hard currency earnings from energy exports during the 1980s will be large, assuming that the world oil price rises and that imports by nations of the Council for Mutual Economic Assistance can be squeezed; and finally

—there is probably little that the United States can do to influence these developments.

HOLLAND HUNTER

Haverford College
Pennsylvania

UNITED STATES

BAXTER, MAURICE G. *One and Inseparable: Daniel Webster and the Union.* Pp. x, 646. Cambridge, MA: Harvard University Press, Belknap Press, 1984. $25.00.

This major new biography of Daniel Webster offers a fully rounded study of the Wester that Baxter calls "this extraordinary man." It covers the entire span of Webster's life and is notable for both its documentation in Webster's writings and its account of the events in which Webster participated.

Webster graduated from Dartmouth in 1801 and as a lawyer and congressman he followed the commercial interests of New England, supporting the Hartford Convention and opposing the War of 1812. But he gradually moved to the nationalism that would distinguish his public career, as he argued for the Bank of the United States, for Dartmouth College, and for Gibbons in *Gibbons* v. *Ogden* before the Supreme Court, where "he was in the first rank of those attorneys who shaped constitutional law." In Webster's dramatic debates with Robert Hayne in the Senate, from which the book's title is taken, he "made a solid case for constitutional nationalism."

Yet the focus of this book is on Webster's life in politics: in the House and Senate in Washington, as a friend of John Quincy Adams's administration, as a National Republican and a Whig, in his shifting relationships to Henry Clay, and in his unending pursuit of the presidency. Political as much as diplomatic aspects are emphasized when Webster served as secretary of state for John Tyler and concluded the Webster-Ashburton treaty with England. Always a conservative, Webster increasingly became a conciliator, opposing the annexation of Texas and the Mexican war and trying to avoid conflict over slavery. His efforts at conciliation, together with his unsurpassed oratorical skills, reached their apex in his speech on 7 March 1850 supporting Clay's great compromise, and they led to a Webster movement for president in 1852, just before his death.

There is much here on Webster's concern for improving his farms, his affection for Marshfield, and warm relationships with family and friends. His land speculation, mortgages, and personal debts, described in detail, defy accounting. And Webster is repeatedly faulted for "serious impropriety" and compromises of character as he served private interest in public office, as in his relations with the Bank of the United States.

Yet Webster's definition of "Liberty and Union" as one and inseparable, writes Baxter, was his supreme contribution to the nation. This outstanding study gives a heightened dimension to Webster's influence on the larger patterns of American development.

RONALD E. SHAW

Miami University
Oxford
Ohio

BOSWELL, THOMAS D. and JAMES R. CURTIS. *The Cuban-American Experience: Culture, Images and Perspectives.* Pp. xiii, 200. Totowa, NJ: Rowman and Allenhead, 1984. $36.50.

The presence in the United States of approximately 1 million Cubans, mostly of recent arrival, constitutes an important demonstration of a contemporary visible ethnic group that in and of itself warrants further study. This is the viewpoint of Boswell and Curtis as they argue that important aspects of this ethnic experience have not been treated within the admittedly growing literature on the subject. Theirs is an effort to offer a broad, systematic overview that incorporates ground previously covered and other aspects that have been neglected.

Analysis of demographic data reveals a few concentrated areas of Cuban Americans, with special emphasis on the Florida community. Thus Boswell and Curtis discuss the attraction of Florida as a result of its climate, along with considerations of proximity to the homeland and the awareness of an earlier migration already established in the Miami area. So dominant has the Cuban migration to this area been that the ethnic group now accounts for 60 percent of Miami's population and 40 percent of Dade County's population. A pattern of replacement of earlier groups in neighborhoods that were becoming depressed followed.

Cuban American politics was preoccupied earlier with ousting the Castro regime; the focus now is on adoption of U.S. citizenship and absorption into American politics. Unlike most Americans of Hispanic descent, Cubans identify largely with the Republican party. In the realm of religion, a small minority are adherents of Santeria—an Afro-Cuban cult—and larger minorities are members of various Protestant denominations; however, the majority are Catholics. In contrast to other Catholic immigrant groups who established their own national parishes, Cuban immigrants are more likely to be integrated into existing parishes. The success of this integration depends on the availability of Spanish-speaking clergy. With respect to family life patterns, Boswell and Curtis describe the traditional preference to respond to strong personal relations rather than impersonal ones such as those that characterize institutions. In this respect, Cuban Americans will have to adjust substantially in the environment of the United States. Boswell and Curtis also adumbrate the significance of the Spanish language to the maintenance and development of a Cuban American culture, describing how language forms the background for the proliferation of Cuban and Spanish-language radio and television programs, musical fare, and *bodegas,* those unique institutions that serve not only economic and grocery needs but also as social and communication centers.

With respect to the family, Boswell and Curtis stress the adjustment problems facing the Cuban immigrants, such as the question of dropping the use of the mother's family name in deference to that of the father, and the changing role of women in a society in which egalitarianism is pronounced. Indeed these dilemmas become particularly acute for second-generation Cuban Americans as they strive to straddle two cultures.

This study correctly acknowledges differences between non-Cuban Hispanics and Cuban Americans, who, unlike other Hispanics, seem well on the way toward social assimilation. It also distinguishes between patterns of European and Cuban immigration. Unfortunately the acknowledgement is not followed by a deeper analysis that, if provided, could be even more meaningful for comparative studies.

In sum, *The Cuban-American Experience* accomplishes what it set out to do—to provide the serious reader with an objective understanding of the multifaceted experience of this Latin group in our midst. Demonstrating a sturdy knowledge of the subject and a complete familiarity with extant studies in the field, Boswell and Curtis proffer a fine nonpolemical coverage of the subject.

SALVATORE J. LAGUMINA

Nassau Community College
Garden City
New York

COLE, DONALD B. *Martin Van Buren and the American Political System*. Pp. xiii, 477. Princeton, NJ: Princeton University Press, 1984. $45.00.

This important biography of an important man will be valuable to specialists, but it will not likely be bought by many others. Well written and lucid, it contains a magnificent bibliography, but it is priced at $45 and is as dry as its subject.

A teacher at Phillips Exeter Academy, Cole pursues the unsuprising theme that Van Buren was the chief architect of America's second two-party system, which he based on the already sanctified Virginia-New York axis. By exhaustive documentation, Cole carries the Sly Fox down the tortuous paths he followed to preserve that coalition during intensifying sectional disputes. Van Buren shifted from local interests to become a central character in the new nationalism but nevertheless maintained his allegiance to Jeffersonian principles of states' rights. He moderated Andrew Jackson's nationalism, mediated regional disagreements, and even after his 1848 Free Soil candidacy could not break with the South but clung instead to bankrupt ideas like popular sovereignty. Van Buren did everything after 1827 for his Democratic party, which Cole proves was a fragile, unreliable alliance.

But Van Buren does not come alive here. Cole admits that the man was uncolorful, despite his spicy nicknames. He was just about sinless, under perfect control in the face of *ad hominem* attacks, and all that could be said about his personality was that he was amiable. In a word, he was boring.

Although this book about him is not boring, neither is it exciting. It covers some of the greatest moments of our history matter-of-factly, without pizzazz. Cole analyzes the Van Buren historiography, sometimes to criticize other historians who more successfully made this man and his capers come to life in print. But this biography depicts Van Buren less as an interesting man and more as a cold statue, a symbol of democratic Northerners who shifted from agrarianism to industrial and urban concerns, or as a monument to the forlorn hope of patching over the bitterness leading to civil war. Even word pictures of his blonde hair turning white do not make Van Buren flesh and blood in this book.

Maybe nothing could. The man was dull, a characteristic that made him a loser in the eyes of both his contemporaries and historians, as author Cole correctly judges. But that fact, and the price, will likely make this book not well read.

W.T. GENEROUS, Jr.

Choate Rosemary Hall
Wallingford
Connecticut

EPSTEIN, DAVID F. *The Political Theory of the Federalist*. Pp. ix, 234. Chicago: University of Chicago Press, 1984. $22.00.

FURTWANGLER, ALBERT. *The Authority of Publius: A Reading of the Federalist Papers*. Pp. 151. Ithaca, NY: Cornell University Press, 1984. $14.95.

These two books represent divergent approaches to and understandings of the *Federalist Papers*. David Epstein, in *The Political Theory of the Federalist,* provides a detailed textual analysis of key parts of *The Federalist*. At the outset he assumes that there is a coherent political philosophy underlying the work, that the arguments contained in it reflect the beliefs and values of its joint authors, that there is no difference between the ideas of Hamilton and Madison, and that the arguments contained therein are as relevant today as they were when first presented in 1787 and 1788.

Building on these assumptions, Epstein argues that the economic interpretation of *The Federalist,* which emphasizes the degree to which the Constitution built a political system assuming that people would act politically in pursuit of their own economic interests, is flawed. Instead he argues that Madison in particular in Federalist 10 and Publius throughout *The Federalist* recognized the crucial role of a variety of other political impulses including the love of fame, the ambitious desire for power, and the egocentric partisan's pride in his or her own opinion. The extent to which the constitutional order built on these assumptions of human behavior allowed the framers, in Epstein's analysis, to create and defend in *The Federalist* a "strictly republican" government that is uniquely constituted to serve the public good.

The strength of Epstein's argument is based on the validity of his assumptions. Albert Furtwangler, in *The Authority of Publius*—quite correctly, I think—draws most of those assumptions into question. Furtwangler argues that *The Federalist* does not reflect the leading ideas of its authors, or of the founders generally, does not contain a rigorous political theory, and is inconsistent within the contributions of individual authors and among the three contributors. From there he goes on to argue the importance of the form of the essays in the evolution of a new style of political discourse and to downplay the importance of Federalist 10 to our understanding of either *The Federalist* or the constitutional order it undertakes to defend. Finally Furtwangler argues that although *The Federalist* offers no indelible solutions to the nation's problems, its authority lies in its example of the level of intellectual discourse that is the key to finding those solutions.

If Furtwangler's argument is the more persuasive of the two, only one thing detracts from it. Furtwangler argues that Federalist 10 is not only overemphasized, but that it was the result of a collaboration so extensive as to make it a dual-author essay. He argues this despite the fact Hamilton never claimed authorship—Madison did—and despite the fact it "is impossible to show [that is, prove] this in detail."

Despite this detraction, Furtwangler's book is an important corrective that should be carefully considered by the many teachers of Federalist 10 in particular and of Publius generally.

STEVEN R. BOYD

University of Texas
San Antonio

HESS, STEPHEN, *The Government/Press Connection: Press Officers and Their Offices*. Pp. xvi, 160. Washington, DC: Brookings Institution, 1984. $22.95. Paperbound, $8.95.

The Washington correspondent has long fascinated students of journalism and politics, but the press officer, seemingly regarded as distant and slightly disreputable kin, has not excited much interest. In writing his previous book, *The Washington Reporters,* Hess built on several studies that preceded it. In writing about press officers, Hess found that no such foundation existed. This book is the first comprehensive examination of Washington press officers, though works on government publicity and propaganda have mentioned them in passing.

Hess observed the press offices at the Food and Drug Administration, the White House, and the Departments of Defense, Transportation, and State, spending one to three months at each. He followed the press officers every day, read their memos, queried them about their calls, and attended most meetings, save those at which personnel matters were discussed. Hess did not promise confidentiality, and except for one person all were willing to go on the record. His observations extended through the first year of the Reagan administration.

Unfortunately, Hess provides little more than a page of historical background. He views the development of the press office as a means to help the media deal with an increasingly complex government. Contrary to occasional reports that tell of a huge federal information bureaucracy, Hess finds that the entire press apparatus of the government is relatively modest.

Ironically, reporters have a low regard for most press officers, often viewing them as failed journalists who try to manipulate the news. This is unfortunate, Hess points out, because press officers are often journalists' only advocates within agencies, prying information out of reticient bureaucrats. At the same time, press officers are not fully accepted by the agencies for which they work. In the bureaucratic social system, press officers have less status than other personnel of the same rank or grade.

The most valuable chapter in this book deals with the routine activities of press offices. Hess estimates that press officers spend about half their time gathering information and answering inquiries from the press, including running interference for journalists within the agency. Part of this function involves monitoring media coverage. At the State Department and White House, the clipping service is rather extensive. Not surprisingly, the *New York Times, Washington*

Post, and a handful of other media organizations appear more frequently in the daily compilations than the size of their circulations might indicate. Overall, press officers and reporters attend to the same media.

Hess found that manipulation of the press is not a central objective of most press offices. The typical press office, he estimates, spends only a fourth of its time preparing press releases and staging events. The major exception is the White House, which devotes a large part of its effort to staging events, especially for television. The White House's emphasis on the visual media is atypical; most agencies gear their work for print journalists.

Government press officers do not set the news agenda, in Hess's estimation; they are reactive, responding to the demands of the media and perhaps their own agencies. Although agencies vary little in the basic conduct of their press operations, differences in strategies and structure can have noteworthy consequences. For major news events, the State Department constricts the flow of information, funneling it through a few spokespersons. The Defense Department, on the other hand, opens the spigots as much as national security will permit. The result, according to Hess, is that the State Department forces reporters to seek information from Congress and other sources over which it has no control, whereas Defense succeeds in getting more of its message into print.

Two chapters detract slightly from an otherwise serviceable book. The one on informal communications tells little that is new, probably because press offices are mainly a formal channel of communication. Informal communications, such as leaks, usually originate from political appointees, sometimes bureaucrats, but rarely press officers. The other chapter, a discussion of communication during crises, dwelled excessively on a few incidents at the expense of offering usable generalizations. Only one crisis occurred during Hess's fieldwork, which might account for the limited view.

Although much has been written about reporters and sources in the last few years, little has focused on professional sources—press officers. The existing literature has concentrated on how politicians and political appointees interact with the press. Hess suggests that press officers, especially career personnel, differ in important respects

RICHARD B. KIELBOWICZ

University of Washington
Seattle

KLINGMAN, PETER D. *Neither Dies nor Surrenders.* Pp. xiii, 233. Gainesville: University of Florida Press, 1984. Paperbound, $12.00.

LAMIS, ALEXANDER P. *The Two Party South.* Pp. x, 317. New York: Oxford University Press, 1984. $25.00.

Southern politics has spawned a bevy of books and articles concerned with the description and explanation of the political history and culture as well as the government form, structure, and style of this region. Rebellion, racism, religious and politcal intolerance, rurality, Republican party exclusion, extreme poverty mixed in some areas—for instance, Texas—with equally extreme wealth, and often intriguing, if not bizarre, candidates and elected officials have stimulated enough academic interest and research to constitute a unique subfield in the study of American political behaivor. These two books continue in this tradition, although each paradoxically carves a niche in this literature through its insight into actual and potential change in the politics of old Dixie.

Peter D. Klingman presents a straightforward historical account of the fluctuations in fortunes of the Republican party in Florida from Reconstruction to the early 1970s. Commissioned by a Republican partisan to set the record of the GOP in the Sunshine State right, Klingman deftly avoids the trap of bias and delivers a carefully documented treatment of a neglected topic. His narrative is replete with several interesting points including the courtship and abandonment of blacks by the party, the patronage role played by a minority party in a federal system of government, and the constant, almost ruinous, factionalism that has haunted Republicans in Florida. Although rich in detail, Klingman's work suffers from a lack of substance that a comparative state analysis or a solid theoretical grounding would have provided.

In contrast, Alexander P. Lamis's book is far more ambitious. Contemporary electoral politics in each of the southern states is covered. The overarching theme is that a major transformation in electioneering and campaigning has spread across the region. Resurgence of the Republican party coupled with the disintegration of racial antagonism and acrimony has precipitated this change. To be successful, candidates—especially those running under the banner of the Democratic party—must build a coalition of black and white voters in the new South. An analysis of recent congressional and gubernatorial races suggests that the leadership skill of politicians is the key variable that determines whether a ground swell of popular support for victory is achieved. The data base for this investigation is a combination of combing countrywide returns in each southern state for discernible voting patterns, reviews of journalistic accounts of campaigns, and personal interviews with a sample of candidates, elected officials, and their aides.

Lamis's argument is most persuasive in its handling of elections in the Deep South. In the other southern states exceptions fast become the rule. One problem with this approach is that the leadership variable—posited as an explanation of voting behavior counter to reasons offered by sociological models—is developed in a theoretical vacuum. Little effort is put into conceptually or operationally outlining who the effective leader is, or what he or she does. Consequently, at times the constant emphasis on leadership becomes strained, almost contrived. Additionally, there are some major methodological flaws here. County voting information is not strong enough for the interpretations made from this source. The sample of persons interviewed is relatively small and absolutely nonrepresentative. The heavy reliance upon newspaper accounts to retell the electoral story of the changing South not only creates a distance between the author and his material; it also raises serious questions about accuracy and reliability. No systematic decisional criteria as to who and what was read are invoked; thus availability and selectivity loom large. To be sure, Lamis is perfectly correct in asserting that the investigation of state politics is incumbered with data-retrieval difficulties; however, this problem is not unique to this subject and should spark innovative and creative research endeavors, and not border on being an excuse.

Both of these books contribute some to the literature on southern politics. The field for a more comprehensive understanding of political changes in this region is still wide open, however.

JAMES W. LAMARE

University of Canterbury
Christchurch
New Zealand

LINK, ARTHUR S. et al., eds. *The Papers of Woodrow Wilson*. Vol. 47, pp. xxvi, 651; vol. 48, pp. xxvi, 674. Princeton, NJ: Princeton University Press, 1984-85. $40.00 and $45.00, respectively.

As intervention increased, and the war abroad drew greater numbers of American troops and agents swarming in England and France, but active in Italy, Switzerland, and elsewhere on the Continent, Woodrow Wilson's directives and associated materials expanded in detail and more often carried the word "urgent." The present volumes cover the period 13 March to 17 July 1918, when no end of the war was in sight.

Wilson himself never before seemed so evidently good and distinguished. His followers sincerely saw him as inspired in words and action. He stayed calm among crises that extended from home debate to the front lines in Europe, where Germans not only maintained strength but seemed likely to make free with the resources of Russia, which was reported to Washington as disintegrating and all but prostrate under Bolshevik rule.

In hindsight it can be seen that Wilson's evenhandedness at home was made possible in spite of a vast, quelled opposition of German and Irish Americans, socialists, friends of the Bolsheviks, and numerous terrorized pacifists of all shades; but the fact is not reflected in the pages of Wilson and his associates. They deplored brutality at home, but, fixed on war to the uttermost, saw limits to tolerance of dissenters.

Still, Wilson's concern for equity and democratic processes is impressive. He fended off flattery from meat packers, mine owners, telephone executives, and others of business stature. He asked for the facts involving war service and fairness between laborers and industrialists. He resisted former President Taft, who would have made his aggressive League to Enforce the Peace a vehicle for the anticipated League of Nations. The Overman Bill gave Wilson unprecedented power to organize or reorganize wartime agencies, yet he looked for representative persons to fill them and solicited advice on proper candidates.

His son-in-law, William G. McAdoo, was admittedly capable and valuable to the war effort as secretary of the treasury and director general of the government-owned railroads. However, he presented problems in cooperation. Wilson weighed his threatened resignation objectively. It is amazing to note Col. E. M. House's coequal status with the president himself. As House recorded in his diary, given McAdoo's possible retirement from government:

> Let [Franklin K.] Lane become Director General of Railroads; put [David F.] Houston in the Treasury; make Vance McCormick Secretary of Agriculture. I thought Lane's appointment would be applauded by the public because of his long experience on the Interstate Commerce Commission . . . [and] because he is not eligible for the Presidency and therefore could not play politics, which was a great temptation to anyone in that position.

McAdoo did not resign, however, and other such crises passed also. Wilson, for example, came to view women's suffrage as inevitable and urged fearful legislators to join him in passing the constitutional amendment. Wilson resisted superpatriots who wanted military trials for individuals charged with disloyalty, everywhere subject to malice and bigotry.

Yet all such pressures were subordinated to those produced by the worldwide war on land and sea, which promised to continue indefinitely. The German Spring Offensive carried long-range guns within 40 miles of Paris. In the East, the Bolsheviks seemed less a threat to Wilson than the German divisions that might cut up demoralized Russia into areas dominated by figureheads who would provide them with food and war materials. Wilson's view that the Russian people would soon create a democratic regime and join the Allies in resisting the Germans was one of the great illusions—encouraged by American observers—of the time.

English diplomats continued to influence Wilson. They urged him not only to send more troops—already numbering a million—to the western front, but also to Siberia, where Czech, German, and other prisoner-of-war groups, Czarist, and still other elements fought for dominance. A mighty problem, mulled over and over again in these volumes, was possible Japanese help in protecting the Trans-Siberian Railroad from seizure or sabotage. The evidence is clear that Wilson had no plans for intervening in Russian affairs. Herbert Hoover, made famous as food administrator, was being groomed as head of a Russian Relief Commission. Wilson pondered commercial relations with the Bolshevik regime and even entertained possibilities of War Commissar Trotsky's raising armies to help hold down the German divisions and prevent them from being freed to build up German forces in the West. The several thousand American troops sent to Siberia were clearly there to keep watch over the Japanese, who might be tempted to seize Russian territory for themselves.

Wilson's responsibility for the breakup of the Austro-Hungarian and German Empires is evident in these *Papers*. Both nations, through American channels in Switzerland and mediators in the Netherlands and elsewhere, put out feelers and proposals looking toward peace, which, in view of German successes east and west, furnished bases for serious negotiations. Wilson rejected them as insincere and as interfering with the alleged democratic aspirations of minorities, especially in the Austro-Hungarian sectors. Once again, as before intervention, Wilson's flimsy sense of what democracy might mean to peasant and nationalistic elements betrayed him. His abstract visions of free peoples in no way comported with those of the British and French, whose first thought was full victory as due payment for their wartime sacrifices. Wilson's belief that all inequities would be countermanded by a League of Nations composed of freedom-loving delegates would not be long receiving tests.

LOUIS FILLER

The Belfry
Ovid
Michigan

ZUCKERMAN, EDWARD. *The Day after World War III: The U.S. Government's Plans for Surviving a Nuclear War*. Pp. 407. New York: Viking Press, 1984. $18.95.

This is a well-researched and well-written book, interesting for a great number of the facts and historical illustrations it brings out. It is even entertaining at many points, despite its fundamentally pessimistic theme. The title is a trifle misleading, for an important portion of the book is devoted to the history of the earlier development of nuclear weapons and to the awesome destructive capabilities they introduced to international relations.

The book's strengths also produce its weaknesses. Although well-written and engrossing, it has a rambling and chatty style that stands in the way of its being used as a text in any basic course on international security problems. The tone of the book tends throughout to be sneering toward anyone who takes civil defense preparations seriously; a student who regards nuclear war as a danger that we can never escape—Zuckerman certainly does not offer any method by which the world could ensure itself against all the risks of nuclear war—might wonder why every bit of planning to reduce the damage in such a war is to be mocked. Preparations to reduce the suffering in a nuclear war are surely to be condemned when they actually increase the risks of such a war or when they cost tremendous amounts of money. But what of the preparations that do not have these risks and costs? Zuckerman offhandedly suggests that Soviet civil defense preparations are exaggerated—I would agree—but he does not discuss such preparations in Switzerland or Sweden.

The manner in which the book's organization jumps around occasionally leaves some serious misimpressions. For example, it is suggested that immediately after the Japanese surrender in World War II, the United States began stockpiling large numbers of nuclear warheads; indeed, quite the opposide occurred, through 1946 and 1947. Elsewhere the book interestingly suggests—probably unintentionally—that the atomic bombings of Hiroshima and Nagasaki were indispensible to getting a Japanese surrender in 1945, that conventional bombings might otherwise not have brought peace for 1946 and 1947. Could the same bombs, and the precedent set in 1945, get the credit for a more general deterrence of any repeats of World War II?

The bottom line of Zuckerman's book is offered much more in its overall tone than in any explicitly stated conclusions. As such, the book misses many of the complexities of the subject, the case where doves might be disagreeing with each other, or hawks might be doing the same. Most of the book was clearly drafted some time before its 1984 publication date, as it does not assign attention to the nuclear-winter study or to the Roman Catholic bishops' statement.

GEORGE H. QUESTER

University of Maryland
College Park

SOCIOLOGY

BULMER, MARTIN. *The Chicago School of Sociology: Institutionalization, Diversity, and the Rise of Sociological Research.* Pp. xix, 285. Chicago: University of Chicago Press, 1984. $29.00.

This book of the Heritage of Sociology series by Morris Janowitz states that "Chicago was the leading center of the social sciences throughout the world in the 1920s." Established in 1892 in a city that counted 503,185 inhabitants in 1880, the University of Chicago experienced not only an inflow of teachers, but also less interdepartmental estrangement than other educational institutions did. Sociology there was developed by W. I. Thomas, who brought Florian Znaniecki from Poland and wrote *The Polish Peasant in Europe and America* with him. A methodological innovation of the time was to collect and analyze hundreds of letters written by the Polish immigrants in Chicago to their families in Poland.

Martin Bulmer, a senior lecturer at the London School of Economics and Political Science at the University of London, observed that Thomas and Znaniecki appeared not to be influenced by Max Weber and other social scientists in Germany, though quite a few University of Chicago scholars studied or obtained their degrees in Germany. Nor did Thomas and Znaniecki appear to echo Durkheim's anomie when discussing the four wishes of personality of Polish immigrants.

The second focus of the Chicago school of sociology resulted from Robert E. Park and Ernest W. Burgess's human ecological studies. Not only a theory of invasion, in which "isolation" and other human ecological terms were used, but also a new analysis of data in terms of the census tract was initiated by Burgess. This focus included not only the human ecological concern with urban population but also Burgess's concern with racial and criminological phenomena. Characteristically, two outstanding black sociologists, Charles S. Johnson and E. Franklin Frazier, obtained their doctoral degrees in sociology at the University of Chicago.

A third characteristic was an increased emphasis on the problem of measuring social phenomena. This development was associated with William F. Ogburn's joining the sociology department in 1927. Ogburn was more concerned with aggregated data, whereas Paul Lazarsfeld, who came from Vienna to Columbia University in the thirties, focused on individual data derived from a sample.

A fourth characteristic of sociology at Chicago was expressed in terms of symbolic interaction presented by Herbert Blumer in his lectures and participant observation method employed by students led by the Canadian Everett Hughes. I was fortunate to sit in Blumer's classes in which he explained well George Herbert Mead's theory of taking the role of others.

The sociology department at Chicago established good relationships with the department of political science, headed by Charles Merriam, whose students were H. Gosnell, Leonard D. White, and H. Lasswell. Henry Schultz in economics and L. Thurstone in psychology were others who cooperated with the sociological group, who favored the use of mathematical methods.

One can agree or disagree with Bulmer in regard to his high evaluation of sociology at that time at Chicago. He felt, for example, that the Harvard faculty teaching sociology in no way rivaled Chicago. However, if one enlarges sociological concern to other territorial and historical societies, P. A. Sorokin, who joined Harvard in the thirties, certainly could be a comparable scholar.

There is one critical observation. Bulmer stated at the very beginning of his book that he would not include George Herbert Mead as part of the Chicago school. In my judgement, it is a pity, because Mead had the original conception of social interaction. When I read also that Park later in his life was influenced by a biology colleague to develop a more mechanistic model of society, I feel a regret that Park's as well as Burgess's epistemology of social phenomena was not discussed. I evaluate this book positively, though I would encourage a further epistemological analysis, perhaps by Bulmer himself.

JIRI KOLAJA

West Virginia University
Morgantown

COSER, LEWIS A. *Refugee Scholars in America: Their Impact and Their Experiences.* Pp. xviii, 351. New Haven, CT: Yale University Press, 1984. $25.00.

Cruelly uprooted from central Europe by the advent of Nazism, thousands of intellectuals—predominantly but not exclusively of Jewish origins—made their way to the United States between 1933 and 1945. Whether they chose to see this country as an adoptive homeland or merely a temporary refuge, many of these émigrés made invaluable contributions to American higher culture. Some became tragic or pathetic failures, unable to adjust their aspirations to the institutional needs and the parochial disciplinary as well as social prejudices of American academic and professional life.

By selecting 48 of these displaced intelligentsia for biographical treatment under seven broad fields of the social sciences and humanities, Lewis Coser fashions a poignant and panoramic account of their professional attainments and personal experiences. His book is a first-rate contribution to the sociology of knowledge in twentieth-century America and in the cosmopolitanization of American intellectual life by means of import-led growth, as it were. Luminaries of the likes of Erik Erikson, Bruno Bettelheim, Erich Fromm, Ludwig von Mises, Paul Lazarsfeld, Karl Deutsch, Hans Morgenthau, Hannah Arendt, Thomas Mann, Vladimir Nabokov, and Paul Tillich occupy center stage, along with institutions that owed both their existence and their vitality to émigré talents, such as the Institute for Social Research and the New School for Social Research. Yet Coser also dwells upon the careers of those who were unable to transfer their status and prestige to alien shores, or who received recognition belatedly as American intellectual currents altered in the postwar era. Numbered among these less fortunate are writers such as Hermann Broch, the psychologists Charlotte and Karl Buehler, as well as sociologist Alfred Schutz and philosopher Aron Gurwitsch, whose phenomenologically oriented research initially met with a frigid reception from native cognoscenti.

In an introductory chapter as well as brief prefatory remarks appended to the biographies, Coser seeks to explain why certain individuals and professional groups not only adapted to their new surroundings but flourished in them, while others failed dismally on both counts. Intellectual success was, of course, conditioned by personality factors, but it was also significantly affected by social networks of support and, more important, by the prevalent intellectual climate at the time in one's chosen field—expatriate German writers languished in the crassness of Hollywood, while psychoanalysts were lionized by eagerly receptive New Yorkers and Bostonians.

If any criticism of this book is justifiable on the part of a reviewer who is confessedly neither a sociologist nor a historian of modern American culture, it hinges on the issue of representativeness. How typical were the careers Coser examines? What of the far more numerous lesser lights laboring in relative obscurity throughout American academe? But the answers to these questions would require a rather different study from the excellent and broadly informative one that Coser has given us here.

ROBERT P. GARDELLA

U. S. Merchant Marine Academy
Kings Point
New York

GERSTEL, NAOMI and HARRIET GROSS. *Commuter Marriage.* Pp. x, 228. New York: Guilford Press, 1984. $17.50.

Commuter marriage is the latest structural adaptation made by the nuclear family in response to the needs of the economy and the tensions generated by modern marital arrangements. According to Gerstel and Gross, this newest familial form represents a forced choice made by dual-career couples who wish to pursue their individual career needs without sacrificing family goals. Consequently, these couples establish separate geographic residencies and spend at least three nights per week apart. Using the traditional family and its underlying requisite of shared residence as a frame of reference, Gerstel and Gross examine the impact of ongoing geographic separations and reunions on these individuals' psychological, social, and material lives.

Contrary to what might be expected, commuters do not pursue their careers for material gain but rather for social and psychological gains in prestige, status, achievement, and the like. Most interesting, though, are the beneficial side effects—increased self-sufficiency, self-esteem, work satisfaction, and a breakdown of sex-segregated family roles that leads to a more egalitarian marital arrangement—that counterbalance the disadvantages of commuting, such as decreased daily interactions, social isolation, and loneliness. These benefits, however, accrue mainly to women. In fact, women are not only more satisfied with the commuting arrangement but also more likely to increase work involvement compared with their male counterparts.

It should also be noted that none of the individuals in this study embrace commuter marriage as the new, improved marital form, and that this arrangement produces its own unique set of tensions and problems. For example, the majority experiences an effect—called a stranger effect—during reunions that requires an adjustment period of refamiliarization with one's spouse. The time needed for readjustment is mediated by temporal factors and is most strikingly presented in Gerstel and Gross's interviews with Merchant Marine families who spend nine months separated while the husbands pursue their sailing careers.

The value of this study is twofold. First, Gerstel and Gross delineate the differential perceptions and experiences of women and men involved in commuter marriages so that it is clear that women psychologically benefit under this new structural marital arrangement. Further, the data support the notion that a more egalitarian division of domestic labor can occur without the anticipated consequence of dissolving the modern nuclear family. Of course, the long-term permanent effects of commuting remain to be investigated. It is hoped that the changes these individuals experience in terms of a more equitable relationship will continue throughout their lives should they return to a more traditional marital structure.

MARIANNE S. MILLER
University of Kentucky
Lexington

GOLANT, STEPHEN M. *A Place to Grow Old: The Meaning of Environment in Old Age.* Pp. xi, 421. New York: Columbia University Press, 1985. $40.00.

Golant, of the University of Florida, has made an important contribution to the ongoing significant Columbia Studies of Social Gerontology and Aging. In contrast to the large body of research devoted to the elderly who are poor, disabled, or extremely disadvantaged, Golant has been

> especially concerned about the environmental well-being of what [he terms] the mainstream elderly population. These are relatively healthy, intact persons who live independently in their own homes in ordinary, average houses and apartments in urban and rural communities across the United States (p. ix).

In a broader frame of reference, Golant has paid special attention to research constructs previously neglected: (1) how the qualities of the place of residence impinge on the experience of growing old; and (2) the diversity of the American elderly population.

The book is the culmination of collaborative research based on a three-year program funded by the National Institute on Aging, "Adult Lives and Patterns of Aging in an Urban Setting", consisting of four component studies having in common their concern with the patterns of social and psychological adaptation of older people living in the social context of a large metropolitan area of Chicago. Golant's study focused on community ecology and the adaptation of older persons, with attention to the environmental well-being of persons age 60 and older in the community of Evanston, Illinois. The major data for Golant's study consist of responses by 400 persons age 60 and older to an interview that averaged 98 minutes and that was administered in their homes. The data collected from these structured interviews faciliated two sets of empirical analyses.

The first, primarily descriptive, ascertained the likelihood that elderly people would experience particular outcomes or consequences from their environmental transactions. The second set, primarily explanatory, determined which individual characteristics influenced the occurrence of these environmental experiences.

Golant's investigation makes clear that social scientists should be wary of making generalizations about the consequences old people experience in the course of living in a place.

> The environment impinges on an elderly population's well-being through its positive *and* negative aspects, its minor *and* major stimulations or assaults, its habitual *and* spontaneous events, its social *and* physical qualities, through its more specific, detailed parts *and* its larger, system components, and through its effects on overt *and* covert behaviors (p. 335).

Clearly, a full appreciation of an environment's impact on old people requires an understanding of its multidimensional fabric.

Golant is to be congratulated on significant research, meticulously conducted, in social gerontology; his work has importance not only for teachers, sociologists, and urban planners, but most crucially for policymakers in an area of evolving critical need.

FRANCESCO CORDASCO

Montclair State College
Upper Montclair
New Jersey

GOODSTEIN, PHIL H. *The Theory of the General Strike from the French Revolution to Poland.* Pp. xi, 337. Boulder, CO.: East European Monographs, 1984. Distributed by Columbia University Press. $30.00.

TAYLOR, STAN. *Social Science and Revolutions.* Pp. v, 176. New York: St. Martin's Press, 1984. No price.

The Theory of the General Strike, which is divided into three parts and an epilogue, examines the overall "history of the *idea* of the general strike," its meaning, its typologies, its relationship to class struggle, and its use by people as an instrument of social change. Part 1, "Radicalism and the General Strike," traces the latter idea and its relationship to radicalism and anarchism from the beginning of the eighteenth century to the second decade of the twentieth, when the theory and practice of the phenomenon under study "came into its own in syndicalist and democratic movements." Part 2, "Syndicalism and the General Strike," has its primary focus on France, Spain, and Italy; and part 3, with emphasis on Germany, Belgium, Sweden, and Russia, discusses social democracy—which then comprehended Marxism—and the "mass strike." The epilogue considers general strikes since World War I, including some in Nicaragua, Iran, and Poland.

Through a thorough examination of actual strikes, attempted ones, primary sources—in English, French, and German—debates at congresses, and discussions in magazines and journals, Goodstein concludes that the general strike—whether revolutionary or reformist—has failed to effect the social change its advocates have sought. And he attributes this failure to the use of the strike more as a "conditioned reflex of workers . . . to what are considered . . . unfair conditions, than as a theoretical-political weapon" consciously employed "to bring about revolutionary change."

Although the seminal theoretical focus in *The Theory of the General Strike* is the "how" of the revolutions—whether such strikes can bring about a revolution, whether they should serve as a supplement to revolution, whether they should be organized or spontaneous—Stan Taylor's *Social Science and Revolutions,* the central concern of which "is the exposition and evaluation of the major contributions among" the post-1960 studies of revolutions, asks why revolutions occur.

Taylor's work succeeds well. After explaining the reasons for the period chosen, it brings under one cover what are, I think, the most outstanding recent contributions in the social sciences—the "rational choice" paradigm in economics, for example—to the study of revolutions. Indeed, this study, which goes beyond A. Cohen's *Theories of Revolution*, suggests some possible answers for the failure of the general strike.

Both studies, although limited in the amount of space accorded to certain important details, should be a must for undergraduates as well as postgraduates in the areas of social change and revolutions.

WINSTON E. LANGLEY

University of Massachusetts
Boston

GREER, GERMAINE. *Sex and Destiny: The Politics of Human Fertility*. Pp. xv, 541. New York: Harper & Row, 1984. $19.95.

Provocative ideas are the fascination of intellectuals and dilettantes, because provocation can stimulate the rethinking of old concepts, patterns of thought, or world views. But provocative ideas must be minimally credible and clearly expressed to be taken seriously. Producing such ideas is a rare and valued talent. Germaine Greer demonstrated that talent in her early, best-selling book, *The Female Eunuch*, where she presented, clearly and forcefully, a case that women had suffered castration as a result of sexual repression. Her writing in that book was bold, challenging, and full of wit. Her argument fit in with some of the feminist literature of the time, but it charted an interesting and stimulating route that differed from that literature.

In an apparent reverse in her views about sex and repression, Greer's most recent book, *Sex and Destiny*, shows great effort and voluminous reading, but does not carry the level of credibility, clarity, or humor that characterized her earlier work. It may be unfair to compare an author's major early achievement with later works, although that is a common practice in literary reviews; but without that earlier best-seller it is unlikely that this book would have gotten much attention.

Greer has a gift for language and jolting generalization, which makes the book interesting to read. She uses a vast spectrum of material from diverse areas like medicine, anthropology, demography, and women's studies to try to make her case for a "new intellectual order," comparable to the new economic order. But she rambles, overstates, and argues for ideas already well expressed in literature that questions Western imperialism, high technology, racism and sexism in family planning, and women's rights. Unfortunately, she does not add to that literature because of her inadequately supported gross generalizations, her confusingly romantic view of primitive life reminiscent of counterculture writers but couched in a nearly Victorian view of sexuality, and her unexplained bitterness.

For example, her claim that current Western society is "profoundly hostile to children" fails to account for such anti-child practices as infanticide, child selling, and child slavery in many other times and places. That absence does not make us right; it makes her argument less credible. She accepts a local act of cutting umbilical cords with dirty sickles—a way to "cull the newborn"—but she cannot condone hospital childbirth. She argues for old-fashioned abstinence, chastity, and sexual restraint, citing examples from other cultures but not explaining how these fit in with the sexual liberation she argued for in the 1970s.

It is clear from this book that Germaine Greer has changed her mind about sex and society, but there is no clear sense of why. It seems that she attempted to present a provocative idea to create this new intellectual order, but the new order is stillborn.

JACK L. NELSON

Rutgers University
New Brunswick
New Jersey

HIRSCH, ARNOLD R. *Making the Second Ghetto: Race and Housing in Chicago, 1940-1960.* Pp. xv, 362. New York: Cambridge University Press, 1983. $24.95.

The dynamics of demographic and political changes affecting housing in Chicago are examined in detail by Arnold R. Hirsch, who places heavy emphasis upon the role of government in creating and maintaining what he terms the second ghetto. In particular, he is critical of federal housing programs that facilitated the flight of the white middle class from the city and the federal urban redevelopment and renewal programs that resulted in the displacement of many blacks.

Hirsch levies a major attack upon the acculturation theory enuciated by Chancellor Lawrence Kimpton of the University of Chicago, who described the problems of blacks in Chicago as similar to the problems European immigrants faced, although he acknowledged that racial prejudice made the problems more severe for blacks. Hirsch wrote that "the facts of black in-migration to Chicago and Hyde Park did not support" the theory, as the proportion of city blacks born in the South was decreasing significantly. In his view, the theory provided its advocates with "psychological comfort" and "justified the defensive action taken."

This volume contains the results of an exhaustive search of Chicago records from the period 1940-60. A major issue that Hirsch did not face directly is the question of what was politically possible during the study period, which ended as the civil rights movement of the 1960s was emerging as a major force. Although it is difficult to quarrel with the evidence Hirsch mustered to support his conclusions relative to the role of the so-called political elite in causing the development of the second ghetto, one wonders whether any other course of action was politically possible given the views and actions of white ethnic groups described in the book.

Hirsch treads on swampy ground in his epilogue—"Chicago and the Nation"—and falls partial victim to the danger of overgeneralizing upon the basis of Chicago experience supported by selected references to other cities. For example, one must base conclusions relative to New York City's experience on more evidence than the cited book by Robert Caro entitled *The Power Broker,* which is highly critical of Robert Moses.

Hirsch holds that "in a locally initiated and controlled program, the intentions of legislators in Washington are of less consequence than those of the people directing the various local endeavors." He summarily dismisses the conclusion of the National Commission on Urban Problems—chaired by Senator Paul H. Douglas of Illinois—that the urban renewal program was a failure and charges that the commission believed "that the sole purposes behind the federal legislation [urban renewal] were those expressed within it."

Unfortunately, Hirsch failed to note that the commission wrote, "It is hard to see how Congress could have done more at that time to protect the basic purposes of the program without clamping down conditions and requirements that would have amounted to a straight jacket on local action or would have killed the program."

JOSEPH F. ZIMMERMAN

State University of New York
Albany

HOCHSCHILD, JENNIFER. *The New American Dilemma: Liberal Democracy and School Desegregation.* Pp. xvi, 263. New Haven, CT: Yale University Press, 1984. $27.00. Paperbound, $8.95.

Ronald Reagan, read this book! You, too, James Coleman!

Indeed, this is a must book not only for those who have lost—or never had—a vision of school desegregation as a necessary tool for the elimination of racial inequality in our society; it is also a compendium of guidelines and supporting evidence for those who remain committed to this vision. The level of scholarship is monumental, with references to approximately 500 different written sources, including books, journal articles, meeting papers, unpublished manuscripts, and court decisions. And the logic and forcefulness of Hochschild's arguments seem inescapable.

Hochschild juxtaposes two contrasting views of the nature of race relations in this country. First is the anomaly thesis, most prominently advanced by Gunnar Myrdal in his classic 1944 study, *An American Dilemma.* The anomaly is that racial discrimination is contrary to American ideals of justice; simply living up to our professed ideals can solve our racial problems. In contrast is the symbiosis perspective, which views racism as a central product and critical component of our system of liberal democracy.

Hochschild focuses on school desegregation in drawing conclusions that generally support this second view. She shows how conventional political processes have been antithetical to a programmatic change—namely, desegregation—that, under optimal conditions, has contributed substantially to the goal of racial equality and improved race relations. The white majority, middle class and poor, even with moderating general racial attitudes, fears the loss of privileged position that radical change in education might produce. Popular control, then, leads to an incremental, or piecemeal, approach to desegregation at best; and this, Hochschild compellingly documents, is least likely to produce positive effects and most likely to produce negative effects, such as heightened racial conflict and white flight.

After critically, but not unsympathetically, examining two possible alternatives—the present muddling-along policy and a serious attempt to upgrade schools for minorities without recourse to desegregation—Hochschild concludes that rapid and complete desegregation mandated by authorities not directly subject to popular control is the best hope for achieving quality and equality in education with minimal disruption. She calls for plans that are metropolitan-wide, only secondarily concerned with the amount of busing, and seriously committed to changing practices and presumptions within the schools that produce unnecessary biases favoring white students and culture.

My only complaint about this excellent book is editorial. It needs a straight list of references in addition to—or, perhaps, as partial substitution for—the 50 pages of bibliographic notes at the end of the text. Searching for the original complete listing of a work when one comes across a later partial reference is akin to looking for a needle in a haystack.

M. RICHARD CRAMER
University of North Carolina
Chapel Hill

KAMINER, WENDY. *Women Volunteering: The Pleasure, Pain and Politics of Unpaid Work from 1830 to the Present.* Pp. xiii, 237. Garden City, NY: Anchor Press, 1984. $15.95.

"From the beginning," writes Wendy Kaminer, "volunteering has both liberated women and kept them in their place." An examination of this complex phenomenon is the task of Kaminer's book, a long overdue addition to the rather sparse literature offering insight into "the pleasure, pain and politics of unpaid work" over the past 150 years in the United States.

In 1981 Colette Dowling publicly established the existence of women's hidden fear of independence and called it the Cinderella complex. Women traditionally were not educated for independence but for a submissive role. The dependent pattern, not autonomy, was termed appropriate female behavior.

Kaminer adds to this psychodynamic grasp of the female's wish to be protected by providing perspectives on problems created by a family system based on rigid sex roles that support paid work for men and "unpaid housework, community work, and economic dependence for women." Volunteering, defined as any freely chosen, unpaid activity and stereotypically seen as a housewife's vocation, certainly did not empower women. It provided them with neither an income nor professional status, but it did serve to relieve the "domestic isolation" of leisure-class women without jeopardizing their family roles.

These middle- and upper-class ladies created unpaid jobs for themselves outside the home by volunteering in cultural activities, moral reform, and social service. Service volunteers became interested in public affairs and joined the ranks of the women's suffrage movement, and notable abolitionist women became feminists. Eventually the feminist movement became responsive to the problems of working-class women. The significant club movement organized women to address questions of social welfare, and black women of all classes began to organize societies to improve education and health care in their communities. Volunteering has always been highly valued in the black community and crucial to its survival.

A resolution issued by the National Organization for Women in 1971 encouraged women to volunteer exclusively to effect social change and to desist from working for free with individuals in need. This attack on service volunteering, now viewed as demeaning work, came largely from middle- and upper-class white feminists and not from the working-class and minority women. The confrontation was for equity.

In the 1980s volunteering has gained a new respectability. There exists a viable place for volunteering in a feminist world wherein the volunteer tradition is integrated in a complementary way with paid professionalism for women. Although economic equality is essential, so is the chance to "do your own thing" through some volunteer work of one's own choice. The goal is to have options.

About a third of this book is devoted to profiling—via direct interviews with a cross section of volunteers—different types of volunteers characterized as survivors, pioneers of transition, the new generation, the casualties, and the coming generation. A social worker, Elizabeth L. Moore, conducted these interviews, which produced some revealing vignettes of personal encounters with volunteering. A limitation of the book is that this sample of volunteers admittedly was not scientifically analyzed and focused exclusively on women living in the northeastern section of the country.

Women Volunteering is a significant book to add to the reading lists of students of social work and women's studies, among other disciplines. It covers the evolution of women's movements, the creation of women's organizations, women's progressive leadership and activism, and women's changing perspectives of themselves as volunteers.

Finally, the book serves to point up the need for sociological research of a more comprehensive nature. Kaminer, who lamented the lack of available statistics on volunteering, suggests that either the U.S. Labor Department compile such statistics or that the national census in the future include some survey of volunteers, which was not done in the 1980 census. Volunteering activities appear a promising area for further research.

FLORENCE P. ENGELHARDT
Arizona State University
Tempe

PANEM, SANDRA. *The Interferon Crusade.* Pp. 109. Washington, DC: Brookings Institution, 1984. $22.95. Paperbound, $8.95.

For more than a decade the National Institutes of Health has promoted scholarly investigation of the potential curative properties of interferon. The infusion of millions of dollars in federal funds for the study of interferon was prompted by a belief that it would become an effective anticancer drug. Between 1972 and 1983, interferon research became a cause celèbre, promoted by funding agencies, biomedical researchers at academic institutions, and major pharmaceutical companies because of interferon's perceived, although unsubstantiated, remedial qualities. Although interferon has not lived up to its expectations as the cure for a highly emotional and dreaded disease, interferon research has still promoted biomedical innovations having far-reaching consequences for further unraveling the mysteries leading to a cure for cancer.

The Interferon Crusade is not a book chronicling the development and production of a potential drug for the treatment of cancer. The primary objective of this brief volume is to provide "a case study to analyze policy issues on the choices and pursuit of biomedical research within the context of a technical revolution." In so doing, Panem is able to address critical policy issues related to the rapidly growing field of biomedical engineering. Some of the very fundamental questions that this volume addresses are related to the level of responsibility of the federal government for funding biomedical research, and the relationship between academic researchers and their affiliated institutions to private industry. The answers to these questions are becoming alarmingly critical in light of budgetary constraints imposed by the Reagan administration.

This book is composed of five chapters in which Panem succinctly outlines the historical and political dynamics surrounding research and development of interferon. Panem's analysis addresses several major topics: the historical development of scientific interest in interferon, funding of interferon research, public policy issues prompted by interferon research, and lessons learned from this experience. In each chapter Panem not only presents a fascinating historical overview of critical factors leading to interest in and promotion of interferon research; she also analyzes the social and political dynamics that prompted the infusion of millions of federal dollars over a ten-year period. In so doing, she raises a series of questions rather than providing easy solutions. "The issues raised . . . concern the future of the American biomedical enterprise and its academic, commercial, and federal sectors."

This book is a fine example of policy analysis using a qualitative approach, but it can also be viewed from a theoretical perspective that Panem may not have originally intended: diffusion of innovation. Like the computer chip, which has facilitated the development of a variety of high-technology industries, interferon research has served as a primary catalyst promoting new technologies related to genetic engineering. I believe this volume should be widely read by individuals concerned with the social, political, economic, and ethical considerations related to research and development of high technology in America today.

STUART W. ZISOOK

Blue Cross and Blue Shield of Illinois
Chicago

PITKIN, HANNA FENICHEL. *Fortune Is a Woman: Gender and Politics in the Thought of Niccolo Machiavelli.* Pp. ix, 354. Berkeley: University of California Press, 1984. $24.95.

Pitkin investigates the importance of gender and politics in the works of Machiavelli in order to understand the meaning of his ideas, both in his time and in ours. Rather than offering causal explanations, Pitkin seeks an interpretive and enriched political understanding through an examination of the relationship between the personal and political. What she discovers is that Machiavelli's ambivalance in matters of political thought are inextricably linked to his views of women, relations between the sexes, family life, and relations between generations. An exclusively male world appears to be the focus of Machiavelli's political writings, but in actuality, an ever-present threat of domination by a powerful female other is evident.

According to Pitkin's analysis, males experience dependency anxiety and they fear the feminine other within themselves. Ambition, greed, and developing sexuality motivate boys to escape maternal domination, but early dependency anxiety is imported into their later political lives. As a result, grown men are afraid to trust and nurture, and desire omnipotence.

In this interpretation, men rely on virtu, which connotes effectiveness and energy required for manliness and independence. But even a man with great virtu may be deprived of eventual recognition because of Fortune, who favors the young, the bold, and the manly. Fortune wants to control and command men and to have her power acknowledged.

> Fortune afflicts in his infancy a man destined to be great precisely so that his eventual glory will come not from his virtu or prudence but from her power, so the glory will be set not to his credit but hers (p. 58).

Fortune is capricious and envious of men, and she may decide to make trouble for no more reason than that she is bored with the way things are. She is occasionally benevolent with her favorites, but even they are required to overcome obstacles. Success is contingent upon adaptability to situations and times, but Machiavelli concludes that humans are incapable of changing and thus are not prepared to adapt as Fortune intentionally varies life situations. Fortune, as seen by Machiavelli, has superhuman powers over the outcome of events in the world of men.

The power of ordinary women, like that of Fortune, is mysterious and dangerous to men, both personally and politically. Personal danger for men exists through the possible contagion of negative female qualities that may be transmitted by mere association. In addition, male self-control may be threatened through the seductive techniques used by women. Political dangers attributed to women are both direct and indirect. Women may privatize republican citizens in the confines of the bedroom, thus causing internal conflict, political division, and eventually weakened patriarchal and political bonds between men. Older women are particularly dangerous politically, for they are both hostile and active. They control sexual access to their daughters, thereby obtaining power to further their ambition. Indirect political dangers exist in times of war when women, as possessions, are sexually abused by conquerers. The abuse solidifies the political resolve of the conquered man to avenge his honor, because women represent both property and honor.

In explaining Machiavelli, Pitkin utilizes the works of Dinnerstein, Arendt, Freud, and Marx, to a name a few. She uses textual analysis, psychological theory, and sociological history to illustrate how Machiavelli's failure to come to terms with the "otherness" of women as being different, yet of this world, rather than mysterious, dangerous, and uncanny, has profound consequences for his philosophies. In the final chapters, Pitkin examines the ideas of Machiavelli as they are related to historical divergence and makes suggestions regarding the relevance of Machiavelli's ideas for our time. One of the outstanding synopses of the difficulty of Machiavelli's understanding of adulthood, masculinity, and humanness is incorporated by Pitkin into this sentence: "Men who deny the humanity of women are bound to misunderstand their own."

Fortune is a Woman falls in the category of a powerful scholarly work that has the added effect of causing the reader to marvel at the brilliance of the author.

LES LEANNE HOYT CROFT
Arizona State University
Phoenix

ECONOMICS

GENEEN, HAROLD with ALVIN MOSCOW. *Managing*. Pp. x, 297. Garden City, NY: Doubleday, 1984. $17.95.

The pervasive theme of business management books—some of them best-sellers—is that managerial shortcomings are responsible for low productivity, poor competitiveness, and other deficiencies. *Managing* is in this genre. Its 14 chapters present principles for upgrading the "mediocre performance" of "befuddled and bewildered" big business. Alvin Moscow welcomes us to Geneen University, a droll hyperbole given the scope and contents of this book.

Harold Geneen held accounting, financial, and managerial positions before selection in 1959 as ITT's chief executive officer, and, later, chairman of the board. His management philosophy developed from what he learned and accomplished. In growth—mainly acquisitions—and profits his ITT achievements were impressive but their ultimate results were mixed.

Sharply critical of management theories and business schools, he relied on experience and "God-given common sense" for "Theory G on Management." His style included systematic review of "unshakable facts"; frequent meetings; "cluttered-desk executive"; obsessive rationality; and singleness of purpose. Executive hubris is egotism, not alcoholism. Freeing bright people facilitates entrepreneurship. Because boards of directors are an "archaic, creaking contraption," they should be replaced only with outsiders.

A workaholic—one who works after 5 p.m.—forthright and convinced that his strategies were sound, Geneen has written a readable, but unconvincing, narrative. His criticisms of scientific management and business courses need airing, but his principles lack depth, useful interpretation, and analysis. Opposed to organizational politics, he never focuses on this critical factor, nor does he discuss labor-management relations, as if these were not relevant. In Geneen's claim that ITT's success was due to his management, other possible explanations are ignored.

Annoyingly unanswered are questions relating to ITT's political scandals. Geneen scarcely provides a balanced treatment of his conflicts with the Department of Justice over proposed acquisitions. He defends bigness and argues that unrelated enterprise can be managed profitably by concentrating on financial controls and profits.

No management techniques, even his, work in all contexts. Making money for shareholders determined his strategies. Even if ITT stock did better than the market index—it did not—is this the sole aim of management? Should corporations not also have responsibilities to employees, communities, governments, and acceptable norms? Geneen emphasizes profits as beneficial to society.

Nevertheless, he offers some perceptive views about the limits of scientific management and the importance of experience, intuition, leadership, and risk taking. Although academics and practitioners should read the book skeptically and balance it with *Geneen* by Robert J. Schoenberg—written without the subject's cooperation—it is modestly useful in providing one chief executive officer's management philosophy and personal credo.

BERNARD SAMOFF

University of Pennsylvania
Philadelphia

HARRINGTON, MICHAEL. *The New American Poverty*. Pp. xii, 271. New York: Holt, Rinehart & Winston, 1984. $17.95.

NAVARRO, PETER. *The Policy Game: How Special Interests and Ideologies Are Stealing America*. Pp. xii, 340. New York: John Wiley & Sons, 1984. $18.95.

Imagine the United States with virtually no poverty. Or the political system with very few special-interest groups. These two visions of the future are examined in new books by Michael Harrington and Peter Navarro. As the authors point out, poverty and the role of special interests are at the heart of many policy debates today. Harrington—scholar, activist, and teacher—has written a sequel to his path-breaking book of the early sixties, *The Other America.* He argues that poverty today is different from poverty in the past and that current solutions to eradicate it remain problematic. Navarro, economic researcher and journalist, argues that many major policy issues are influenced by special interests that transcend a particular set of needs that the participants may have been pursuing.

Harrington believes that American poverty is elusive and removed from the center of people's lives. The impersonal nature of the new poverty means that less attention and fewer resources have been directed toward solving the problems of the newly impoverished. In this group he lumps not only the historically impoverished—welfare receipts, single-family households, blacks, women—but the recently afflicted workers—such as steel workers—from traditional strongholds of industry. Jobs have been lost in the manufacturing sector as the focus of economic activity has shifted more to the service sector. Harrington brilliantly traces the plight of these workers from Maine to Detroit to Appalachia and Indian reservations. His compassion for the poor and his understanding of their position in American society makes him one of our foremost analysts of the poor in the United States. In addition he critiques the debate on poverty—statistical and definitional—and pinpoints the weaknesses and strengths of various analyses of the so-called reduction in the incidence of poverty. Harrington suggests that in fact poverty has substantially increased and now affects income classes that previously were somewhat insulated from experiencing downward economic mobility. His solution to poverty involves moving toward a full-employment economy and accounting for the consequences of structural changes in the international economy that make poverty more international in scope than before.

Navarro believes that politically motivated actions by special-interest groups have left the political process in shambles. His book is a who's who of special-interest groups. In the current economy, he argues, special interests are the norm and objective policymaking remains a thing of the past. The future lies in our capacity to frame questions and derive results from a model of political and economic behavior that focuses on the capture-ideology approach. Simply put, we have to identify who the players are—special-interest groups; understand their respective ideologies—conservative or liberal; examine the economics of the issue to see who—that is, which special-interest group—has benefited; and calculate the costs of misguided ideologies and parochial special-interest groups on the economy. Navarro uses statistical tests to demonstrate the weaknesses of special-interest groups in the areas of rent control, protectionist trade policies, farm policy, electric utilities, the Equal Rights Amendment, and the weapons sweepstakes. He ends by arguing that "special-interest politics must fall before the force of a well-informed and better-organized citizenry, and blind ideology must yield to more pragmatic solutions, solutions that begin with the basic insight that constructive policy reforms can make us all better off."

Harrington's book might well be viewed as a special-interest manifesto by Navarro. It is precisely this kind of lobbying that he rails against in his book, though he does not directly address the issue of poverty. Throughout his book Navarro assumes that solutions can be derived that are based on "pragmatism" and "constructive policy reforms," but it is unclear what he means by those terms. His statistical work relies heavily on neoclassical economic theory, a body of economic knowledge that many commentators have argued makes assumptions that cannot be replicated in the real world. He neglects to explore the implications of connecting such theories to political debates. Furthermore, what he considers a pragmatic or a constructive policy reform, someone else might argue is an ideology. "Pragmatism" is a trendy word; however it is not useful to conjure up images of pragmatic or objective research when the model relied upon is not a reliable assessment of reality.

Harrington's book is neither objective nor necessarily pragmatic. But he does address the wider issue of how ideological debates have shaped and influenced the policy debate around poverty. Unfortunately he does not provide sufficient sources. There are no footnotes; individuals and institutional studies are mentioned in the text, but it would be very hard to trace the sources he uses. This was, I believe, quite appropriate for his earlier book; but it makes it hard for others to pursue his insights further.

Both books deserve a careful reading and attention despite their drawbacks. It remains to be seen whether the role and influence of special-interest groups will wither, or if poverty will be reduced. Working toward a vision of such a world remains a more fruitful pursuit than not working toward such a vision.

LOU FERLEGER

University of Massachusetts
Boston

HAYES, ROBERT H. and STEVEN C. WHEELWRIGHT. *Restoring Our Competitive Edge: Competing through Manufacturing*. Pp. vii, 427. New York: John Wiley & Sons, 1984. $19.95.

This book joins a fairly lengthy list of publications concerned with the decline in international competitiveness of the U.S. economy, or industry, or manufacturing. The last of these three is the topic of this book, but the book's value relates to a broader scope.

The book was designed, by either the authors or the publisher, for service as a textbook in management classes. This detracts from its readability, but not disastrously. There are 14 chapters and a good, lengthy index. The first 3 chapters are somewhat introductory in character, and the general reader might wish to turn to chapter 11, "German Approaches to Manufacturing Management," and chapter 12 on Japanese approaches. Then the reader might go back to the more detailed textbook presentations in the middle of the book, of interest to the specialist or management student, or go directly to chapter 13, "Learning from Your World Class Competitors," and chapter 14, "Building Manufacturing's Competitive Potential."

The chapters on Germany and Japan make it glaringly obvious that in comparison, the United States' manufacturing has become fat and lazy, particularly since World War II. Not just owners, management, laborers, or labor organizations, but society at large in those two countries has grasped the desirability or utter necessity of focusing on long-run productivity at moderate profitability, with workers genuinely involved or integrated into the process of production-distribution-consumption, with craftsmanship well regarded as a social value. Managers as well as workers spend years learning technical aspects of production processes, making possible an almost obsessive concern with quality. The career craftsman in manufacturing, meaning one who learns the technical details, not too surprisingly perceives himself or herself as a success in life, quite often staying with one company, and taking pride in the production of quality products. The contrast with the United States' manufacturing, on average, is pronounced.

FLOYD B. McFARLAND

Oregon State University
Corvallis

KRAUSS, MELVYN B. *The New Protectionism: The Welfare State and International Trade*. Pp. xxiv, 119. New York: New York University Press, 1978. $20.00. Paperbound, $9.00.

Countries are different. Location, labor quality, environment, natural resources, and level of development are but a few of the myriad factors leading to interarea heterogeneity. At least since the Heckscher-Ohlin theory, economists have pointed out that this heterogeneity heads to trade relations that, because of gains from trade, result in higher incomes for all nations. In this book, Krauss is not only a strong advocate of this process, but goes on to claim that any government intervention is necessarily bad, because it either hampers trade directly or affects comparative advantage by influencing the production process.

The arguments are presented in five chapters, all in a sense building upon each other. Chapter 1 sets the stage by cogently yet nontechnically reviewing trade theory, illustrating not only the welfare gain from trade, but the welfare losses associated with various types of government intervention. Chapter 2 defines the problem. In the 1970s an increasing number of trade-restricting actions were taken. These included the traditional tariff type of measures, but expanded to include "labor subsidies, capital controls, cartel agreements, subsidized loans, regional development grants, investment grants, price-fixing arrangements, production subsidies, consumption subsidies. . . . " Not all were motivated by trade considerations. However, according to Krauss—in chapter 3—all "significantly affect" trade in a detrimental way so that not only do the perpetrating countries suffer, but the impact of their so-called domestic welfare policies is exported even to free-market countries that must respond, as seems to be the current case between the United States and Japan. Chapter 4 deals with the possible responses, and chapter 5 with the inherent economic stagnation that presumably results from a welfare-type policy in the first place.

The concluding paragraph of the book provides an excellent summary:

> The long run implication . . . is that the welfare state is self-destructive. It both depends on economic growth and destroys it. . . . It is perhaps the essential irony of the welfare state. The attempts to insure one's economic position serve only to insure the opposite (p. 118-19).

Krauss's tone in the book is that of a partisan proponent. Thus to judge the book one must judge whether the arguments are convincing. To this end I do not believe Krauss succeeds. The book is far too abstract, and too few examples are given. The fact is that all welfare policies have two faces: costs and benefits. Even I, a sympathic reader, was not convinced that in all cases welfare-type benefits fall short of the costs. Not allowing the Concord to fly into Kennedy International Airport does reduce trade, but which poses a greater cost, the lost gains from trade or the resulting noise and air pollution? Temporary quotas on Japanese auto imports increase automobile prices, but are these more or less costly than the governmentally mandated unemployment benefits for the auto workers? Notions of second best, or short-run versus long-run considerations, are not broached.

The reader, however, need not despair. Krauss's subsequent book, *Development without Aid*, provides a more convincing story that extends ideas of the free-trade argument further to notions of unfettered capitalism as a stimulus for economic development. I recommend this newer book, which gives concrete examples comparing economic development of typical Third World countries to the so-called free-market Gang of Four—Hong Kong, Singapore, Taiwan, and South Korea.

SOLOMON WILLIAM POLACHEK
State University of New York
Binghamton

SCHWADRON, TERRY, PAUL RICHTER, and JACK CITRIN. *California and the American Tax Revolt: Proposition 13 Five Years Later*. Pp. iv, 194. Berkeley: University of California Press, 1984. $19.95. Paperbound, $6.95.

The passage in California of Proposition 13 in 1978 signaled the first shot in the tax revolt. In the next several years, Californians passed two more tax-reduction measures, and a host of other states followed. The campaign on Proposition 13 was marked by predictions of fiscal disaster or supply-side prosperity. This book argues that both sides were wrong.

Five years after Proposition 13's passage, the *Los Angeles Times* supported an extensive effort to assess its effects. The paper engaged Price Waterhouse and mobilized a team of 18 reporters, many of them specialists, to probe Proposition 13's fiscal and political impact. The results were published in the *Times* in 1983. Those articles, along with an introduction by political scientist Jack Citrin and supporting materials, form the book.

Citrin's long and thorough introduction is the most explicitly social scientific chapter. Citrin is concerned with the national diffusion of the movement, specifying its targets and goals, examining the correlates of successful or unsuccessful tax-cutting measures, and generalizing about "decremental budgeting." The chapter may be read by itself or as introduction to the remainder of the volume, though perhaps inevitably the chapter reads as if it were grafted onto the rest of the book rather than an outgrowth of it. Citrin's analysis of the correlates of the success or failure of tax-cutting measures and his discussion of the highly political process of decremental budgeting are especially interesting and suggestive.

Successive chapters deal with the response of local government, how various state and local agencies dealt with new political and fiscal realities, and with the diffusion of the revolt. The most useful of these for most scholars is the chapter on the responses of state and local agencies. Although not as extensive as one might like, each of the many topics addressed is a mine of conclusions and hypotheses. Taken as a whole, the book is a readable mix of academic analysis and journalistic detail, though the volume is not as fully integrated as one would like. It is a fine source of both what we know and what we might further want to know about the consequences of tax revolt.

Several themes are worth noting. Although Richter and Citrin argue that both opponents and proponents of Proposition 13 were wrong in their predictions, one can easily imagine both camps citing the book in support of their positions. The sheer complexity of events, the difficulty of inferring causality, and the critical role played by changes in the state's economic health all permit interested parties to claim they were right about Proposition 13's effects. Whatever value Proposition 13 had as a quasi-natural experiment, however, was vitiated by the recession-recovery cycle California underwent in the wake of the proposition's passage. Sifting out these effects is especially difficult on the fiscal side, where one can find conflicting evidence of the incidence of Proposition 13's effects, including equity effects. In contrast, political effects are much clearer: decreased local control, and the shift in the fortunes of state political actors that accompanied the movement of fiscal control to Sacramento as the state took over local functions.

Inevitably, there were unanticipated consequences. Renters were largely denied promised rent reductions, which doubtless spurred several rent-control movements statewide, resulting in greatly enhanced political mobilization by renters' groups. Radically different assessments being applied to identical homes, depending on date of purchase, may set the stage for another round of initiative activity, with equity as its new goal.

The decrease in funds that followed Proposition 13's passage radically changed budget politics; the goal became maintenance, not growth, and the costs were borne disproportionately. A number of short-term coping strategies were adopted, and once again muddling through became the order of the day.

One comes away from the wealth of detail and analysis in this book impressed with the extent to which the fiscal changes that followed Proposition 13's passage were genuinely systemic and, therefore, difficult to trace, but also with the rapidity and predictability of the political response to it. The book is an excellent analysis of both these kinds of effects.

PHILLIP L. GIANOS

California State University
Fullerton

YOFFIE, DAVID B. *Power and Protectionism: Strategies of the Newly Industrializing Countries.* Pp. xi, 282. New York: Columbia University Press, 1983. No price.

It is widely believed that the developing countries' weakness in their trade relations with rich industrial nations stems primarily from the latter's control of their own import markets. Historically, such controls existed as tariffs and quotas. In recent years, however, the industrial nations have been moving in the direction of new protectionism—bilateral agreements in the form of voluntary export restraints (VERs) and orderly marketing agreements (OMAs) that put quantitative restrictions on selected imports. According to the U.N. Conference on Trade and Development, the widespread use of VERs and OMAs in Europe and in the United States has been seriously damaging to the world economy and especially to the economies of the newly industrializing countries of Asia and Latin America.

In this analytical study of new protectionism, Yoffie concludes that the structural weaknesses of VERs and OMAs enable newly industrializing countries to successfully exploit them under certain conditions. Indeed, several industrializing countries like Korea, Taiwan, Hong Kong, Singapore, Brazil, and Mexico have penetrated the barriers of new protectionism and have, in the period between the early 1960s and late 1970s, "almost doubled their share of the world's industrial production, tripled their share of OECD imports and expanded their share of world exports by 170 percent". According to Yoffie, such successes stem from the developed nations' use of VERs and OMAs mostly as ad hoc, short-run political policies and not as well-conceived tools of industrial intervention.

The book consists of six chapters. In the first chapter, Yoffie considers the political underpinnings of international trade and concludes that, given factor mobility in exporting countries and short-run protectionist policies in importing countries, the newly industrializing countries can exploit the structural weaknesses in new protectionism by following a "long-term oriented, loop-hole seeking strategy which can be supplemented by other tactics." In chapters 2-5, the book explores the process of bargaining and the implementation of protectionism in the postwar period in four East Asian exporters: Japan, the Republic of Korea, the Republic of China—Taiwan—and Hong Kong. The four country studies are organized around four products: textiles and apparel, footwear, color televisions, and automobiles. Whereas chapters 2-4 focus on a detailed account of the U.S.-Japanese negotiations and efforts to limit Japanese export of textiles, chapter 5 deals with negotiations of OMAs with Taiwan and Korea in their exports of footwear. In chapter 6, Yoffie considers patterns of protectionism in color televisions and automobiles and provides a general summary of his findings. After studying about 15 of the more than 50 negotiations in these four sectors, Yoffie concludes that the countries that followed a "strategy of upgrading, bargaining for loopholes, cheating, and exploiting transnational ties, especially if the latter policies are done on a small scale and without much fanfare" have benefited much more than those that resisted pressures from the United States for VERs and OMAs. Although Yoffie expects the protectionist environment of VERs and OMAs to continue in the near future, he is fairly optimistic that the newly industrializing countries can turn such adversities into advantage by following appropriate long-term accommodating policies.

The book is well written and it poses a very important challenge to the classical theories of international trade. Although many of Yoffie's specific claims are not clearly proven empirically, he provides a useful analytical framework for further investigation.

P.I. MATHEW

U.S. Coast Guard Academy
New London
Connecticut

OTHER BOOKS

ALFORD, JONATHAN, ed. *Arms Control and European Security*. Pp. viii, 147. New York: St. Martin's Press, 1984. $22.50.

APEL, KARL-OTTO. *Understanding and Explanation: A Transcendental-Pragmatic Perspective*. Pp. xxii, 293. Cambridge, MA: MIT Press, 1985. $25.00.

ARJOMAND, SAID AMIR. *The Shadow of God and the Hidden Imam*. Pp. xii, 356. Chicago: University of Chicago Press, 1984. $28.00.

ARONOFF, MYRON J., ed. *Cross-Currents in Israeli Culture and Politics*. Pp. 115. New Brunswick, NJ: Transaction Books, 1984. $29.95. Paperbound, $12.95.

BARDO, JOHN W. and JOHN J. HARTMAN. *Urban Sociology*. Pp. vii, 401. Itasca, IL: F. E. Peacock, 1982. No price.

BILSON, JOHN F. O. and RICHARD C. MARSTON, eds. *Exchange Rate Theory and Practice*. Pp. ix, 528. Chicago: University of Chicago Press, 1985. $58.00.

BLACKWELL, JAMES E. *The Black Community: Diversity and Unity*. Pp. xvi, 398. New York: Harper & Row, 1985. No price.

BROWN, LESTER R. et al. *State of the World*. Pp. xvii, 301. Washington, DC: Worldwatch Institute, 1985. Paperbound, $8.95.

BULMER, MARTIN, ed. *Sociological Research Methods: An Introduction*. Pp. xv, 351. New Brunswick, NJ: Transaction Books, 1984. Paperbound, $12.95.

CAMPBELL, BERNARD. *Human Ecology*. Pp. ix, 198. Hawthorne, NY: Aldine, 1985. $19.95. Paperbound, $8.95.

CASTELLANOS, DIEGO. *The Best of Two Worlds: Bilingual-Bicultural Education in the U.S.* Pp. xii, 287. Trenton: New Jersey Department of Education, 1984. No price.

COOPER, RICHARD and RYLAND CRARY. *The Politics of Progress: Governor Leader's Administration 1955-1959*. Pp. vii, 211. Harrisburg, PA: Penns Valley, 1982. No price.

CRONON, WILLIAM. *Changes in the Land: Indians, Colonists, and the Ecology of New England*. Pp. x, 241. New York: Hill and Wang, 1983. Paperbound, no price.

CURTIS, LYNN, ed. *American Violence and Public Policy*. Pp. xi, 263. New Haven, CT: Yale University Press, 1985. $23.00.

DANN, URIEL. *Studies in the History of Transjordan, 1920-1949: The Making of a State*. Pp. x, 127. Boulder, CO: Westview Press, 1984. Paperbound, $13.50.

DENNETT, DANIEL C. *Elbow Room: The Varieties of Free Will Worth Wanting*. Pp. x, 200. Cambridge, MA: MIT Press, 1984. $19.95. Paperbound, $8.95.

DIAMOND, PETER A. *A Search-Equilibrium Approach to the Micro Foundations of Macroeconomics*. Pp. 74. Cambridge, MA: MIT Press, 1984. $7.50.

DIBB, PAUL, ed. *Australia's External Relations in the 1980s: The Interaction of Economic, Political and Strategic Factors*. Pp. 227. New York: St. Martin's Press, 1984. $25.00.

DRAKE, FREDERICK C. *The Empire of the Seas: A Biography of Rear Admiral Robert Wilson Shufeldt, USN*. Pp. xv, 468. Honolulu: University of Hawaii Press, 1984. $29.95.

DUFF, ERNEST A. *Leader and Party in Latin America*. Pp. ix, 177. Boulder, CO: Westview Press, 1985. Paperbound, $15.95.

DUNN, KEITH A. and WILLIAM O. STAUDENMAIER. *Military Strategy in Transition: Defense and Deterrence in the 1980s*. Pp. x, 225. Boulder, CO: Westview Press, 1985. $26.00.

FARMER, RICHARD E., LYNN HUNT MONAHAN, and REINHOLD W. HEKELER. *Stress Management for Human Services*. Pp. 96. Beverly Hills, CA: Sage, 1984. Paperbound, $9.95.

FREDRIKSEN, JOHN C., comp. *Free Trade and Sailor's Rights: A Bibliog-*

raphy of the War of 1812. Pp. xii, 399. Westport, CT: Greenwood Press, 1985. $45.00.

FREY, R. G., ed. *Utility and Rights*. Pp. ix, 245. Minneapolis: University of Minnesota Press, 1984. $29.50. Paperbound, $13.95.

GARAY, RONALD. *Congressional Television: A Legislative History*. Pp. x, 195. Westport, CT: Greenwood Press, 1984. $27.95.

HANDEL, GERALD. *The Psychosocial Interior of the Family*. Pp. xiv, 520. Hawthorne, NY: Aldine, 1985. $49.95. Paperbound, $19.95.

HANLEY, D. L., A. P. KERR, and N. H. WAITES. *Contemporary France: Politics and Society since 1945*. Pp. xii, 372. Boston, MA: Routledge & Kegan Paul, 1984. Paperbound, $17.95.

HANSTEN, PHILIP D. *Drug Interactions*. Pp. x, 460. Philadelphia: Lea and Febiger, 1985. Paperbound, $22.50.

HARGROVE, HONDON B. *Buffalo Soldiers in Italy: Black Americans in World War II*. Pp. viii, 199. Jefferson, NC: McFarland, 1985. $18.95.

HILL, ROBERT A., ed. *The Marcus Garvey and Universal Negro Improvement Association Papers*. Pp. lviii, 811. Berkeley: University of California Press, 1985. $38.50.

HOY, CALVIN M. *A Philosophy of Individual Freedom: The Political Thought of F. A. Hayek*. Pp. ix, 144. Westport, CT: Greenwood Press, 1984. $27.95.

HYFLER, ROBERT. *Prophets of the Left: American Socialist Thought in the Twentieth Century*. Pp. x, 187. Westport, CT: Greenwood Press, 1984. $29.95.

IMPERATO, PASCAL JAMES and GREG MITCHELL. *Acceptable Risks*. Pp. xix, 286. New York: Viking Press, 1985. $15.95.

JUDSON, C. FRED. *Cuba and the Revolutionary Myth: The Political Education of the Cuban Rebel Army, 1953-1963*. Pp. xi, 294. Boulder, CO: Westview Press, 1984. Paperbound, $22.50.

KAVANAGH, DENNIS and GILLIAN PEELE, eds. *Comparative Government and Politics: Essays in Honour of S. E. Finer*. Pp. viii, 247. Boulder, CO: Westview Press, 1984. $32.50.

KIRBY, ANDREW, PAUL KNOX, and STEVEN PINCH, eds. *Public Service Provision and Urban Development*. Pp. 420. New York: St. Martin's Press, 1984. $35.00.

KITANO, HARRY H. L. *Race Relations*. 3rd ed. Pp. xiv, 286. Englewood Cliffs, NJ: Prentice-Hall, 1984. $24.95.

KITZINGER, SHEILA. *Birth over Thirty*. Pp. ix, 182. New York: Penguin Books, 1985. Paperbound, $5.95.

LEFEBVRE, HENRI. *Everyday Life in the Modern World*. Pp. xxiii, 206. New Brunswick, NJ: Transaction Books, 1984. No price.

LEVY, LEONARD W. *Emergence of a Free Press*. Pp. xxii, 383. New York: Oxford University Press, 1985. $29.95.

LEWIS, PAUL G., ed. *Eastern Europe: Political Crisis and Legitimation*. Pp. 202. New York: St. Martin's Press, 1984. $25.00.

LOEWENBERG, PETER. *Decoding the Past: The Psychohistorical Approach*. Pp. xviii, 300. Berkeley: University of California Press, 1985. Paperbound, $9.95.

LOWE, MARIAN and RUTH HUBBARD, eds. *Woman's Nature: Rationalizations of Inequality*. Pp. xii, 155. New York: Pergamon Press, 1983. $27.50. Paperbound, $12.50.

LYNN, JOHN A. *The Bayonets of the Republic: Motivation and Tactics in the Army of Revolutionary France, 1791-94*. Pp. xii, 356. Champaign: University of Illinois Press, 1984. $24.95.

LYNN, NAOMI B., ed. *United Nations Decade for Women World Conference*. Pp. 93. New York: Haworth Press, 1984. $19.95.

MACKAY, ALFRED F. *Arrow's Theorem—The Paradox of Social Choice: A Case Study in the Philosophy of Economics*.

Pp. ix, 143. New Haven, CT: Yale University Press, 1984. Paperbound, $6.95.

McDONALD, TERRENCE J. and SALLY K. WARD, eds. *The Politics of Urban Fiscal Policy*. Pp. 176. Beverly Hills, CA: Sage, 1984. $25.00.

McNULTY, PAUL J. *The Origins and Development of Labor Economics*. Pp. viii, 248. Cambridge, MA: MIT Press, 1985. Paperbound, $7.95.

MEISTER, ALBERT. *Participation, Associations, Development, and Change*. Pp. xviii, 268. New Brunswick, NJ: Transaction Books, 1984. $34.95.

MILLER, JAMES. *Rousseau: Dreamer of Democracy*. Pp. xii, 272. New Haven, CT: Yale University Press, 1984. $25.00.

MILLER, STEVEN E., ed. *Strategy and Nuclear Deterrence: An International Security Reader*. Pp. xiii, 297. Princeton, NJ: Princeton University Press, 1985. $32.50. Paperbound, $8.95.

MORLEY, JAMES WILLIAM, ed. *Japan's Road to the Pacific War*. Pp. xi, 410. New York: Columbia University Press, 1984. $35.00.

MORRIS, ROBERT. *Social Policy of the American Welfare State: An Introduction to Policy Analysis*. Pp. xi, 276. New York: Longman, 1984. Paperbound, $16.95.

MOSS, ROBERT. *Moscow Rules*. Pp. 389. New York: Random House, 1985. $16.95.

MUELLER, FRANZ H. *The Church and the Social Question*. Pp. 158. Washington, DC: American Enterprise Institute for Public Policy Research, 1984. No price.

NEELY, ALFRED S., IV. *Ethics-in-Government Laws: Are They Too "Ethical"?* Pp. 58. Washington, DC: American Enterprise Institute for Public Policy Research, 1984. Paperbound, $4.95.

NORTON, AUGUSTUS RICHARD et al. *NATO: A Bibliography and Resource Guide*. Pp. xiii, 252. New York: Garland, 1985. $50.00.

ORNSTEIN, NORMAN J. et al. *Vital Statistics on Congress*. 1984-85 ed. Pp. xxiii, 261. Washington, DC: American Enterprise Institute for Public Policy Research, 1984. No price.

PERTSCHUK, MICHAEL. *Revolt against Regulation: The Rise and Pause of the Consumer Movement*. Pp. x, 166. Berkeley: University of California Press, 1984. $12.95. Paperbound, $6.95.

PETERI, GYORGY. *The Effects of World War II: War Communism in Hungary*. Pp. x, 229. New York: Columbia University Press, 1984. $25.00.

PLANO, JACK C. and MILTON GREENBERG. *The American Political Dictionary*. Pp. ix, 606. New York: Holt, Rinehart and Winston, 1985. Paperbound, no price.

REVEL, JEAN-FRANCOIS. *How Democracies Perish*. Pp. vi, 376. New York: Doubleday, 1984. $17.95.

ROSS, BERNARD H. and MURRAY S. STEDMAN, Jr. *Urban Politics*. Pp. x, 336. Itasca, IL: F. E. Peacock, 1985. No price.

ROSSI, ALICE S. *Gender and the Life Course*. Pp. xxi, 368. Hawthorne, NY: Aldine, 1985. $34.95. Paperbound, $14.95.

ROWE, WILLIAM T. *Hankow: Commerce and Society in a Chinese City, 1796-1889*. Pp. viii, 436. Stanford, CA: Stanford University Press, 1984. $39.50.

SALAS, RAFAEL M. *Reflections on Population*. Pp. xv, 240. Elmsford, NY: Pergamon Press, 1984. $30.00.

SCHUSTER, MICHAEL H. *Union-Management Cooperation: Structure-Process-Impact*. Pp. xiv, 235. Kalamazoo, MI: W. E. Upjohn Institute for Employment Research, 1984. $17.95. Paperbound, $12.95.

SHAVER, PHILLIP, ed. *Review of Personality and Social Psychology*. Pp. 312. Beverly Hills, CA: Sage, 1984. $28.00. Paperbound, $14.00.

SPURLIN, PAUL MERRILL. *The French Enlightenment in America: Essays on the Times of the Founding Fathers*. Pp. xi, 203. Athens: University of Georgia Press, 1984. $20.00.

STEWART, WILLIAM H. *Concepts of Federalism*. Pp. 239. Lanham, MD: University Press of America, 1984. No price.

STREIKER, LOWELL D. *Mindbending: Brainwashing, Cults, and Deprogramming in the '80s*. Pp. xvii, 218. New York: Doubleday, 1984. $14.95.

STUECK, WILLIAM. *The Wedemeyer Mission*. Pp. x, 177. Athens: University of Georgia Press, 1984. $18.00.

TEPLIN, LINDA A., ed. *Mental Health and Criminal Justice*. Pp. 320. Beverly Hills, CA: Sage, 1984. Paperbound, $14.00.

TOOL, MARC R., ed. *An Institutionalist Guide to Economics and Public Policy*. Pp. xii, 337. Armonk, NY: M. E. Sharpe, 1984. $30.00. Paperbound, $13.95.

WALKERMAN, ELYCE. *Father Loss: Daughters Discuss the Man That Got Away*. Pp. xvi, 291. New York: Doubleday, 1984. $15.95.

WHYNES, DAVID, ed. *What is Political Economy?* Pp. ix, 243. New York: Basil Blackwell, 1985. $29.95. Paperbound, $11.95.

WILLIAMS, WILLIAM APPLEMAN et al., eds. *America in Vietnam: A Documentary History*. Pp. xii, 345. New York: Doubleday, 1985. $19.95. Paperbound, $9.95.

WILLS, JOHN E., Jr. *Embassies & Illusions: Dutch and Portuguese Envoys to K'ang-hsi, 1666-1687*. Pp. xi, 303. Cambridge, MA: Harvard University Press, 1984. $20.00.

WINN, MARIE. *The Plug-in Drug: Television, Children, and the Family*. Pp. xiv, 288. New York: Penguin Books, 1985. Paperbound, $6.95.

WINSON, JONATHAN. *Brain & Psyche: The Biology of the Unconscious*. Pp. x, 300. New York: Doubleday, 1985. $16.96.

INDEX